Some notable appreciati

"A book proclaiming the victory of the Church and the heroism of her priests."

— Radio Vatican

"These events can well be placed alongside those of the first three centuries of Christianity for use in apologetics and religious instruction."
— † Franziskus Cardinal König, Archbishop of Vienna

"I have just been reading *Christ in Dachau* — the most shattering but uplifting book I have read in my life. This book proves to us that the spirit of faith and love and the readiness to make the supreme sacrifice that inspired the early Christians is still alive today, among both priests and laity."
— † Michael Buchberger, Archbishop of Regensburg

"I congratulate you on this book ... which will become a standard work of Christian apologetics."
— † Josef Hilti, Suffragan Bishop of Regensburg

"So exciting in places that I couldn't put it down."
— † H. Roloff, Suffragan Bishop of Munster

"The unique contents of this book have led me to recommend it on every possible occasion."
— † Josef Zimmermann, Suffragan Bishop of Augsburg

"A book that should be available in every parish library."
— *Speyer Diocesan Journal*

Christ in Dachau

Aerial photograph of Dachau camp

1. Kitchens and stores, 2. Parade ground, 3. Prisoners' barracks 1–30, 4. Plantation, 5. Peppermill, 6. Crematorium, 7. SS barracks, 8. Garages, 9. SS pay office, 10. SS headquarters, 11. SS officers' quarters, 12. Magazines (photo: Stephanus heute, Fr. Pies).

Fr. John M. Lenz

Christ in Dachau

SOPHIA INSTITUTE PRESS
Manchester, New Hampshire

Copyright © 2023 by Sophia Institute Press

English translation by Countess Barbara Waldstein formerly published in 1960 by Missionsdruckerei St. Gabriel, Mödling Bei Wien, Austria.

Printed in the United States of America. All rights reserved.

Cover design by Updatefordesign Studio.

On the cover: Dachau Concentration Camp (CW6B7G) © Photo 12 / Alamy Stock Photo; Dachau Concentration Camp Memorial Site(FB0160) © Images and Stories / Alamy Stock Photo.

Scripture quotations are taken from the Douay-Rheims edition of the Old and New Testaments.

No part of this book may be reproduced, stored in a retrieval system, or transmitted in any form, or by any means, electronic, mechanical, photocopying, or otherwise, without the prior written permission of the publisher, except by a reviewer, who may quote brief passages in a review.

Sophia Institute Press
Box 5284, Manchester, NH 03108
1-800-888-9344
www.SophiaInstitute.com

Sophia Institute Press is a registered trademark of Sophia Institute.

paperback ISBN 978-1-64413-890-8

ebook ISBN 978-1-64413-891-5

Library of Congress Control Number: 2023940025

First printing

Contents

Introduction to the English Edition
by Barbara Waldstein

When he came out of Dachau, Fr. Lenz was asked by his ecclesiastical superiors to write an account of his experiences. He was not asked to write a history of Dachau or an indictment of the concentration camp system but simply an account of his personal experiences. Fr. Lenz being the man he is, however, this task could not end there. A priest interned among other priests, all victims of the struggle between godless Nazism and Christ's Church, he could not but see his internment and that of his fellows in the light of this struggle, and so this book — which began as a simple factual account of the experiences of one man — in fact became the saga of this one particular phase, restricted in time and in space, of the unending struggle between good and evil.

Priests in Dachau were, as everyone knows, not accorded the same sort of treatment as that given to the criminal prisoners, or even to other political prisoners. They were, for the most part, segregated, and the treatment they received, not only at the hands of their Nazi jailers but also from the godless fellow prisoners who were often appointed as their "bosses," was, in the main, even more brutal, more pointedly sadistic. Yet this was not always so. Part of the time, they did, in fact, receive preferential treatment. This was all part of the curiously paradoxical system. The important thing to remember, however, is that they were dealt with as a class apart, as a particular menace to the Nazi ideology, and, therefore, that their particular story, their reaction to the whole struggle, is doubly significant — first, because they were priests of God, professional champions of Christ's Church, and second, because their jailers recognized in them the representatives of the most powerful enemy of Nazism.

To grasp the significance of this book, we must turn away from the word *Dachau* with its connotations of oppression, injustice, brutality, and hatred, and look to the other word of the title: *Christ* — *Christ in Dachau* — and to the subtitle, *Christ Victorious*. It is a story of victory, of a victory that was the modern counterpart of the victory of Calvary, the story of how this victory was won for Christ and with Him by the thousands of priests from a score of countries, from every kind of home background — parish priests and prelates, monks and friars, teachers and missionaries.

In his preface, the author disclaims all literary merit. The book is intended as a document and not as a literary tour de force.

It has not been the translator's task to change the author's concept of his work or his style or, in any way, to tint the glasses through which English-speaking people will read the document. Certain editorial changes, it is true, have been made with the consent or at the suggestion of the author, but *Christ in Dachau* in the English version remains essentially the book as it was originally written.

A Tribute to Dachau Town

A small medieval town on the banks of the Amper, Dachau was probably unheard of outside its own immediate neighborhood until Hitler's decision to site a concentration camp there brought it a place in world headlines — not fame but infamy.

Inevitably, the very name Dachau calls to the minds of strangers only the concentration camp and the inhuman crimes committed there, and inevitably some of the horror they feel attaches to the town that had the misfortunate to have a suitable camp site.

Not only is this unjustifiable, but the exact opposite is true. Readers of this book will learn of the efforts of the parish priest on behalf of the first prisoners and later on our behalf and will also learn something of the cooperation and sympathy extended to the prisoners by the town and by its inhabitants of all classes and ages. But only a tithe is recorded here of the help we received, help in the form of gifts, help in the form of providing communication between the camp and the world outside — all done at the risk of their own lives and liberty.

The people of Dachau did not forget us in their prayers. Let us not forget them in ours.

— Fr. John M. Lenz

Preface

Thy kingdom come, Thy will be done on earth as it is in heaven.

— Matthew 6:10

What we priests were forced to endure under the Nazi regime, especially in Dachau concentration camp, is no more than a cup filled from the vast sea of human suffering in the world today. It is not this suffering as such that is important. The important thing is to show those who have crosses of their own to bear in life just what the grace of God can do for those who follow faithfully in the footsteps of Christ the Crucified. It is no less important to reveal the wickedness of Hell.

That is why I have written this account of our experiences, the original German version of which was published eleven years afterward. May this book have God's blessing. It is a record, both for the world today and for posterity, of the life, the suffering, and, above all, the victory of the Church during this satanic era.

Dachau has become notorious throughout the world. For us, Dachau recalls memories as diverse and full of contrasts as the world itself. Dachau was unique in the opportunities it afforded to get to know human nature, unique in the chances it offered to gain experience of the world as it really is, unique in the countless burning questions it presented — and in the answers — and in the stimulus it gave to face these problems. Only when I started to work on this book did I begin to realize all this to the full. The book aims to provide an answer to these manifold questions, an answer inspired by the true Catholic spirit. It is my sincere hope and prayer in all humility that God may use this book to further His kingdom.

Dachau means something else too. It is a terrible warning to us all, not only for today but for tomorrow. God alone knows how real and present the lessons of this book may yet be for us. The prisons and concentration camps of Soviet Russia are terrifying parallels enough. Those who once sat among the judges at the Nuremberg Trials are now the new criminals, the new hangmen. For it is possible to profit from the bitter lessons of the past only if these events in the history of the world are viewed with the eyes of true Christian faith.

The book lays no great claim to literary merit. Its prime concern is to present straightforward facts, to give an absolutely truthful account of our experiences. Events and episodes recounted within the inner structure of the book follow, in the main, in chronological order. The book is not a novel but a piece of contemporary evidence; it bears witness to an encounter with Christ, to a recognition of Christ at a time of the bitterest suffering, the fiercest combat with the forces of evil. It is an inspiring story of priestly devotion and heroism at a time when the Church of God was subjected to danger and persecution. The power of the Catholic Church — a power that has no need to resort to arms — emerged victorious, just as it will always be victorious, as Christ Himself proclaimed. Only through Christ and His Church can the world be saved, as this book also shows.

This is a book written for everyday people about everyday people. It is a book about life, about priests in the service of God. It is a book about Christ Himself. May it bring light, strength, and joy to all who read it.

Christ the Victor is the subtitle of the book, and fittingly so, for it was Christ the Victor who inspired me to write it.

The many personal experiences that feature in the book have been included at the express wish of a high clerical authority.

I should like to express my sincere thanks to all those who have helped me by their good counsel and by their practical assistance.

For God and His kingdom!

— Fr. John M. Lenz
1960

God's Words — Words of Comfort

I am the light of the world. (John 8:12)

I am the resurrection and the life. (John 11:25)

I am the way, the truth, and the life. (John 14:6)

He who will be my disciple, let him deny himself, take up his cross daily and follow me. (Luke 9:23)

My yoke is sweet and my burden light. (Matt. 11:30)

Do penance, for the kingdom of heaven is at hand. (Matt. 3:2; 4:17)

What doth it profit a man if he gain the whole world and suffer the loss of his own soul? (Matt. 16:26)

It is by endurance that you will secure possession of your souls. (Luke 21:19)

Was it not to be expected that the Christ should undergo these sufferings and enter so into his glory? (Luke 24:26)

We must share His sufferings, if we are to share His glory. (Rom. 8:17)

Your distress shall be turned into joy. (John 16:20)

Christ in Dachau

The sorrows of this world are not to be compared with the glory that shall be revealed in us. (Rom. 8:18)

Eye hath not seen, nor ear heard, neither hath it entered into the heart of man what God hath prepared for those who love Him. (1 Cor. 2:9)

In eating and drinking, in all that you do, do everything as for God's glory. (1 Cor. 10:31)

Keep faith with me to the point of death, and I will crown thee with life. (Rev. 2:10)

Rejoice and be glad, for great is your reward in heaven. (Matt. 5:12)

Then at last the just will shine out, clear as the sun, in their Father's kingdom. (Matt. 13:43)

Book 1

Prelude to Dachau

Charity is the apostle's indispensable weapon in a world torn by hatred. It will make you forget, or at least forgive, many an undeserved insult.... This charity, intelligent and sympathetic even towards those who offend you, does by no means imply a renunciation of the right of proclaiming, vindicating and defending the truth and its implications.

— Pope Pius XI, *Mit Brennender Sorge*, March 1937

1

Why?

A pilgrimage of thanksgiving

It was July 2, 1945, at eight o'clock in the evening. It was time to lock the doors of the shrine for the night, and as I came out of the chapel, I saw that it was raining — soft, summer rain, cool and refreshing after the heat of the day. It was almost symbolic, I thought, as I walked back through the rain to the house where I was staying, my mind filled with memories of the past dark years from which we had been so mercifully delivered by the grace of God and His Holy Mother. All through those six nightmare years spent in Dachau, I had never ceased to trust and hope in Our Lady, and I had made a solemn vow then to make a pilgrimage to her shrine at Altötting if I ever came out alive. I did come out alive, and my first visit outside the camp was to Altötting in Lower Bavaria, a fitting place for such an act of thanksgiving, for it is one of the oldest and most honored shrines of Our Lady in the whole of Christendom.

For centuries, Christian pilgrims have made their way here to lay their troubles and their joys, their special petitions and intentions, before the Mother of God. Convinced that she would help them, they were never disappointed. The countless inscriptions on the walls, both inside and outside this holy place, and the many votive paintings are proof enough of that. "Our Lady, come to our aid!" "Mary will never fail us!" "Our Lady, Refuge of Sinners!" These words found an echo in my own heart, for I knew what Our Blessed Mother had been to us in the horror of Dachau, and I was quite convinced that it was through her intercession that I had come out alive.

Christin Dachau

It was hard to believe in those tranquil summer days that the dark satanic era of Nazi domination that had plunged Europe into war and misery for so long was over at last. Hitler's regime of terror and godlessness had finally been broken. Christ had triumphed over the powers of Hell. We of His Church had never doubted that He would emerge victorious in the end, but the way to victory had often seemed intolerably long and hard, a veritable Way of the Cross for those of us who suffered the horrors, the privations, and the sheer grey monotony of life in a Nazi concentration camp. There were, in fact, not very many who did survive the experience in comparison with the countless thousands who died. For those of us who came out alive, our survival was indeed a miracle. Mary had come to our aid, and it was only right and fitting that I should come to honor her in humble thanksgiving at her great shrine.

I shall never forget those long, peaceful summer days in Altötting, days of quiet prayer and meditation, days of rest after the strain of six long years behind barbed wire and the strenuous weeks that had followed our liberation by the Americans. There had been much to do in the camp in those days, for an almost superhuman task of organization had awaited us in helping the authorities to cope with the chaos in the camp. It had taken weeks to effect the discharge of the prisoners, but there were still many who were homeless or destitute or too sick to be moved, and my days had been filled in helping to care for them. I could see that it would take weeks, perhaps even months, before they were cleared, and I knew that they could not be left without a priest.

"Come back to us after your pilgrimage to Altötting, Father," beseeched one old man who was dangerously ill. "You've just got to come back! You can't leave us alone!"

So I went back to Dachau after a few days, refreshed and strengthened by my stay in Altötting. I was very impressed by what I saw there, by the countless groups of devout pilgrims led by priests and religious, fine men and women who had no illusions about the mammoth task confronting them of helping to build up a new Germany and a new Austria out of the shambles left by the war, but who were confident of God's help and, above all, fired with enthusiasm and zeal for the work that lay ahead. I knew only too well from experience how much depended on the spiritual qualities of our priests and religious as fearless champions of Christ and servants of His Church here on earth. I came away from Altötting reassured and strengthened by the knowledge that we had priests and religious of this caliber to lead our people along the road to God. I thought back to the dark days of the rise of the Nazi party and the spread of its godless doctrines. There had been intrepid champions of the truth in those days too, but we could have done with more. If our Catholic Faith had really been something living, something vital to our very existence, it is doubtful whether even a proportion of our people would have fallen prey to the Nazi pseudo-religion. We had been too lukewarm; our religion had become something conventional and had lost its living quality, so it was easy for many to lose sight of the essential values, to become blind to truth. So much depends on our leaders, the men and women who are Christ's servants as priests and religious, whose duty it is to fire those in their care with a new enthusiasm for Christ, to keep His teachings perpetually before their eyes, to strengthen, uphold, and protect, so that their flock should never again lose sight of the eternal truths manifested in the teachings of the Church.

"God save Austria!"

I thought a great deal about the early days of the Nazi regime in Austria during my stay at Altötting. Now that the era of Hitler's terror was finally over, I felt it was necessary to take stock, as it were — to review the situation objectively, if only to form a basis for a new line of action in the troubled and chaotic time that certainly lay ahead for all of us. As an Austrian, I was fully aware that there were many who, in all good faith, believed that my country had accepted, indeed welcomed, the Hitler regime. I knew that this was not true, but I determined to examine the situation again for myself in absolute honesty and in the light of my own experiences at that time.

March 12, 1938, is a day that no Austrian is ever likely to forget. It was a perfect day, the sort of spring morning when one's heart sings for sheer joy over the first really warm sunshine. But my mood changed abruptly as the news reached me that Hitler had marched into Austria! Despite the shock, it was no great surprise really, for the recent political events had served as warning enough. We had all been secretly dreading this moment, knowing it to be inevitable yet steadfastly refusing to believe that it would come. But when this moment did come, it brought the end of Austria.

March 12, 1938. The end had virtually come the evening before with the parting words of Dr. Kurt von Schuschnigg, the Austrian chancellor: "God save Austria!" This was certainly his unceasing prayer throughout the long years of his imprisonment by the Nazis. And God heard his prayer. Austria has risen again and will remain under God's protection. Back in 1866, Cardinal Othmar Rauscher wrote the following words in a pastoral letter issued in Vienna: "More than once, Austria has seemed to be standing on the verge of destruction. The end seemed near. But Austria has always endured in the devotion and faith of her people and under the protection of the Almighty." An old and true expression of the spirit of Catholic Austria.

"God save Austria!" A review of the last twenty years of Austria's history before 1938 shows that the new small Austria that emerged after the peace treaty of the First World War was never lacking in good men to guide her. True greatness and patriotism cannot be judged by the yardstick of party politics. There is only one lasting value by which statesmen can be judged, and that is by their contribution to their country's spiritual recovery, to its religious revival. Those who choose to leave God out of all their dealings and encourage others to follow them are certainly only undermining their country's fortune. "The salvation of our Fatherland lies on the road to eternal life," as Paul de Legard says.

A great deal has been written about the ovation that greeted Hitler's troops as they marched through the streets of Vienna. The picture of cheering crowds waving Nazi flags and shouting "Heil Hitler!" is, however, very deceptive. For all the thousands who lined the streets, there were thousands more sitting at home behind locked doors, mourning the fate of their country. Too great importance should not be attached to the misleading demonstrations in the streets, for many of those who clamored for Hitler and the Nazis were just unfortunate dupes of the ruthless propaganda. Many were simply carried away at the moment by the tide of excitement, unable to resist the flags and the music and the crowds. There were others, too, paid organizers of the party entrusted with the task of creating the right sort of atmosphere for a triumphal entry into the capital; and there were many citizens of Vienna forced to participate in the demonstrations by threat of reprisals against their families.

Why?

Incidentally, the official figures of the postwar census of Nazis in Austria are revealing. They show that for the whole of Austria, 536,000 persons were liable to be registered as members of the NSDAP;[1] of these, 98,000 were "illegal" — i.e., had belonged to the party before the Anschluss,[2] while it was still illegal. Considering that the population of Austria at the time of the Anschluss was some 6½ million, these figures are the clearest proof of how small the number of real Nazis was during those fateful days of 1938. We of the clergy have no need of such statistics, for we saw how the situation was for ourselves. We saw the way the wind was blowing for a long time, and we knew that all true Austrians protested against the shameful rape of their country by a man who had no place for God in his heart. There were many who were guilty of passive acquiescence, too lukewarm or too cowardly to resist, but we, the priests, knew from the hundreds who thronged our churches and sought us out in desperation in our rectories and monasteries and friaries — we knew that there were many who thought quite differently.

Let us look back for a moment in all honesty. Who were the willing victims of the Nazi propaganda, foolishly carried away by the fine-sounding words of a handful of men at the head of a movement that utterly rejected the teachings of Christ? What about those who were guilty in their own way too, those who offered no real resistance?

St. John tells us that without faith all is vain, for faith overcomes the world. There were many who had no faith in those days, who, having once fallen away from the Church, were an easy prey to Hitler's substitute for religion. Where there was no living religion, the thorns of the Nazi doctrine grew up like the thorns in the parable. Only those who lived in the light of faith could recognize the danger behind the Nazi propaganda, harmless enough though it might at first appear, and could see the power of the devil behind Hitler.

January 30, 1933, the day Hitler came to power in Germany, was an evil day for the whole of Europe. I remember the grief and shame I felt at the thought of Germany in the hands of such a man. All we could do was to pray. "O Lord,"

---

[1] Nationalsozialistische Deutsche Arbeiterpartei, or National Socialist German Workers' Party.
[2] The uniting of Germany and Austria in 1938.

Christ in Dachau

I prayed that day, "look down in mercy and providence upon the countless thousands who still remain faithful to Thee in this fine land." I was working on a book about astronomy at the time, and I gave vent to my feelings in the following passage:

> The power of the Almighty is invincible. The Rock of Peter can never be conquered. It stands firm against all challenge. Ever since the earliest days of the Church, the struggle has been unremitting, and it will go on to the end of time. Mankind has never ceased to dare to defy the Almighty; mankind — though nothing but a swarm of ants in God's great creation — has openly dared to oppose His will. Yet what pitiful little creatures we really are in God's universe! The so-called lords of the world, the great dictators and the petty tyrants, are only to be pitied in their pride and vainglory. They cannot submit in humility to the one great God, their Creator, but are blind and willing slaves of the devil himself in his perpetual battle against God. But they are pitting their forces in vain against the laws of God; they are attempting to storm the Rock of Peter, only to fall back in the end, shattered and broken.

"Everything depends upon God's blessing," as an old German proverb so truly reminds us. No one in his senses could expect good out of evil, or happiness and prosperity at the hands of a man who denies God. Yet there were many who were blinded by the new ideology, by the dangerous new religion of power. Even "good Catholics" were led astray, for their religion had long ceased to be something that really inspired their lives, and they had lost sight of the truth. Put to the test, their faith simply folded up — and the rest was easy. We all know how easy it is in life to lose even the most important, the most precious things. They can be lost in a moment, unthinkingly, as a child might play with a shining precious stone and then suddenly find it was no longer there, that it had slipped through his fingers, lost, irretrievable. The dark Nazi era should be a warning to us priests, for religious leadership lies in our hands, and it is up to us to make our faith a living thing, something that will inspire in our flock a new enthusiasm for Christ and His will on earth. We were the shepherds of our flock in those dark days too, and if we are honest with ourselves, we must admit that we often failed in our duty as fearless champions of Our Lord. Let us remember this now in these new troubled times when our responsibilities are no less heavy.

The truth should be told!

As the Bible declares, there is "a time to keep silence and a time to speak" (Eccles. 3:7). For years, we were condemned to silence. Yet in point of fact, those years were a "creative pause," as it were. It seemed as though God were using this period of silence to prepare us for speech. For a long time in the camp, any form of religion was taboo, and religious discussion of any kind with our fellow prisoners was met with heavy punishment. Biblical texts were even censored in our letters home. We priests were forced into silence. It was God's will, yet it was a silence imposed by the wickedness of man.

It goes without saying that there are still many who would be glad if we were to "keep silence" — in their own interests. The truth about the "death mills" of the concentration camp can only serve to their further indictment. If, on the other hand, they have turned back in sincerity to God, then here is their chance to prove their sincerity and accept their penance. It is, after all, a very light penance compared with the gravity of their sin!

Would it not be better to put an end to the matter and cover all this injustice with a comfortable "mantle of love"? By no means. This sort of "mantle" would be only cowardice, even indolence. It is a poor service to the erring to blindfold eyes that are dazzled and to stop up ears that cannot hear. It is not the task of us priests to bolster self-deception. Weak consideration for the evildoers of this world inevitably ends as betrayal of the good.

This book is a straightforward account of facts, and the truth about human beings can never be unadulterated praise. It is not the purpose of this book simply to praise my fellow priests in Dachau. But the Church of truth and those who proclaim her message need never be afraid of the truth. They acknowledge with true gratitude the divine grace, at the same time recognizing, in all humility, their own personal frailty. We priests need never excuse the fact that we are human beings, just as we must never allow ourselves to grow arrogant because God has shown us His grace.

I was asked to write about my experiences in Dachau, the request coming from a high clerical authority. A book about all the priests in Dachau developed.

Christ in Dachau

The book aims to answer, in the light of faith, the countless vital questions with which we were constantly faced in Dachau. It is neither a horror story nor a hymn of hate. It is the simple story of human beings and their spiritual problems, the story of the miraculous ways of God's grace amid the ragings of Hell.

It would be easy enough to be silent. Easy enough simply to pass over the manifestations of God's greatness, to avoid arousing violent recriminations merely out of cowardice. Self-love can always find motives for such evasion. But this is not the right road for us, for on this road, we shall find no courage, no faith, and still less can we win a martyr's crown. The Church of Christ has always chosen the other road.

Much has already been written about Dachau. Hundreds of booklets and pamphlets about the camp have already been circulated throughout the world. Those written by priests shine like beacons in this mass of "horror literature," for the horror was only half the truth, only one side of the story of life in the concentration camp. For those who did not encounter Christ in the depths of the misery and horror of Dachau missed the most wonderful experience of all.

A warning and not an indictment

It is not our purpose simply to expose the guilty. A priest's book should never be a campaign in this sense, nor should it be a settlement of old scores. The book is addressed first and foremost to those who had no part in these crimes: it is intended to bring them comfort and strength by revealing the triumph of good over evil, of truth over falsehood. For this is the real, the final, victory.

Nor is this intended as an indictment of the German people. What is attacked is the godlessness of a totalitarian system based solely on power, a system that could well be enforced again — in any country, in any nation. But just as the noble Russian people and the Bolshevist regime are two quite different things, so must the same distinction be made between the German nation and the Nazis.

Names that figure in the evil chronicles of Dachau have, for the most part, been omitted in Christian charity. Names are, after all, of no great importance to us here. What is important is truth. I can, however, reveal these names at any time, just as I can vouch for the accuracy of all the facts recorded in this book.

Christ in Dachau proclaims the victory of God and His Church. It is further intended to open the eyes of the penitent, to stretch out a warm hand to them in sincerity and heartfelt charity. It is my earnest wish to lead all back to the mercy of God. The priests of Dachau have no wish for retribution, no desire to wound or kill. Their sole desire is to inspire devotion to God, the God of love and of life who saved them so miraculously and so often from almost certain death.

Nor are we looking for acclamation. God and His kingdom — that is all that matters. Ever since the Fall, our ways to God have been paved with suffering. Six and a half years behind barbed wire was a bitter price to pay in order to be able to hold on to God. But for the same result, I would again joyfully face prison, hunger, and death.... Life is not easy; it involves a constant struggle against the forces of evil. It is no mere game; it means putting up a fight, and if we are followers of Christ, we will stand willingly at His side, ever prepared to do battle in the cause of Him who storms the gates of Hell in all eternity and proclaims His victory over Satan and all his works.

God is Love

Yet the mercy of God is boundless. No one need ever despair. "If your sins be as scarlet, they shall be made as white as snow" (Isa. 1:18). That is what the Divine Love offers us. The Son of Man is our Redeemer, the hope of all truly penitent sinners who turn to Him, trusting in His infinite mercy and love. "I have loved thee with an everlasting love, therefore have I drawn thee, taking pity on thee" (Jer. 31:3). "For God so loved the world as to give His only begotten Son" (John 3:16).

We of the Church Militant are doing battle here and now against the enemies of God and His kingdom. We cannot be friend to every man without betraying God. It may well be that the truth for which we stand will give offense to those who still deny God. But it was precisely for them that the Divine Prince of Peace Himself declared, "I came not to send peace, but the sword" (Matt. 10:34).

To men of goodwill, however, the truth can bring nothing but good. For those willing to turn back to God, the truth can help them to find salvation, leading them nearer in love and confident hope, in humility and a true spirit of remorse, to Him who suffered and died for them. It will lead them nearer to God.

Millions of men, women, and children met their end, directly or indirectly, in the concentration camps of Hitler's Third Reich. In the words of Fr. Otto Pies, S.J., "For the sake of those who died and of those who come after us, we are bound to proclaim the truth and to go forward with fortitude on the hard road of life as witnesses of the triumph of the Cross and the Resurrection of Our Lord."

"For God and His kingdom!"

2

Arrested

Dachau is just around the corner

With the Nazi victory in March 1938, a new and dark era had begun for Austria. Our good Catholics were almost heartbroken. They came to us priests in their desperation in the hope of finding some kind of support, some consolation. These men and women were the true patriots of Austria, men and women who remained true to their convictions in the face of the new ideology of the Hitler regime. These were the real Austrians, a heartwarming contrast to the new type of citizen of Hitler's "Ostmark," as our country was now called. They seemed literally to spring up overnight, these new overbearing officials with their Hitler salutes and swastikas and photographs of the Führer. Suddenly they were to be found everywhere, in the streets, in offices, in trams, loud-voiced and arrogant, the new Austrians. These were heartbreaking days indeed.

"You'll be the first of us to be sent to Dachau," prophesied my good friend Fr. Engelbert G. But his own sermons at May devotions had been no less outspoken. Not long after, he received a warning note from the police, but, thank God, no further steps were taken. We knew that it was our duty as priests to speak out fearlessly against the godlessness of the new regime. I felt that it was more than ever imperative at that time to strengthen the belief in God's goodness, to inspire courage to remain true to our Faith. I knew very well that I was in danger of arrest, but I knew, too, that I must obey the Holy Father, Pius XI, who had categorically declared:

> The priest's first loving gift to his neighbors is to serve truth and refute error in any of its forms. Failure on this score would be not only a

13

betrayal of God and your vocation, but also an offense against the real welfare of your people and country.[3]

Dachau! The name was already notorious. Mauthausen, Buchenwald, Sachsenhausen, and many others were to follow. Even back in 1938, there were many prominent Catholics among those interned in the concentration camps of Germany.

At the end of the summer, I was transferred to Vienna, but before leaving my parish in Carinthia — a province in the south of Austria bordering on Yugoslavia — I made a farewell round of my little flock. I took the opportunity to visit a small farmer whom I knew to be a convinced Nazi and one of the pillars of the local party organization. I did my best to make him see reason, pointing out that a godless state system could never be a good one and must inevitably bring evil in its train. The man listened to all I had to say in silence and apparently with the greatest interest.

When I was arrested by the Gestapo a few weeks later in Vienna, this farmer's "denunciation" was read aloud to me by my interrogator, and I was expected to answer the charges contained in it, paragraph for paragraph. I prayed to the Holy Ghost to come to my aid, for the poor misguided peasant had had a great deal to say. Not only had he misinterpreted much of what I had said, but he had invented a whole lot more besides! I answered truthfully everything they asked me, and my answers were recorded verbatim. Finally, my interrogator asked me to define the purpose of my sermons to my flock. I told him that I had felt compelled to warn them that our Faith was at stake, that the Church of Christ was in real danger in the new Austria. I added that I had also spoken to console them with the belief that the Nazi regime could not last forever! The official took down every word I said, and I was glad. Years afterward, I saw the official record of my statement. It included the following words about Hitler: "Never before in the history of the world has any one man been acclaimed with such enthusiasm as Adolf Hitler — and no other figure in the history of the world will be so hated and cursed as Adolf Hitler."

---

[3] Pope Pius XI, encyclical *Mit Brennender Sorge* (March 14, 1937), no. 36.

I was also shown the official document summarizing my interrogation, which was prepared a few days later:

> The accused admits to having talked of the persecution of the Catholic Church and the establishment of a new pagan religion under National Socialism. He further admits to the statement that the National Socialist form of education is atheist and further insists that it is impossible that the Führer himself should not be aware of this fact. He maintains that such anti-Christian teaching can only be enforced with the knowledge and acquiescence of the Führer and the members of his government. On the other hand, he denies having referred to the Führer as the antichrist, stating that he has always contradicted such opinions since, in his view, the antichrist would have to have many more followers — according to what is stated in the Bible.
>
> It is clear that the accused is not conversant with the principles of National Socialism, or he could hardly hold such erroneous views.

It was a sad sign that the new Nazi creed had already seized such a hold upon the population that even our good peasants were corrupted and could go so far as to denounce their own priests. It boded ill for the future.

The Carinthian farmer was not alone in denouncing me. Another man betrayed me too. He still lives in Vienna, and his name has never been revealed to the authorities. Toward the end of November 1938, he handed over a letter I had written to another priest containing a description of the storming of the archbishop's palace in Vienna by a Nazi mob on October 8. A few extracts will serve to illustrate the atmosphere in which we Catholics in Austria lived in those days.

> Friday, October 7. A crowd of Hitler Youth in uniform tried to break up the Catholic youth rally in St. Stephen's Cathedral by chanting, "Our faith is Germany."
>
> On Saturday at 8:30 p.m., organized groups, each of five youths, assembled in front of the palace. At a word of command, a volley of stones smashed the more than fifty windows on both sides of the palace; this to the accompaniment of the German national anthem and the

Christic in Dachau

Horst Wessel song. The main door was forced, and the mob stormed in, reducing the apartments to chaos and throwing furniture, pictures, clothes, and vestments out onto the street below, where they were set on fire. More anthems and the Hitler salute.... The archbishop's private chapel wrecked and desecrated.... By the mercy of Heaven one of the priests had been able to consume the Blessed Sacrament.... Someone telephoned the police when the raid began — but it was forty minutes before they arrived. They arrested one person, allowing the rest to get away unmolested.... A servant tried to take photographs, but the film was confiscated by the police.... In the morning, all the mess was cleared from the street.... Not a word in the Sunday papers.... Everyone was supposed to sign a document undertaking to say nothing about the incident. The cardinal and the clergy refused, but the domestic staff was forced to sign. On Sunday morning the palace was occupied, all rooms sealed, and everyone confined. No one was allowed in or out. The cardinal was a prisoner in his own palace.

The Gestapo had collected sufficient material to warrant my detention in custody. I spent the night of December 5 on the dirty floor of an empty cell in the Gestapo headquarters at the Hotel Metropole. On the evening of the next day, they took me to the Rossauer Lände, a prison in one of the outlying districts of Vienna. I shall never forget how I felt when I set foot inside this prison. It was a terrible yet strangely elevating moment. I reminded myself that I was no criminal but had been sent to prison for my Faith, and I began to recite the Te Deum as I climbed the stone stairway between two warders. But the higher we went, the more slowly the words came, and when I found myself confronted by row upon row of cells behind iron bars, I could not bring myself to finish this wonderful hymn of praise.

At first, we were an exclusively Christian community in our cell, and I could say grace at mealtimes, and we could pray the Our Father and the Hail Mary together. I was even able to hold Bible classes until the day F. came to join us. Although he had been thrown out of the SS, this man was still so imbued with Nazi doctrine that he threatened to denounce this "Catholic propaganda." But I still continued to say grace, even when my cellmates were replaced by avowed atheists. They never made any protest but stood quietly around the table until I had finished.

Christmas in jail

Christmas Eve came. We had hoped in vain for an amnesty. We sat there in our grim cell, hungry, lonely, and homesick, and thought nostalgically of past Christmases. But our happy memories of the Christmas of our childhood days contrasted sadly with reality. Our supper was brought in, no different from the same dreary prison supper we got every evening. There was nothing whatever to remind us that this was Christmas, the feast of Christ's Nativity. As the door slammed behind the departing warder, these grown men suddenly began to cry like children. It was the first time I had seen men really cry. And I found I was no better myself. I sat there with tears streaming down my cheeks. I tried to find a few words of comfort, but it was no use. The bitter reality was too shattering, and nothing I could say or do at that moment could help.

But it turned out to be a wonderful evening after all, an evening that, as we all said afterward, we should remember all our lives. Two of us — S. and I — had been lucky enough to be allowed a Christmas parcel from home. We sat down to our meager supper and opened our parcels — a salami and lots of traditional Austrian Christmas cookies. We shared these gladly with the others, and all of a sudden, our misery was forgotten in true Christmas joy, a joy that was all the greater for our own helplessness. I read the Christmas Gospel aloud, and we sang "Silent Night." Soon we were as happy and hilarious as children under the Christmas tree.

On Christmas Day, we opened our barred window and listened for the bells of the Servite church. Christmas in prison! It was a sad and at the same time a wonderful experience for me as a priest. How rarely at Christmas do we think of the prisoners, prisoners who can cry like children because the locked doors of their cells have opened the door to their own hearts and released memories of the Paradise Lost of their childhood!

"Protective custody"

On January 5, 1939, a Gestapo man presented me with the official red order for my "detention in protective custody." I was to receive a second such order on July 19, 1940. Both of these documents are in my possession today.

In the opinion of the State Police authorities [so runs this first warrant], Lenz endangers the security of the State and undermines the morale of the people by his persistent offensive references to leading figures of the National Socialist movement. There seems every reason to suppose that he intends to persist in this unpatriotic attitude and in his attempts to undermine the confidence of the people in the Government and in the Party.

(signed) Heydrich

The arrival of this document seemed to me to seal my fate. As I saw it, there was no longer any hope that I should be set free. The days seemed interminable; the future looked black in the extreme. January 16 came, the anniversary of my mother's death. I well remember how shattered I had been that day back in 1924 when I first heard the news. Now, in prison in Vienna, I was shattered by my spiritual despair and misery. I longed like a helpless child for the consoling presence of my mother. I began to pray, following the example she had given me throughout her lifetime of unfailing goodness and patience. Prayer provides the answer in every situation, and by prayer I slowly regained my spiritual equilibrium.

February 2, the feast of the Purification, was a wonderful day for me. As a result of a slight accident, I was admitted to the prison infirmary and found myself in the care of good Catholic nursing nuns. It was wonderful to be back in such an atmosphere of peace and dedicated work, to have enough to eat again and a clean and comfortable bed. But it lasted only nine days, and on February 11, I was back in my prison cell.

A few days later, I was transferred to cell number 110 on the first floor — in solitary confinement. I learned that I was shortly due to appear before a "People's Court" on a charge of treason. I was never told the grounds of this accusation, but I knew that my life was in danger. Msgr. Eduard Köck, the good prison chaplain, was no less pessimistic about my chances. It was he who told me that the London radio had announced my arrest. I resolved to make the best possible use of my time and began to study English and to give "talks" on history and geography over the inter-cell "telephone" system. In this way, I was able to maintain contact with many of the other cells. Such practices were, of course, highly dangerous, and the utmost care had to be taken to avoid detection.

Pope Pius XI died on February 10. We had lost a great and holy man. The whole world was waiting to hear who would be chosen to follow him in this unique dynasty founded by Christ Himself. On March 2, one of the warders whispered to me at midday, "Pacelli is the new pope!"

Now and then, we were allowed letters from home. I heard from my sister in Bad Gleichenberg that my first nephew — Josef — had been born on March 2. I wondered if I should ever see him. His good mother wrote to me regularly all through the long years of my imprisonment; when I did finally see Josef, he was already six.

3

Prison in Vienna

Fine quarters

I was soon to change my prison quarters again and so come to cell number 44, which I shared with another priest, Msgr. Josef Enzmann. There I was to spend the spring and early summer of 1939. We learned that the notorious Pruscha murderers had been confined in cell number 44 for nineteen months — until their execution. The inmates of the cells next door were constantly changing, and most of them ended on the gallows. This presented no problem for the prison authorities, for the hangman was resident in the jail itself and was thus available at all hours of the day and night.... We had all sorts of criminals as neighbors — murderers, thieves, and firebrands, what the Nazis were fond of describing as "the scum of society" — and we knew that, in their eyes, we priests ranked no higher.

If I had only known then what awaited me in Dachau, I should have viewed with different eyes my imprisonment in the Vienna jail. I should have been perfectly reconciled, even content. But that is the way of life, for only when we have endured real hardship can we learn to accept the difficult things of life in the right spirit. As it was, I longed desperately for freedom, chafing impatiently at the inactive life I was forced to lead in the dirty little cell where never as much as a ray of sunlight penetrated through the small barred window. But although I would have given anything to be free again and able to devote all my energies to my priestly work in the world, there was always the consolation of prayer and meditation. In this, Msgr. Enzmann was a wonderful comrade and spiritual companion. We began each day together with St. Ignatius's wonderful Suscipe,

21

Christ in Dachau

Domine (Accept, O Lord, my whole freedom …), and before we lay down at night, we would sing the Te Deum in Gregorian chant. We read and prayed together, and we worked on the draft of a plan intended to be developed later for the Catholic youth of Austria. We had to burn such papers afterward, of course, for we never knew when we might be surprised by the Gestapo. Now and again, a friendly warder would allow us to slip in and visit one of the neighboring cells. This not only served to break the monotony of those grey prison days, but, above all, it gave us a chance to help some of the unfortunate prisoners in the condemned cells to make their peace with their Creator. Looking back, it seems to me that, if for no other reason, our detention in prison was worthwhile simply for this. Perhaps some of these men would never have found their way back to Our Lord if they had not had to die in this way. The realization that their end was near made them begin to think about God, perhaps for the first time in their lives. They began to see the seriousness of their crimes in the light of Christ's teachings and to acknowledge their guilt in sincere repentance. We priests were near at hand to hear their confessions and to give them what help we could in their last hours. God's ways are often strange indeed! The death sentence — in the eyes of the world, the greatest misfortune and degradation — was often the greatest happiness on earth for these men, since it brought salvation for their immortal souls.

When war broke out in September, our prison rations were suddenly and drastically reduced. During the summer, prisoners had chucked whole loaves of bread into the courtyard for want of something better to do. Now we found ourselves hungry, really hungry. The prisoners began a hunger demonstration. "Hunger! Hunger! Hunger!" came the organized chant from all sides of the building. But the protest met with little response from the authorities. Our prospects for the future looked grim indeed.

Many of the prison inmates were genuine criminals, really tough gangster types or men who had got into bad company and had been led into committing crimes of every kind. But the state had changed its character since the Anschluss of March 1938, and there were also many among us who could not be numbered among them. The new "Father State" was merciless and unpredictable, more like a beast of prey than an institution to protect human rights, and for many, their detention behind bars — or the death penalty — was a cruel travesty of justice. Yet there was nothing any of us could do to alter his situation. Many of these "political" prisoners were simple workmen, typical Viennese with the quick wit and rather sly but devastating humor that is their birthright. They were fond of composing little ditties in broad Viennese to the tune of some popular song, and these would often resound across the courtyard to be met with the loud laughter of the other prisoners. Most of them met their end on the gallows.

On April 10, I was moved again to share a cell with another priest and good friend, Fr. Anton Pauk, C.Ss.R. Fr. Pauk was a prolific writer and had gotten into trouble with the Nazis over one of his poems. He was later sentenced to eighteen months. All through the hungry years in Dachau, Fr. Pauk kept me supplied, when possible, with parcels of bread through an old retired schoolteacher in Vienna who was a mutual friend.

The nights brought me the freedom I longed for, for in my dreams, I forgot the hardship of the prison life. Sometimes I would dream that I was back in the lovely church in the Lavant Valley where I had so often said Mass, or I would find myself at the altar of the church of St. Peter Canisius in Vienna. Often I would be surrounded by the countless small boys and girls whom I had prepared for their First Communion. My nights were transformed into a joy that sustained me through the long, dreary days. Above all, prayer was my greatest solace. All my life, my heart has gone out to those who cannot pray. I have witnessed so many terrible scenes, both in prison and in the concentration camps, of men and women driven to spiritual despair because they had not yet discovered the solace of prayer in their hour of need. It was a help, too, to know that I was not alone. There were many others who shared my fate, citizens of the true Austria whose faith and convictions were not to the taste of the new regime.

Visitors

Now and then, we were allowed to have visitors. Even today, I look back on these brief visits with a strange mixture of pleasure and pain.

The sound of the warder's footsteps and the clatter of his great bunch of keys as he unlocked the door at some unaccustomed hour never failed to send a shiver down our spines. After all, we never knew just what such an unexpected visit from the warder might portend. Our hearts would begin to beat furiously.

Christ in Dachau

"Lenz is wanted below," the warder would say, indicating the door with his thumb.

I would follow him in silence. Maybe the Gestapo wanted to see me; maybe the prison governor wanted to see me; perhaps he had orders for my release; or maybe ... But usually the summons meant that there was a visitor for me.

Visiting days were, by and large, a communal affair. On such occasions, we would be assembled from our various cells and marched across the courtyard under close guard on both sides. We would try to collect our thoughts and do what we could to improve our appearance, tidying our disheveled hair as best we could and smoothing out our crumpled prison clothes. There was inevitably something of importance to tell or to ask our friends or relatives on such occasions, and we had to take care to find just the right moment when we would not be overheard.

We would be hustled into a small room where we sat silently, each preoccupied with his own personal problems, waiting for the precious five minutes. We had no idea who would be there, how they would look, what news they would bring. The atmosphere in the room was charged with nervous tension.

We were marched in two by two. Warders and prison officials watched every movement of our eyes, our mouths, our hands. A high iron grille divided the room into two. We stood there behind it like caged animals, our eyes searching frantically for the face we had waited to see — until we found it.

Never shall I forget the day my father came to see his priest son in prison. It had been hard enough for him when I had left home to obey God's call to the priesthood. He had certainly never dreamed then that he would come to visit me in jail. His eyes met mine in pleasure and pain. In vain I tried to reach for his old, toil-worn hands through the bars of the grille. He tried to speak, but all he could do was weep bitterly, the tears coursing down the furrows of his weathered countryman's face.

All kinds of people came to see me in prison: relations, friends, fellow priests, members of my flock. I shall never forget their kindness — and their prayers.

People's Court?

"So I am to be judged by a People's Court," I wrote on February 22, 1939, in a letter addressed to "my Judges." "I could ask for nothing better. But choose the people whose priest, teacher, pastor, and writer I once was.... Let these be my judges! I am not alone here. High officials of the old regime, men like Hanisch and Kalossa and Msgr. Enzmann are here in prison with me. If these are the criminals of the new state, then I can only say that it is a crime to be a "decent" citizen and not to be, or have been, in prison!"

It was a dangerous letter, and I knew it. I followed it up with another in the same tone at the beginning of June. As a result, I was formally accused under § 76: The Use of Threats against the Law. But I had already served the maximum sentence for such offenses many times over anyway, and in any case, it was canceled by Hitler's amnesty of September 1, 1939.

At last, a "three-judge senate" met on December 11, 1939, to consider my case. The public was not admitted to the courtroom. My letters were read out loud. A verdict of not guilty was the result, a verdict that was later confirmed by the Supreme Court in Leipzig, on May 3, 1940.

On May 6, I found myself once again a free man after spending seventeen months in jail. The Gestapo apparently raised no objection. It seemed too good to be true.

I resolved to get out of this Hitler prison called Greater Germany, for I knew that my personal liberty, and above all my work as a priest, would be in constant jeopardy. I hoped to be able to slip over the frontier. I procured some civilian clothes, the grey homespun jacket and trousers worn by the peasants in the Austrian province of Styria.... It was in these that I finally arrived in Dachau.

I was arrested again on May 18, and on May 20 I learned that my fears were confirmed. From May 20 to July 6, they kept me in the cells of the Gestapo headquarters in the Hotel Metropole, after which I was sent once more to the Rossauer Lände until August 9. On July 19, I had to sign the second warrant for my "protective arrest."

Not forgotten

Once again, my friends rallied around, and from quite unexpected quarters I received food parcels, writing materials, and even flowers. Above all, I was assured of their prayers.

The feeling that I was not forgotten by all these good people was a great source of moral strength. The months I had already spent in prison, the uncertainty and nervous tension, and finally the shock of rearrest after ten days of illusory freedom —all had taken a toll on my patience and inner equilibrium. At the same time, however, I had never ceased to pray that God would accept these trials in His grace and use them in His own way to lead some of those who had strayed back to Him and His eternal truths.

Book 2

Dachau: The Way of the Cross

Take, O Lord, and receive all my liberty, my memory, my understanding, and all my will, whatever I have and possess. Thou hast given all these things to me—to Thee, O Lord, I restore them: all are thine, dispose of them all according to Thy will. Give me Thy love and Thy grace, for this is enough for me.

— St. Ignatius of Loyola

4

The Beginning

The journey

Never shall I forget that night in the transport cell. They had herded sixty-nine of us into this dirty little room big enough for three at most. We were plagued by lice, and the stench was indescribable. Bugs crawled in swarms over the filthy walls. Early next morning, we were marched off to the station, where we were received by SS guards, their weapons at the ready.

It was August 9, 1940, the day I was sent to Dachau on one of those prisoner transports to the concentration camps that were to become notorious in Hitler's Third Reich. The procedure was always much the same, as is borne out by the accounts of others. Cattle trucks were not always used, and on this occasion, the SS had commandeered ordinary austere passenger carriages for their "specials." The following account of just such a journey is given by Col. Walter Adam, who also spent many years in Dachau and died in 1947:

> No sooner were the carriages full and the roll call taken than patrols of SS noncommissioned officers would appear on the scene. The prisoners were made to stand up in turn and answer to their names and other particulars. This was accompanied by the usual flow of abusive language and often by brutal blows and other degrading treatment. We were made to sit in alphabetical order, our backs straight as boards, our hands laid flat on our knees, and our eyes fixed on the glaring electric bulb in the ceiling. Outside each compartment, an SS guard kept watch with loaded rifle. These guards passed the time on this seemingly endless journey by

hitting us over the head, boxing our ears, kicking us around, and dealing us vicious blows with the butts of their rifles. They were particularly hard on the unfortunate Jews from Vienna, forcing them to do "deep knee bends" and then prodding them mercilessly in the buttocks with their bayonets. Another cruel trick was to order them to open one of the windows and then accuse them of trying to escape, an offense punishable by shooting on the spot. We were soon to learn the methods by which they set out systematically to break every vestige of free will. We were fortunate indeed if we arrived at the camp with no more than broken teeth and bleeding lips.

In his book *1000 Days*, Erwin Gostner describes a journey to Dachau toward the end of April 1938. Here Georg Schelling, a priest who was later to become an outstanding personality in the priests' community in the concentration camp, was subjected to typical abusive treatment by the SS guard. "You black swine!" the man swore at him. "I'd like to know how many of your so-called housekeepers you've —" Then he punched him in the face with his fist. The priest submitted to the blow without a word, only raising his hand to wipe the blood from his lips. This served only to infuriate the guard still more.

Many priests had similar experiences on these prisoner transports. More than once, I myself thought death was imminent. I was quite prepared for anything. Above all, I had no illusions about our reception at Dachau. Dachau! The name already stank, and I knew I had small chance of coming out alive. I made a firm act of faith and placed my destiny in the hands of the Almighty. "Thy will be done!" I knew that, apart from anything else, this was the only way to achieve peace of mind.

It was afternoon by the time we arrived in Munich. Through the window I chanced to see a friend of mine, Fr. Toni Kling, standing on the platform. The window of my compartment was tightly shut, but I shouted "Dachau!" at the top of my voice. That, as I learned in 1945, was how the Jesuits came to know of my whereabouts. Otherwise, I should certainly have been "missing" for months. My shout brought the SS guard rushing in. "Shut your trap, you cur! You priest!" he snarled.

Then we were chained in pairs and driven at bayonet point to the waiting police vans.

After a suffocatingly hot drive, our reception at Dachau was ominous. SS men came at us from all sides, jeering and abusive, kicking and striking us. Word soon spread that I was a priest, for one of the guards had seen me reading my breviary in the train. I did not deny it — I never did, even in moments of the greatest peril. It was the office of the Curé d'Ars I had been reading, and then I had started that of St. Lawrence, Martyr. I knew I was about to face a martyr-dom myself. Would I bear it holily? When would it end, and how? "Lord, Thy will be done!"

"Welcome to Dachau!"

The routine reception procedure now began. First the photograph room. We were lucky here, for there were no SS men around. Other new arrivals were often less fortunate. An "old Dachauer," H. Ferber, describes a typical recep-tion: "The SS guards in the passage set upon us, ruffling our hair, pulling our ties crooked and doing everything possible to make us look like the thugs, the scum of humanity, we were supposed to be."

After they had taken our pictures, we were marched across into the Jourhaus through the great gates with their ironic inscription *Arbeit macht frei!* — Work brings freedom! Here we were stripped of all our clothing and possessions and herded stark naked to the barber, who soon made short work of our hair and of our beards, if any. A quick shower followed, after which the "zebra" prison-camp uniform and the regulation wooden clogs were flung at us. We pulled on the clothing hastily, tentatively trying out the unaccustomed footwear. It was some time before we could bring ourselves to raise our eyes and look at one another. Our glances were almost furtive, and it was hard not to catch one's breath in horror at what met one's eyes. There was a terrible finality about that moment. Our fate had been sealed. We were to look like that for a long time. It was as though these new clothes — convict clothes flung at us so brutally — signified the new "naked" existence that had begun for us, an existence in which everything private, everything individual, was verboten. I was filled then with an indescribable pain, a searing pain that reached to the very depths of my soul....

At long last, the humiliating preliminaries were over. As number 14233, I was marched across with other new arrivals to the camp proper. Block 26 was reserved for new prisoners. There were literally thousands of men there already, each of whom had, like me, been reduced to a mere number. The individual had disappeared. I was later to learn that it was better that way, that absolute conformity was something extremely important in this place. "Never try to be different from the others" sums up the first law for self-preservation in a concentration camp.

A wonderfully warm feeling of consolation came over me at the sight of all these other men. I was not alone: there were other human beings with me here, sharing my plight. And although we were watched all the time, always at the mercy of our guards, we were, at the same time, always under the eye of Providence. The words of the Our Father had never before had such meaning for me. What greater security can we have, after all, than complete reliance on God's providence, on the protection of God, who forsakes none of His creatures in time of need or danger?

The elite of Austria

It did not take me long to discover that I was in distinguished company here. My fellow prisoners were truly fine men, despite their convict's clothing, men who had refused to deny their religious convictions — martyrs for Poland; martyrs, too, for Germany. I found many Austrians, leading Catholics who had played significant roles in the political life of our country, and I was soon to learn that this little group of Catholics had already developed into an active center of spiritual power in the life of the camp. Austria had been the first victim of National Socialist foreign policy in 1938, and it was the Catholic statesmen who remained at their posts up to the end who were the first victims of the concentration camps of the godless dictator. It was these men who personified the best of the real Catholic Austria, who laid the foundation for us priests in the strange and complex world of the camp. There was a strong antireligious element in the camp, and the real atheists and toughs were naturally prejudiced against the priests from the start. But these men, through their personal example, through their fearless daily manifestation of their faith, through their good humor and their Christian charity, paved the way for us among the other prisoners. It was they who really broke the wave of active hatred against us, saving us from countless perils, plots, and traps, protecting us, helping us as best they could in times of hunger or sickness. I was to see all this later for myself.

Hitler lost no time in arresting Austria's leaders. Shortly after the Anschluss, on April 2, 1938, the first batch of political prisoners arrived at Dachau, a batch that included 165 senior officials and leading figures in the public life of Vienna. A second batch followed on May 22 with almost as many. Of a third batch that arrived in June, six were dead on arrival, shot by their guards on the journey.

And so it went on.

Austria's martyrdom had begun, a martyrdom that was to go on for years. The great majority of the prisoners of these early batches did not live to see the day of liberation. Many left the camps as physical wrecks. But thank God we can still say with satisfaction that there were nevertheless some who could not be conquered either by spiritual or by physical hardship, and these are the men who are once more at the helm of our new, liberated Austria.[4]

Among the prominent figures in Austria's public life who were interned in Dachau were: Leopold Figl, Dr. Fritz Bock, Dr. Gerö, Dr. Alfons Gorbach, Dr. Felix Hurdes, and Dr. Ferdinand Graf. The former chancellor, Dr. Kurt von Schuschnigg, was sent to Sachsenhausen. The postwar chancellor, Leopold Figl, was interned in Dachau until September 1943. I often used to take an evening stroll with him down the broad road running through the camp. This kindly man, with his never-failing sense of humor, helped many of his fellow prisoners in the bitterness and monotony of prison life.

The camp

Dachau concentration camp — Konzentrationslager Dachau, or KLD. The initials were everywhere, stamped on the clothing, branded on the tools, and painted on the vehicles. I think they must be branded on the very souls of all Dachau prisoners: KLD.

The Nazis had three types of concentration camp: labor camps, such as Dachau; hard-labor camps, such as Buchenwald; and extermination camps, or

[4] *Kleines Volksblatt*, March 1946.

Christ in Dachau

"bone mills," as they were known to the prisoners, such as Auschwitz, Natzweiler, and others. This book gives a picture of what the "mildest" form was like.

Dachau itself is a romantic old town with a population today of some twenty-five thousand. Half an hour's walk to the southeast is the east gate of the camp, and from there, the "SS Road" leads to the Eikeplatz. During the First World War, there had been a large munitions factory on the site, but when it was demolished in 1919 after the Treaty of Versailles, several of the buildings and huts where the workers had lived had been left standing, and it was these that formed the core of the notorious concentration camp.

The actual work on the construction of the camp began in 1933 and was officially finished on August 15, 1938. By the end of 1933, there were already some 5,000 Germans in Dachau, out of a total of more than 150,000 in camps spread over the whole of Germany. As the late Col. Walter Adam comments significantly, "These carefully planned horror camps, organized with typical German thoroughness, were set up by the NSDAP as a 'contribution to peace.'"

The new town that was Dachau concentration camp — KLD — was divided into three main parts: the prison camp itself, the headquarters and administrative area, and the SS quarters, the last-named a little world of its own. The SS were divided into the Totenkopf, or "Death's Head," SS and the regular SS troops who served with the army. Their quarters in Dachau were modern and equipped with the most up-to-date fittings. The sick bay and punishment-squad quarters were also in this section of the camp.

Behind the kitchens, washrooms, and laundry (a building that might just as well not have existed, as far as the prisoners were concerned) stretched the dreaded "bunker," with its long row of isolation cells used for solitary confinement on the commandant's orders. The east side of our camp was bounded by the plantation and the west side by this SS compound. This section, reserved for Hitler's elite, contained playing fields, a swimming pool, a fishpond, parkland, and a modern hospital, as well as indoor recreation facilities. The whole was bounded on the south by the SS Road, with attractive villas surrounded by flower gardens and the riding school. We were to see this all for ourselves five years later, when the roles of prisoners and guards were exchanged; from July 1945, some twenty thousand SS prisoners were confined in our old quarters, and we were transferred to the SS compound. In September 1945, the SS Road was appropriately renamed the Way of the Cross.

"Work brings freedom!" declared the inscription over the gate, flanked by the SS Death's Head. Dante's words would have been more appropriate: "Abandon hope, all ye who enter here!"

The Nazi authorities spent money enough on the camp, employing the slave labor of the prisoners to carry out their improvements. In this way, a new housing area was built for married SS men and their families, as well as a china factory, a munitions factory, a shooting range, and a large camp arsenal. Later, we were to come to garages, workshops, magazines . . .

Our actual prison compound was rectangular, about six hundred yards long by three hundred yards wide, bounded on all sides by a high wall, an electrified barbed-wire fence, and a moat. Around the perimeter were seven brick watchtowers, several stories high, with heavy machine guns that were trained on the compound. We were often to hear their sinister rattle, especially at night.

The gate of the Jourhaus was the entrance to the concentration camp. The exit? For many thousands, if not tens of thousands, the "chimney" — the crematorium — was the way out.

Inside the gate came the great concrete expanse of parade ground where the prisoners were assembled for roll call. Sixty thousand men could be lined up there. On the right were the clothing depots and workshops. In the center rose the great block of prisoners' kitchens flanked by the laundry and washrooms. On the left were the thirty huts, known in the camp as "blocks," which were the prisoners' quarters.

The huts, about 270 feet long by 30 feet wide, were divided into four rooms and a washroom with lavatories. A broad road lined by young poplars ran through the camp, dividing these rows of huts. On the left were numbers 2 through 30, housing the worker prisoners; numbers 1 through 29, opposite, were for invalids and those unfit for work.

The Punishment Squad

I was assigned to Block 26 — the hut that, six months later, was to be our chapel in Dachau! But on that August afternoon, I could not guess how often I would enter this block later. I found many kindly faces among the inmates, including the

Christ in Dachau

former Austrian vice-chancellor Richard Schmitz from Vienna, who gave me some helpful and practical advice while he set about sewing on my prisoner's numbers and the red patch indicating political prisoners. Hardly had he finished, however, when the door burst open and an SS guard appeared. My name was rapped out sharply. My heart began to race. The beginning, I thought ruefully, had been too good to last. As yet, I had seen only one side of Dachau: I was soon to see another and very different side. I was told to report at once to the commander of the punishment squad. Every priest who was sent to Dachau from 1938 to 1940 was automatically assigned to the punishment squad. Why should I be an exception? Schmitz smiled at me encouragingly and pressed my hand in commiseration. I had no idea what awaited me, but as I followed the guard out of the hut, I resolved to meet it with courage. Once again, I prayed fervently, "Thy will be done!"

Across in the punishment block — Block 17 — I found several prominent Catholic laymen and a large group of priests, including Fr. Fritz Seitz, the first German priest to wear the concentration camp prison uniform. There were priests from all over Austria and many more from Poland. There were a great many Jews, too, as well as gypsies and members of various biblical sects — a motley crew, but harmless enough. There were, however, others: Kü, a really tough gangster type serving a life sentence; a rabid communist who had fought for the Reds in the Spanish Civil War; an ex–Foreign Legionary . . . The proportion of real criminals was high, and it was these men, perhaps even more than our SS guards, who were to make our life a hell. Most of the prisoners in the punishment squad were serving a twelve-month sentence, but the Jews had been given hard labor for life.

A world without God

We sixty-nine new arrivals were ordered to report the following morning, Sunday, August 10, 1940, to the commander of the punishment squad. He was from Saxony and had been a baker in civil life. Not only was he a hardened atheist with a bitter hatred of priests, but he was also a sadist into the bargain. He stood there, undersized and poorly built, taking stock of us with his mean little eyes. His opening words made our position in his squad quite clear.

"You scum!" he spat at us. "You pack of outcasts from the German community!"

A perfunctory examination by the camp doctor followed. It was here that I first saw Dr. K., of the sick bay, and his crony, the head nursing orderly. I could see what sort of a pair they were and was filled with a grim sense of foreboding.

I was beginning to get some idea of the organization of the camp by now. From other prisoners I learned about the functions of the "capos." "Capo" was the camp name for foreman or overseer. The word was printed in black on the yellow armband proudly worn by these functionaries, who were themselves prisoners but had special duties and privileges. These and the so-called block personnel were, in fact, our real masters in the camp. Fellow prisoners, they were, for the most part, willing tools of the SS, who used them to do their dirty work for them. We were completely at their mercy, for they were the lords of life and death as far as we were concerned. Various privileges were attached to their office — above all, that of better food. For this reason, many of them were utterly ruthless, prepared to resort to murder if need be in order to retain their position or get a certificate of good conduct on discharge. There was no limit to which they would not go in their godless, self-seeking practices.

The notorious Capo Christl, senior prisoner of the Jews' block, was a typical exponent of such cold-blooded egoism. The previous Christmas Eve, he had complained of being hungry and asked for permission to speak to the commander of the punishment squad.

"I killed off my ninety-seventh Jew yesterday," he announced proudly in the presence of several others. "Tomorrow I promise to bring it up to a hundred. When can I come and get myself something to eat?"

Those were our bosses, the lords of Dachau concentration camp!

It was Sunday, but there was nothing in this place to remind us of the fact, for God had been banished. Only in the souls of those who stayed faithful to Him through hardship, suffering, and disillusionment did God still remain, in secret. And so in our hearts, we cherished God in sacred loyalty — in the face of Satan and his followers. A world without God must, of necessity, become a hell on earth. But God's justice is still there — and His merciful love. Dachau taught us a great deal, and it taught us quickly. In a very short time, one acquired a spiritual maturity that it would have taken years of hard-won experience to attain in the everyday world. We learned an inner composure, never to be shocked or surprised by anything anymore. It was a hard school, but it taught us a worthwhile lesson. We learned how to hold on to God.

On our way to report to Commandant Z., I noticed a Jew of about thirty years of age who could scarcely drag himself along. He had been subjected that morning to "special treatment" in the gravel pit. The unfortunate man happened to have a rather ugly face und to wear thick-lensed glasses. This had been enough to arouse the wrath of the capo of his group, who had played a despicable game with his helpless victim. They had beaten him up and then covered him with wood shavings and set fire to him. They had not killed him, merely subjected him, body and soul, to the lowest human degradation. The man was a pitiful sight, his hair and eyebrows singed and his face quite black. His body was covered with burns. Worst of all, it must have been clear to him that this cruel game at his expense was only a prelude to his certain murder later on.

He was limping after us with the utmost difficulty, obviously barely able to stand, and I knew that for this very reason, he was in immediate danger of being shot by the SS guards. As it was, they were jeering at him and making fun of his obvious terror. I broke out of the ranks and, running back to him, grasped him firmly under the arms and half-dragged him along with me. The episode could well have ended badly for both of us. I sent up a fervent prayer to the Almighty. I still do not know how we managed to get away with it. But God was there.

We were working in the gravel pit next afternoon when a Jew crawled over to me. He was barely able to stand, but his SS bear-baiters had let him go, having satisfied their sadism for the time being. His face was deathly pale, and he had a great wound in his forehead. He must have been about fifty and had been a singer in a cabaret in Vienna. It was easy to judge from his appearance what sort of life he had led, a perpetual round of pleasure and good living. He had certainly known many good days in the past, but he had never found time for God; he had passed by His mercy and never sought His love. Now he was one of the Nazis' countless victims. For all his worldliness and insensibility, he realized well enough that he was as good as a dead man, yet I could see that in no way was he prepared to face death. I did what I could for him, imploring him to think of the life to come, to consider what his life had been and to seek God's forgiveness and mercy. The man was so sunk in his own misery that nothing I said had any effect. What was more, he had so long been preoccupied with entirely material things that he was completely insensible to spiritual truths. Although my task was made all the more difficult by the presence of the capos and the SS guards, the situation of the unfortunate man half-prostrate beside me and literally in the shadow of death gave my priest's conscience no peace.

But there was still nothing I could say or do to induce him to change his way of thinking. He simply lay there on the gravel before me, a heap of misery without a trace of human dignity, complaining of his misfortune as loudly as he dared. I begged him to consider what could await him after death, but he did not seem in the least concerned. All his life he had lived softly, concerned with nothing but sensual pleasures, and he had long since given up even the pretense of self-respect. Now he was in the hands of other godless men, men who could hardly be called human, who had even less appreciation of true human dignity.

A dangerous situation

August 11, 1940. Midday and glorious Sunday weather. We were working in the gravel pit reserved for the punishment squad. Death was never far away.

We sixty-nine new prisoners had been handed over to Capo J., a short, thickset man with a pair of menacing eyes.

"I'm your capo," he announced by way of introduction. "I may as well tell you from the start that I was human once, but I've been turned into a brute by all I've seen here. Who knows, I might turn human again if you work properly for me! And now, get on with it; don't waste any more time."

We set to work with wheelbarrows of earth and gravel. I was lucky enough at first to find a place some distance from the capo. Once, however, I had the misfortune to pass the under-capo, who recognized me at once as having been the only priest in the last batch from Vienna.

"Hey, you priest, come here!" He filled an enormous wheelbarrow with gravel for me to carry across to the dump. I was totally unfit for heavy work like this. I wondered how it was to end. Very soon, great blisters began to appear on the palms of my hands, but the man still drove me on, kicking me viciously from behind all the time. He forced me to run up the gravel hill with a full load and would then push me over the side at the steepest point, so that I fell and rolled down some eighteen feet, together with my load of gravel. This he did several times, running after me like an evil spirit in pursuit of his victim.

My hands were bleeding, and I was completely out of breath. I was bathed in sweat. I could feel my strength ebbing fast, but still my tormentor did not relent. Driven to the point of exhaustion, I cried out, "You don't have to drive me; I'm working as hard as I can!"

The man looked at me with his terrible eyes, his face dark. "Don't you realize, you miserable priest, that it's your turn to die like a dog today?"

I resigned myself to the inevitable and bent down to take up my wheelbarrow again. My arms had no strength anymore, and I could no longer see the five wounds in my hands through the mist of sweat and tears. I simply went on working — working for my life. Never before had I summoned the last reserves of strength like this. But never before was the image of Christ Crucified so alive in my soul. Never before was His Passion so real to me as in that moment.

The nightmare scene in the gravel pit was indescribable. Everywhere roamed the SS men, goading, abusing, and jeering; the nearer they came, the more frenzied grew the capos. Between the brutality of the SS and the bestiality of the capos, the prisoners had a thin time of it. "The heart of the godless knows no compassion." But deliverance was at hand. It was Sunday, and work stopped at five. I could have jumped for joy when the whistle blew. *Deo gratias!* sang my heart a thousand times over as we were marched back to camp. I was as happy as a child. I had been saved. By six o'clock, it would have been too late.

The good capos

In all fairness and justice, I feel I must make it clear here that not all capos were murderers. Had this been the case, scarcely anyone would have come out alive. Nor would it have been right to take every coarse remark, every form of verbal abuse and severity, at its face value.

"Capo Pospisil saved my life," one priest declared afterward. Another priest told me how this capo, a prisoner from Vienna, had somehow managed to smuggle in for the sick, at considerable risk, fresh vegetables from the garden. He would often volunteer to work on Sunday, for in this way, he could procure pig swill for the hungry priests and Jews in the punishment block.

Later on, as capo of the working squad known as the "Bog Express II," he organized all kinds of services for his unfortunate fellow prisoners, ranging from coal, food, and medical supplies to the organization of a news system. It was he who was responsible for the deliveries of sugar that reached the infirmary a couple of times during the typhus epidemic, fifty-liter pails of it camouflaged on top by a layer of ersatz coffee. The underground "resistance committee" received news and newspapers. Polish priests received the forbidden parcels of altar wine and altar bread from the rectory in Dachau town.

Capo Pospisil was not the only good capo, but he warrants special mention all the same, for there were not a great many like him. Today, every ex-capo is anxious to appear in a good light — they were all "the best of comrades." There are many, however, who can be thankful that they are alive at all and that they have not landed in jail. Justice has not yet caught up with them in this world. Only the voice of their own consciences can reach their Judas souls or remind them of Cain, who slew his brother.

The Austrian capos were especially known for their humanity. There may have been bad ones among them, it is true, but these were real exceptions. This fact must be stated in all truth and honesty and justice. "The Austrian capos stuck together better. They did not abuse their fellow prisoners but did all they could to protect them against the others" (Adam).

The camp plantation had already been laid out in 1938–1939 and covered some 160 acres. For the cultivation of this land, the workers were divided into several "commandos" under twelve capos (with armbands) and twenty-five under-capos (without). The maximum number of workers (1940–1945) was about 1,300 in summer and 400 in winter. The plantation obviously provided the prisoners with the widest and most varied field of activity.

In June 1938, the plantation was already an "Austrian colony." In April of that year, the first plans for it had been drawn up by Dr. Emmerich Zederbauer, a former rector of the University of Vienna. This eminent prisoner impressed even the SS authorities by his quiet, scholarly manner and an astonishing fund of knowledge. The professor saw to it that as many of his fellow Austrians as possible were detailed for work on the plantation.

Work on the plantation had already taken a heavy toll on the prisoners. The work of draining the swamp, carried out, for the most part, by Jews, had cost many of them their lives. The terrible Capo Christl had succeeded in winning the fierce battle for the post of senior capo against his rival Michatsch, but by the spring of 1939, he had been replaced by the Austrian capo Sprung.

Sprung, a Viennese, took care that as many of his compatriots as possible got the responsible jobs, and from then on, there were no further instances of murder on the plantation, and no reports of bad conduct calling for severe disciplinary action ever reached the SS authorities. It even proved possible to "buy" the SS men — after all, they needed vegetables for their families.

"On March 12, 1940, I took over the plantation," writes Hans Gaster from the Austrian province of Styria. "With the assistance of Dr. Egon Hilbert, who indeed must take credit for most of the work, I succeeded in achieving at least tolerable working conditions. During the five years remaining until the end of the war, we were fortunate in being able to save several hundred of our fellow prisoners from being sent off on transports by hiding them in our working commando on the plantation. Needless to say, this often involved us in the greatest difficulties and exposed us to grave personal dangers."

Not every prisoner in a privileged position in the camp was necessarily a favorite with the SS authorities, and many of these good capos trembled more in their shoes than we ordinary prisoners when the SS officers arrived unexpectedly on a tour of inspection. Woe betide him then if his block, his quarters, or his clerical work were not in apple-pie order. The crueler his SS chiefs were, the more difficult it was for him to get out of the situation without using us as scapegoats. That was just the way things were. But he could still remain a good comrade for all that, and it was not difficult to tell which of the capos were loyal to us at heart and which of them were simply willing tools of the criminal SS overlords. There were good capos and bad capos in Dachau, just as there were in any other concentration camp. For the bad capo, things were easy, for as the unofficial hangman of his fellow prisoners, he enjoyed the favor of the SS. Life was much more difficult for the good and loyal capo or the senior prisoner of a block, for they could keep their positions, hard-won to start with, only by sheer hard work and efficiency. The Nazis were no respecters of persons, still less of human dignity and truth.

The camp bosses

The "ruling class" among the prisoners themselves formed a sort of aristocracy, though they were mostly far from noble. Most of them were of low origin and were really mean characters, often with a streak of real brutishness. These were the camp bosses — the senior prisoner of each block, the oldest prisoner in the camp, the head capos, the labor capos, the block clerks, and all the other petty tyrants. These were the men with privileged positions.

We all had to kowtow to them, and woe betide us if we ever dared to assert our own rights. The charge of "mutiny" was punishable with the severest disciplinary measures, and there was no question of appeal or vindication.

There were various motives that prompted these low-minded men to aspire to such positions in the camp. Most of them got a brutal satisfaction out of being able to browbeat their fellows while toadying to the SS. Such jobs afforded the best possible outlet for the sadists or those whose thwarted complexes clamored for a chance to wield power, to strut about with a capo's yellow armband and a new uniform. Maybe some of the old Prussian military drill also played some part in forming the characters of these men.

"In spite of everything, these years of enforced proletarian existence were undoubtedly a most valuable experience — especially for us priests," writes Fr. Georg Schelling. It was interesting to note that the very men who, in normal life, would have loudly boasted of their proletarian origin now seized every opportunity here in the camp to lord it over the others. As soon as they had managed to climb even one step higher in the camp's social scale, they immediately became the "camp bosses"; and not only did they expect special deference to their rank, but they were also completely ruthless in the methods they used to retain it.

I often used to think of the truth of the old German proverb "The nobleman knows how to ride. But if the beggarman once gets into the saddle, then woe betide the horse!" The true character of these men was apparent at once, for unless they were truly noble at heart, they very soon sank to the level of the beasts and lost every trace of self-respect.

God's justice

"The worst of our block personnel and capos in Sachsenhausen are dead! They wanted to kill us — but we've come out alive!" These were the words of a priest friend of mine in 1941. He had been interned in Sachsenhausen up to the previous year and had only been saved by a miracle. One of his capos had taken his own life, another was killed by a bomb, a third had met his end in the dreaded "bunker." "The mills of God grind slowly."

One day, for instance, Capo H. had a stroke of bad luck. The man he had been about to kill off proved a less easy victim than he had anticipated and succeeded in taking refuge in the sick bay. He had already lost one eye. An SS doctor took pity on him and saw to it that H. — who already had a murder record — got eight years' hard labor.

It was always a dangerous thing for any prisoner to know too much about the SS crime machine; the privileged position of capos exposed them to just this danger. Equally if the outside world got to know of his own crimes … They could never be quite sure, these men.

Old S. suddenly fell foul of the SS authorities. No one knew why, but all at once, he was very much out of favor. The green patch for criminals replaced his red one, and he was packed off to Mauthausen. In the quarry there, a gypsy "accidentally" dropped a heavy block of stone on this mass murderer. "His body was laid beside those of his own victims of that same morning. We gave the gypsy a whole loaf of bread for having rid us of this monster" (E. Gostner).

Among the SS block commanders was one from Hamburg; he was known throughout the camp as the "blond beast." One day, as he was rummaging among the belongings of one of the priest prisoners, he found a card announcing the death in action of the priest's friend, who had been a Catholic army chaplain. "Another black dog dead" was his sole comment. Shortly afterward, he himself was sent to the front — and returned a cripple.

H., more usually known as "the killer of Dachau," used his riding boots on a priest and a few days later was thrown off while riding and broke his leg.

S., a prisoner who had more than once betrayed his comrades, denounced three priests to the camp commandant on a charge of "politicizing." The priests were severely punished, but their betrayer also got his due. He found himself in the "bunker" and got "twenty-five" — twice. Shortly after, he was sent to Mauthausen, where his fellow prisoners killed him.

Fr. Bettendorf was betrayed by the senior prisoner of his block for having two pullovers. This brought severe punishment. But the betrayer found himself in the "bunker" for forty-two days and twice "25." Later, he repented and was filled with remorse.

There are countless such stories, and not only in the camps — stories particularly of those who betrayed their priests only to end themselves later in prison or in a concentration camp.

A miraculous escape from death

August 12, 1940. Work started for us at 6:00 a.m., and we had to get up two hours before. I said a fervent prayer as I took my place in the column, but my heart was heavy as we were marched off to work. What was this day to bring? My experiences of the previous day were still only too vivid.

But to my surprise, the dreaded foreman left me in comparative peace. Fr. Mayr had intervened on my behalf. I was still put to work on the wheelbarrows, however, and the foreman took good care that they were always filled to capacity. All the time, the air was ringing with the sharp commands of the SS men.

I saw a young man in front of me desperately trying to keep his wheelbarrow from toppling over. It was obvious that his strength was almost exhausted. He was tall and slightly built, with a lean, intelligent face. He must have been about twenty, and I took him for a student. I could see that he was at breaking point. He turned and caught sight of me.

"I can't go on, Father," he panted. "I just can't! There's no hope for me, I tell you. I'm going to run into the lines. I just can't stand it anymore!"

Our working area was surrounded by a close line of SS. Anyone attempting to break through that line was shot on the spot. In two days, six men had met death that way, running in despair against the guns.

"For God's sake, don't do that!" I called to him softly. "Try to stick it out, at least the first day. After that it's easier. You'll see!"

"I can't go on," was all he could say. "I just can't!"

No one else had heard him.

It must have been about eight o'clock when an SS man who was our block commander and was responsible for the work detail caught sight of me. He flung me to the ground, for no other reason than that I was a priest, and began kicking me, jeering, and calling me names. I had to submit to all this in silence, but at least I could lie still for a few moments on the gravel and rest. But not for long. I soon had to get back to work with my wheelbarrow.

Before long, my strength began to ebb again. I paused for a second to look quickly at my hands: fifteen open wounds. If only my arms had not been so limp and helpless … The fear that this was to be my last hour summoned my last reserves of strength.

"O Jesus, how Your steps must have faltered too after the terrible scourging when You had to carry Your Cross! How heavy it must have been!"

I simply could not go on any farther. I had to rest after every second step. I was no longer capable of even setting down my heavy load; the wheelbarrow simply fell out of my hands. One of the SS men who had seen this happen came over and began to shout at me, "You swine! You cur! You priest! It's no good trying the 'go slow' policy here. Sabotage! You're just refusing to work, that's all. I'll soon teach you!" And he reached for his revolver.

"O Jesus, mercy! Mary, help! I can't go on!"

Suddenly, a shot rang out. Someone must have run into the sentry line, probably the young student, for I never saw him again. God have mercy on him. He was driven to this death by sheer desperation. Seven prisoners now within two days … The SS sentries found it fair game, but for us it was a terrible warning.

The shot fired at that very moment proved to be my salvation. The SS man left me standing there and hurried off in the direction of the shot, anxious not to miss anything. He had forgotten all about me in his anxiety to see who had been killed off this time. I was safe, at least for the moment.

Capo Kü came across to where I was working, and I decided to risk the consequences and show him my bleeding hands. He took me by the arm and led me into the control hut. Behind the desk sat the SS man who had been kicking me around only a few hours before. The capo showed him my hands. Without a word, he produced some iodine and quickly brushed it over my hands. As I winced with pain, he began to curse me, but finally he let me go and I was put on lighter work, raking and weeding in the garden.

"Fall out, Jews and priests!"

As we were lining up on the square for our midday meal, we found Commandant Z. waiting for us. He halted the column and ordered Jews and priests to fall out.

What could this mean? Jews and priests! Invariably we were coupled together, for in the eyes of the camp authorities, we were the scum, the cast-outs. Not until 1942 did the situation change in this respect. But in 1940, Jews and priests still personified the worst kinds of criminals in the eyes of these men who knew no God. To them, we were scum, and they viewed it as their duty to exterminate us as quickly and as unobtrusively as possible.

The machine guns on the watchtowers began to rattle ominously. The camp authorities deliberately organized this sinister rehearsal whenever the prisoners were assembled on the square for roll call. It was meant to terrify us. And it did terrify us. The deadly rattle was earsplitting now as Jews and priests obeyed the terse command. We fell out and waited, fully prepared. We knew that as long as we had the courage to stand true to God, we could count on His protection. "If God is with us, who can be against us?"

One thousand men were picked for a transport, Jews and priests — the scum of the camp. They were looking for stonemasons, too, which suggested that we were wanted for work in the quarries. Men from other blocks were brought across to join us. Word spread that we were to be sent to Mauthausen and Gusen.

That evening, we were herded into Block 19, the transport block, designed to accommodate 250, though we were four times that number. Here we were kept for three days, supposedly to give us a rest. It was not humanity that prompted this consideration, however, but rather the naïve hope that we might make a better impression on their Mauthausen colleagues as being fit for work in the hard-labor camp.

Morituri, vos salutamus! The comrades we left behind in Dachau said goodbye to us, convinced that they would never see us again.

The previous year, a similar transport had left Dachau for Mauthausen. "1,650 prisoners were sent to Mauthausen on September 26, 1939. By the end of January 1940, some 950 of these men had already died of hunger or cold or had been killed" (W. Ferber).

No doubt the camp authorities intended to send us to our death too, and their murderous plan very nearly succeeded.

For three long days, we sat in this overcrowded space, tormented by hunger, waiting for the transport.

Christ in Dachau

"Haven't you even a crust of bread for me, Father?" begged an old school-master from the Tyrol. He was weak to the point of collapse. It was a hopeless plea, and he knew it. None of us had anything whatever. We all shared the same helpless misery.

Among us was a young gypsy from South Tyrol who had a fine singing voice. He began to sing our lovely old folksongs, one after another. I shall never forget how we sat there in silence, our eyes fixed gratefully on the young singer. We had no way of repaying him for the strength and comfort he gave us.

At last, we got orders to start. I asked a Polish priest to hear my confession, for I wanted to prepare for death. And I made a solemn vow to Our Lady.

"Holy Mary," I prayed, "if you will help me this year out of my misery and imprisonment, I promise that my first journey shall be to your shrine at Mariazell."

Every year in autumn, I renewed this vow. I waited and prayed and hoped that Our Lady would hear me and that I would soon be free. But instead, she was to give me other and far more valuable proofs of her intercession: spiritual strength and courage to endure those hard years. God is indeed good.

5

Gusen

Prison transport to "Murderous Mauthausen"

August 16, 1940. A goods train bound for Mauthausen with one thousand men packed into cattle trucks. I shall never forget this journey. The doors were locked, of course, and there were no windows. It was forbidden, on penalty of immediate shooting, to open the tiny peephole. Two of the priests in our truck were suffering from diarrhea and had no way of getting out.

We had long since finished the packet of food they had given us to last the whole journey — so little that we might just as well have eaten nothing. Our hunger was intense. We sat there trying to find solace for our grim situation in silent prayer, placing our whole trust in the mercy of God. It was indeed a terrible journey, a journey that was to lead to death for many of us. It grew dark outside, and someone began to sing. We joined in, in a desperate attempt to keep up our spirits.

The journey seemed interminable, and our hunger increased. No one really knew where Mauthausen and Gusen were, so we had no idea of our whereabouts. At long last, the train came to a standstill and the doors were flung open. We had arrived at Mauthausen station.

A group of SS guards was waiting for us and herded us out of the train like cattle intended for the slaughterhouse. "Thy will be done!" I prayed again as we were goaded into a long column. I can still picture the terrible scene — one thousand prisoners surrounded on all sides by SS guards wildly gesticulating and unceasing in their vile abuse. They were heavily armed and equipped with bicycles and torches.

Christ in Dachau

Mauthausen — camp of terror and of horror. Today a great marble memorial pays tribute to "the 122,766 prisoners who were brutally murdered" there. Many thousands more were simply killed on arrival — there is no record of their names.

It must have been between ten and eleven at night when we arrived at Mauthausen, the dreaded forced-labor camp with its notorious quarry. My heart began to beat furiously as we were driven up the steep steps on the left of the high wall of the quarry. I counted 143 steps and wondered how many times that number of lives had been lost there. The steps were hewn out of the face of the rock and were extremely irregular and difficult to negotiate. At the top, they turned sharply to the right toward the camp gates. This was the point at which the unfortunate prisoners — God knows how many of them — were loaded with heavy stones and then driven down, very often to their death.

At one point, just above these stone steps, almost five thousand men were shot in cold blood during the course of three years. It was by no means exceptional for prisoners to be loaded with stones weighing two hundred pounds or more — a new and unique death sentence. It took four men to lay this burden on the shoulders of the victim.

As we were marched through the gates of the camp, another company of SS received us with the usual flow of vile language and the usual rough treatment. Some of the other prisoners told us later that they often set their dogs on new arrivals. I shall not easily forget that night in Mauthausen, a nightmare scene lit by the merciless glare of searchlights under a starless sky.

At long last, we were given some thin potato soup, which at least served to take the edge off our gnawing hunger. Then we lay down, utterly exhausted, packed side by side like sardines on the floor of an empty wooden hut. The room was far too small for us all. Early next morning, we were driven out onto the square for roll call. Five hundred were chosen to remain in Mauthausen; the remainder were to go to Gusen.

"Name?"

"Johann Lenz."

"Occupation?"

"Priest."

The SS man eyed me sharply. It had been my earnest prayer that I be sent to Gusen.

"You're no use to me," he snapped, passing on to the next prisoner. I suppose he thought I was not strong enough for the sort of work he wanted done. For me, my prayer had been answered.

My heart was full of gratitude to God. Little did I know then that, at that time, Gusen was even more terrible than Mauthausen. Gusen was nevertheless to be my salvation, for when the order came later from Dachau to transfer me to the punishment squad, Mauthausen would almost certainly have meant my death.

Worked to death

The camp at Gusen was actually a branch of Mauthausen. Work on this camp had been started in the winter of 1939–1940, first of all with the construction of the high walls and barbed-wire entanglements that formed the boundaries and then on the wooden huts for the prisoners.

This work had cost hundreds of lives, for the prisoners who were driven down from Mauthausen to work each morning very often returned in the evening on the point of death, if not already dead, from hunger, cold, and overwork. "Anyone who had the good fortune to survive that terrible winter must have been saved by a miracle of God!" That is what some of those who did survive told us afterward.

Stories of these horrors had even reached me in prison in Vienna. On December 3, 1939, the camp register recorded 3,120 prisoners at Mauthausen. On April 19, 1940, only 1,234 still survived. On a single day, as many as forty corpses had been brought back from the quarry. These unfortunates had spent the day in the hardest form of forced labor.

The situation was not very different in Gusen. Some 150 men were sent down from Mauthausen every morning — a march of one hour, and a quick march at that. Every evening, the dead and the dying would be collected and brought back to Mauthausen in a truck. They were simply tipped out inside the gates, the dead and the dying together in one heap of bodies. The horror of this place that they had to face anew every day inevitably soon robbed even normal human beings of every feeling. Each of the prisoners had more than enough to do to keep his own body and soul alive. Their main concern was to keep death at bay at all costs.

Christ in Dachau

A new ordeal begins

Gusen was not much more than a name to us at that time. We had heard that conditions there were primitive in the extreme, but we were still not prepared for what confronted us when we arrived there. All the way down, I had an SS man behind me who had derived the greatest pleasure from kicking me. He seemed to regard it as a sort of trial of strength. Tired and desperately hungry, we stood on the square at Gusen waiting for orders. It was the afternoon of August 17, 1940. We had had neither breakfast nor a midday meal, and now we were expected to work for four hours in the summer heat.

It was not long before the camp commandant appeared.

"Fall out, all priests!"

The old command again! I wondered what they could want with us this time. About fifty men fell out. We were prepared for the worst, but even so, fear struck at our hearts. But apparently, he only wanted to know how many of us there were.

In fact, no discrimination was made between priests and laity in this camp, at least as far as the authorities were concerned. Everyone was subjected to the same sort of ill-treatment. Nor was it forbidden to pray, to go to Confession, or to hear confessions. In this respect, things were very different from Dachau.

The number of prisoners at Gusen rose by August 1940 to seven thousand — twice the number registered at Mauthausen in that month.

In Gusen, as in Mauthausen, the "greens," as those with the criminal's green patch were called, were the bosses among the prisoners. Gusen was, after all, the concentration camp for criminals, and they were the firstcomers. They felt they had a privileged position over us others and sought every opportunity of enforcing this. They were lords of the camp, as we were to see before very long, for no sooner had we arrived than they surrounded us like a pack of hyenas. They forced us to hand over any money we had, together with stamps and valuables of all kinds. Robbed of all we had, we were then detailed to the various blocks. The senior prisoner of my block — and hence, my boss — openly boasted of twenty previous convictions. As he told us that evening, he had been doing a flourishing business before his arrest as the proprietor of a notorious brothel in Innsbruck.

Another of our prisoner bosses was a man called Martin. He laughingly told us that same evening of his experiences robbing churches. He found one incident especially entertaining. "I stuffed the chalice and the monstrance into my rucksack," he told us with a broad grin, "and the ciborium, after emptying it on the floor first, of course! It must have been around midnight when I was interrupted by the sacristan. 'What are you doing here?' he asked. I can tell you, those were his last words!" Theft, sacrilege, . . . and murder.

There were many such characters at Gusen. We "reds" — political prisoners with the red patch — were subjected to the most incredible treatment at their hands. The priests had a particularly hard time, for they used us in every way as doormats, and it was more than our lives were worth to offer any resistance. Murder meant nothing to these men. They had nothing more to fear.

No hope for the sick

For those who had the misfortune to fall ill, things were very hard indeed. There was virtually no one there to care for them; no one who wanted to help. If you were sick and managed to get admitted to the infirmary, you might possibly recover; if not, there was no other course but to go on working — and very likely die. Not that the infirmary was safe either. The prisoner orderly in charge of the diarrhea ward had openly stated that any priest admitted to his charge would come out a corpse. The man hated all priests as he hated God. It was small wonder that we avoided the diarrhea ward — but the cases of this sickness increased.

One of the victims was Fr. Marcell Leeb, a good and kindly man and a fine priest, from Carinthia. He suddenly developed the severest form of diarrhea and could retain nothing whatsoever. We had no change of underclothes, nothing but the thin camp rags under the striped prison uniform.

I nursed him as best I could, washing out his underwear in a hand basin, while the unfortunate priest lay there in his prison stripes on the lousy straw pallet. He was desperately ill, and I was quite sure that he was going to die. What if the underclothes did not dry overnight?

That night, a shot suddenly rang out in the darkness. I rightly guessed that one of the prisoners had in desperation tried to make a getaway. They had shot him on the spot. I began to shiver violently and crept further down under my dirty blanket. It was cold, for it was raining outside. Horror pictures of these last few days rose before my eyes like a sequence in some terrible film. It was almost more than I could bear.

Christ in Dachau

Helpless victims

In the morning, we had to report for work. I volunteered for stone carrying. Little did I know what this would mean. The stones were heavy, and we never knew when the terrible SS guards would appear. They might well have found the stones too small. It took us a full quarter of an hour to reach our destination each time. Not only were we weak from hunger, but we were without protection from the weather — be it hot or cold or pouring rain.

Worst of all, perhaps, we were never safe from the criminals. During the first few days, one of the so-called nursing orderlies from the sick bay came into our hut. He began to talk to Fr. L'Hoste, and when the latter happened to contradict him on some completely unimportant point, he struck him a savage blow above the heart. Father L'Hoste collapsed in agony on the spot and lay there gasping for breath, convinced that he was going to die. But the orderly simply left him there and strolled down the room, talking to other prisoners as if nothing whatever had happened.

In due course, I managed to change my job of carrying stones for work on another site, where things were made somewhat easier for us priests by a friendly capo. Although himself a pantheist and a convinced communist, the man had a fundamental respect for "intellectuals" — and we priests fortunately fell into this category. Some of the prisoners said he had been a murderer, but he was our unfailing friend and protector. This was another example of the inscrutable ways of God. In Dachau in the summer of 1940, we learned that he, too, had met a violent death.

But on the whole, the capos at Gusen were no better, if not worse, than the SS men themselves. Their power in the camp was virtually unlimited. For instance, a prisoner who had fallen into disfavor could be "recommended" to the capo in the quarry. This man's life was then in the foreman's hands; it was up to him to decide whether he would send him back alive or dead that evening. The man might have a wife and children waiting for him at home. This made no difference. His name would appear in due course on the casualty list as having been killed by a fellow prisoner.

The camp commandant

It is difficult to say whether the camp commandant was more to be feared when he was drunk or when he was sober.

We were regaled on arrival with the story of the "Polish massacre." This had taken place on August 13, only four days previously. The authorities took infinite pains to impress upon us the way things were done in Gusen.

It seems that the labor squad had reported as usual at midday and was formed up on the square. The commandant had then appeared and given the order for all Germans, above all the capos and block personnel, to set upon the Polish prisoners and beat them up.

Only a few days before that, an old Polish priest had been murdered. He had been suffering from severe diarrhea and had gone off to the latrine and had not returned in time. Perhaps he had collapsed from sheer weakness, or perhaps he had just forgotten the roll call. In any case, the capos and block personnel were sent out after him. They found him and beat him nearly to death. As a punishment, he was ordered to stand upright in the blazing sun for four hours. That was too much; he collapsed and died.

The "Polish massacre" must have been terrible indeed. Poles who had narrowly escaped death told us about it afterward. The German capos had special orders to go for the intellectuals — priests, doctors, and schoolteachers. Anyone who looked in any way intelligent or who wore glasses was virtually damned.

In this connection, several people advised me to stop wearing my glasses. "They'll only get you into trouble," they warned me. "They've a special grudge against all intellectuals." But I was quite unable to do without my glasses, and I am glad to say I was able to keep them all the years I was interned. They were knocked off, of course, on the numerous occasions when I got my ears boxed or my face slapped, but, thank God, they never got broken. It was vital to be able to see well in the camp, for with good eyesight, it was often possible to avoid a dangerous situation. I have often been asked how I managed to survive at all with glasses. I asked God's protection here too.

Our Polish comrades told us that when they were marched onto the square for the usual roll call that evening, they had found the place strewn with bodies. Thirty Poles had been killed outright, thirty had lost an arm, and another thirty were to die in the next few weeks. Among them was the Polish priest Msgr. Troska. His body was one mass of wounds and bruises.

Another "joke" of the commandant's was the surprise night inspection of the various blocks. It was reputed that he came only when drunk. He was invariably accompanied by a guard of several stalwart SS men armed with truncheons. He would appear suddenly and switch on the glaring electric light, whereupon we all had to spring out of bed, as we were, and stand to attention. Anyone who had the misfortune to be caught wearing underpants was doomed. It was strictly forbidden to wear them at night and failure to comply with this regulation was automatically interpreted as attempted escape. It sufficed for one culprit to be found, and we were all turned out into the road in our shirts and beaten up by the light of the searchlights. Not even at night were we safe. Worn out by the heavy burden of the day, we would creep into our straw sacks in fear and trembling, never sure what the night might bring. Most prisoners obeyed the "underpants rule," but not all. There were always some who were prepared to jeopardize the others, so the nocturnal visits continued.

Death at any moment!

We had to be prepared to face death at any moment, for we were in constant danger — *in proximo periculo mortis,* as we often reminded one another. Any day, we might be sentenced to the dreaded punishment of "twenty-five" or "hanging," or we might be sent to the punishment squad. We never knew. How long could we endure this sort of existence?

Prayer was the only thing that saved us. "If God does not save us by a miracle, then we are indeed lost!" We realized the truth of this more forcibly every day. And yet miracles did happen, day and night. We implored Our Lord and His Blessed Mother to help us, and we silently invoked our guardian angels.

I, too, was suddenly seized with diarrhea. I was really ill, and my situation was desperate. I was certainly incapable of marching to work in the quarry, and it was out of the question to chance the diarrhea ward in the sick bay. Nor could I expect my comrades to help me. I got up at two in the morning and succeeded in getting myself a job in the kitchens. While there, I asked a fellow prisoner, a member of the Communist Party, to give me a hand with a heavy crate of potatoes. He flew into an unaccountable rage and began to set about me with his feet. His language was indescribably vile.

A few days later, I saw him outside our block with some of his party friends. I went up to him and, with a few kindly words, reproached him for his harsh treatment of me in the kitchens. Shortly afterward, I learned that he had approached the under-capo of my squad, making all sorts of promises if I could be "disposed of" at work.

At one time, I was detailed as "clerk" for the working party assigned to the Westerplatte of the quarry. I caught sight of our good old Fr. Leeb working away at a particularly dangerous spot, constantly under the eye of the SS guard. As clerk, I more or less belonged to the administration, and I took it upon myself to go over to Fr. Leeb, who was utterly exhausted, and move him to a less exposed place, where he would be able to rest a little. The SS guard noted my action in a report to the camp commandant, and only the intervention of the head capo saved me from severe punishment.

At the end of October, Fr. Leeb, who could no longer stand, was forced to resort to the diarrhea ward. Whether or not he knew beforehand of the grim warning of the orderly in charge, I never discovered. At all events, twenty-four hours later — the evening of All Saints — he was dead. We were convinced that this fine priest had been murdered.

In November 1940, a large number of Polish prisoners was discharged from Gusen. Hope began to spring up throughout the camp. But things turned out rather differently. The men who were picked out on the afternoon of the appointed day were simply taken by truck to Mauthausen and shot.

One day, I was working on the cesspool installations with some other prisoners when a young SS man came along. He was drunk. He knew that I was a priest and forced me into a religious controversy. I answered his attacks fearlessly, and he very soon saw that the game was lost from the start. He drew his revolver and pointed it at me menacingly. Then he lowered it and left. "That took guts!" commented the communists nearby. But I nearly paid for it with my life.

The weather was our enemy too

Although winter was a long way off, it could still be intensely cold, especially at night when it was raining, and we would shiver under the one thin blanket issued to us. We were abnormally susceptible to cold, perhaps because we never got enough to eat. There was always the danger of catching a chill or falling sick. Later on, in November, we were given more blankets, and things were a little better.

Christ in Dachau

Bad weather in any form made life doubly hard for us, and a single rainy day might mean death for as many as thirty to fifty prisoners. Hunger and sheer misery had robbed many of us of the last vestiges of self-confidence and, indeed, of resistance of any sort. We were not issued with waterproofs, and no shelter was provided, nor had we any means of changing into dry clothes. We would thus be soaked to the skin in a matter of minutes, the water would run out of our trouser legs and shoes, and our teeth would begin to chatter. Only when the rain gave no sign of letting up would the whistle give the signal to down tools. Even so, we still had to carry stones back with us. No matter what sort of weather it was, we all — the capos excepted, of course — had to carry great stones home on our shoulders.

Our shoes, shirts, and trousers had, in any case, to dry on us. We often had to stand in the pouring rain for long periods, lined up waiting for roll call, wet to the skin and shivering with cold.

Diarrhea and pneumonia were the dreaded illnesses. Only faith in God's providence and sheer willpower could save us here. "Whatever happens, I mustn't get sick! No, I'm not going to get sick!" We repeated the words over and over again. "If I get sick, then it's all up!" It was this final inner resistance that really counted. If you gave up, then you were indeed lost. Those of us who clung to God and trusted in His providence found a new strength.

Sent to the punishment squad

September 10, 1940. Bad news indeed! Our friend Stepan, who was then working as a clerk in the camp administration office, had seen an order received from Dachau: Fr. Mayr and I were to be transferred to the punishment squad. We never discovered why.

Dr. Karl Maria Stepan was a wonderful friend to us. He never failed to help us, particularly the priests, in every possible way. He was one of those who had miraculously survived the terrible winter of 1939–1940 in Mauthausen and had helped to save the lives of many of his unfortunate comrades. He was discharged from Gusen on October 2, 1940, but he was rearrested in the autumn of 1944 and sent to Dachau.

Stepan's inseparable friend and compatriot Doleschal, an official of the Austrian provincial government, also deserves special mention here. This little man, an ardent Catholic and the very best of comrades, was discharged from Gusen together with Stepan. He broke down as he said goodbye to us, overcome by the sight of the human misery he was leaving.

The day we heard we were to be sent to the punishment squad was a day of incessant rain. We priests had taken shelter as best we could in our deep sandpit. We had dug this pit ourselves, and our capo saw to it that we were allowed to work there in comparative peace. We had to be on our guard all the time, of course, for at any moment, the dreaded SS man D. and his assistants K. and S. might appear. In this pit we used to pray together, reciting the prayers of the Mass by heart and singing psalms and hymns. We carried out the work required of us here, too, and were, to some extent, protected in bad weather.

The same evening, Fr. Mayr and I were moved over to Block 16A, which was both a punishment block and Jews' quarters. All the Jews in the camp, together with the camp criminals, were accommodated in Dormitory A.

We were gotten up at the crack of dawn the next morning for "latrine carrying." This meant carrying heavy barrels and containers slung on long poles over our shoulders, four men for each load. It was terrible work, not only on account of the stench — you just had to get used to that — but because the weight was so crushing that we often thought we must collapse on the spot. Each trip meant an uphill climb of a quarter of an hour to the cesspool, with armed SS guards posted at regular intervals along the route.

In the meantime, new cesspools were being dug, ready to be filled by the Jews and the camp convicts. It often happened that prisoners, particularly Jews, were pushed or thrown into these pits. A Polish prisoner told me how he had succeeded in rescuing one Jew who was on the point of suffocation — a risky undertaking. The Poles had an especially hard time. I once saw one of the capos of the punishment squad kill a Polish prisoner who had stopped to pick up a cigarette butt. A few days later, I saw the body of a Polish priest lying on the way to one of the cesspools. He had been shot by the guards simply because he had been unable to work anymore.

New latrines were installed during the second half of November in a separate blockhouse built for the purpose. Now, if we required to relieve ourselves at night, we had to go out in the cold in nothing but shoes and our shirts — a cruel journey, particularly for those whom the cold had already afflicted with bladder trouble.

Life in the punishment squad grew almost unbearable. Whenever there was anything especially hard or unpleasant to be done, the men of the punishment squad would be detailed. Now that the latrine problem had been solved by the new installations, we were available for many other kinds of hard labor. Never shall I forget those seemingly endless forced marches, carrying heavy burdens of all kinds. We were made to walk in long columns, one behind the other, so that it was quite impossible to stop even for a moment's rest. Sometimes we were so weak that we could scarce place one foot in front of the other. Often we had to carry great slabs of stone on our bony shoulders.

One thought alone preoccupied us all the time: When would we be free again? This yearning for freedom filled our days and haunted our dreams at night. A rumor went around that the camp was to be closed. All kinds of dates were forecast; hopes were roused and shattered — and built up again. We all lived in the desperate hope that our salvation would come before long. But the days and the weeks passed, and nothing changed.

A camp of prayer

I often thought back nostalgically to the months of prison in Vienna. I think I would have given anything to be back there again. How I had chafed in those days at the inactivity and frustration behind the bars of my cell! But there had been time to read and to write, time for quiet meditation and for prayers.

But in Gusen there was time for prayer too. Indeed, Gusen was literally a camp of prayer in those autumn days of 1940. Whether it had been like this in the early days, or whether things changed later on, I do not know. At that time, however, there can scarcely have been another concentration camp where so many of the prisoners prayed — and a great many of them were not priests either. Work, life, and death — everything was accompanied by prayer; everything was consecrated by prayer. For all its horror, the "death mill" of Gusen was a true community of prayer.

It was, above all, the Poles and their gallant priests who inspired this spirit of prayer. The elite of Poland's intellectuals was interned in Mauthausen and Gusen. Few of them can still have been alive by the time the Americans came in 1945.

I shall never forget the sight of those Poles praying in Gusen. I can see them now in their long slave columns, each pitiful procession headed by a capo. The "stone brigade" on their way to the quarries, each man bearing a great stone on his right shoulder, or the "earth brigade" bound for the earthworks, passing slowly in pairs, carrying great buckets of earth slung over poles.

Trusted prisoners who happened to pass these long columns of men would hear the murmur of their fervent prayers. If an SS man or a dangerous capo appeared on the scene, however, cries of "Uwaga!" (Take care) or "Woda!" (Water) would replace the Hail Marys and Our Fathers as a general warning signal. The procession would then lapse into silence until the danger was past, and only the reverence and inner serenity of the tired faces would reveal the devotion of the praying men.

As a rule, we did not have to work on Sunday, and just as our work during the week was sanctified by prayer, so we began Sunday with religious devotions. We had no Mass in Gusen, despite the numerous priests there were in the camp, but these Sunday devotions were held in almost all the huts where there were Poles. These Poles were to be found everywhere, gathered around one of their priests, praying together and singing their old Polish hymns, and listening devoutly to the Gospel. For many of the sick and dying among them, these Sunday services were very often their last religious consolation on earth.

Camp mosaic

"Father, will you hear my confession? My brother died three days ago, and I shan't last much longer myself." The young man who had come to me was one of two brothers called Alt from Vienna. The fact that they were Jews had been enough to condemn them to death. Starvation had carried out the sentence, bitter hunger combined with hard labor, and the lice.

I did what I could to help him. I took him along with me next morning for the usual roll call, leading him gently by the arm. The man was a walking skeleton, but his eyes began to shine as I told him of the promises of Our Lord and of the eternal joys of Heaven. I traced the Sign of the Cross on his brow and gave him my blessing. He died two days later. We had lost two of our best comrades far too soon.

Christ in Dachau

We had no means of administering the Last Sacraments to the dying, for we had no altar in Gusen, no Mass, and no Holy Communion. Not even the sound of a church bell reached us in our banishment. And yet there were some 150 priests in the camp, priests who lived and suffered and died with their fellow prisoners — without the Body of Our Lord. In this place of penance, only the sacrament of Penance remained for us. We priests availed ourselves frequently and joyfully of this holy sacrament, our hearts full of gratitude to God. But not only priests came to Confession; many of the other prisoners came too.

The sunrise was often indescribably lovely at Gusen, rose-fingered dawn, just as Homer described it. And the sunsets were no less beautiful. We learned to watch the sky with a new awareness. It seemed as though we had had to come to this place in order to learn to appreciate to the full the beauty of God's creation and to realize our Father's goodness to us — a new lesson that "God is love."

The countryside around Gusen had a peculiar beauty of its own, although down in the camp, on the Danube, the range of vision was limited. Up on the Westerplatte, however, it was possible in good weather to see across to the spires of the abbey church of St. Florian. I could never look across to the church without an indescribable sadness, a sadness and a desperate longing for freedom — for a church in which to celebrate Mass again, for home.

The containers from the latrines seemed heavier than ever, and I was terribly hungry. A comrade gave me a bit of tobacco to chew in order to take the edge off the pangs, but it made me feel so sick that I had to spit it out. It began to rain heavily. We would have liked to take shelter for a few moments, but the SS guards were never very far away. They drove us on again with curses, blows, and kicks. On again, despite rain, hunger, and ever-failing strength. "Lord, Thy will be done!"

At midday, we would file in, one block at a time, to collect our meal. The capos and block personnel had already fished up such fragments of meat and bones as there were from the bottom of our pail. The tidbits were always reserved for these men, a group of unscrupulous criminals. The soup was thick, made with potatoes and turnips, and to us it tasted just wonderful. The only thing was, there was never enough of it. There was no proper canteen, and we had to take our soup out onto the road, which was not yet finished. We would sit on the rough stones to eat our soup and have a few minutes' rest. At the end of an hour, we had to fall in again for work. We also had to make use of this time to delouse our shirts as best we could. We were then marched back to work, past the SS sentries at the gates. We never forgot our "good intention" for the second half of the day: short prayers imploring God's mercy and protection gave us new strength. We never forgot Our Lady and the holy angels.

One day, it was announced that photographers were coming to Gusen. It seemed they were keen to take pictures of the camp and of the prisoners at work. Unfortunately for them, a fog came up and spoiled the good business they might have done afterward at the expense of our misery. Another day, an SS commission from the concentration camp at Sachsenhausen arrived. The title of capo was exchanged for that of "foreman," and prisoners in this privileged position were forbidden to ill-treat the other prisoners or to administer corporal punishment. Both "improvements" were futile, however, for the new regulations were observed for half a day at most.

Our life on this earth is like a mosaic, a pattern made up of many stones. Formed by God's master hand, this mosaic becomes a spiritual image of God Himself, the most precious work of art in creation. Without the hand of God, however, it is no more than a chaotic heap of stones, without sense or order. Everything makes sense if God is part of our lives. There is no sense in anything if we refuse to acknowledge God's wisdom. There were plenty of instances of this in our daily life at Gusen.

"The sufferings of this time …"

"Lenz, they've stolen my bread ration again today! I can't stand it anymore, I tell you!" W., a schoolteacher from Tyrol, was a pitiful figure indeed. The man was a devout Catholic and was unusually gifted in many ways, but he was addicted to drink. Even in the camp, he somehow managed to get hold of liquor. He died that winter, a pitiable wreck. Men who drank or who were addicted to smoking had the hardest time of all, for alcohol and nicotine had a particularly toxic effect on bodies weakened by semi-starvation and less resistant to disease. Such prisoners were invariably the first victims of every epidemic. It was a bitter lesson, but worth learning.

N. was one of those who had been caught smoking by an SS man. He was given "twenty-five" and sent to the punishment squad. Nonsmokers were at least spared some of the dangers of camp life. There were many who died of starvation, having exchanged their last crust of bread for tobacco, and many even resorted to stealing, only to be beaten to death when the theft was traced by the prisoners they had robbed.

Orders were received for a crematorium to be built at Gusen, and the punishment squad began work carrying bricks. One day, I got brief leave of absence from this work, for I had heard they were issuing "new" shoes, and there was just a chance that I might be able to exchange my own almost useless clogs for another pair. On my way to the clothing store, I saw one of the brutal prisoner nursing orderlies at work out in the open on an old Polish prisoner with a scrubbing brush and a pail of icy water. The poor old man was cowering there, stark naked, shivering in the cold autumn air. "*Mi Bosche! Mi Bosche!*" cried the old man, nearly dead from cold and exhaustion. But the prisoner-nurse only intensified his vicious treatment.

One day when we were lining up for supper, dead beat after the day's work and longing only for something to eat and then our straw sacks, we were greeted by the block capo. His face was dark with rage.

"Nothing to eat for any of you, you won't even go into the cookhouse, until that —— C reports here!"

From a hut across the road came the sound of blows and cries of rage and pain. The absentee was receiving "twenty-five" at the hands of the block capos. Another case of bread stealing. This time the thief paid dearly for his bread — with his life.

Some of the prisoners used to save part of their supper bread for their soup in the morning. This took a lot of willpower. If you ate your miserable few ounces of bread at once, your hunger was at least staved off for an hour or two longer — and there was also nothing for the bread thieves to get their hands on during the night. If you made the heroic decision to keep some bread till the next morning, you had to tie it firmly to yourself before lying down for the night. This meant just one more task to be added to the ritual precautions that preceded going to bed in Gusen. Shoes, jackets, and caps were all liable to disappear or be exchanged in the night. For this reason, most of us used these articles of clothing as a pillow. By the time we had deloused our shirts and underpants — as far as this was possible — there was not very much time left for sleep.

I well remember those still, frosty November evenings, the dark sky sprinkled with stars. They shone down on us in our prison camp, a steadfast consolation. The stars, like the sun and God's fresh air, were things that no one could take away from us. Timeless, ageless, unchanging, the stars proclaim how short this earthly life of ours really is — and how soon our misery in this world is over. Only God remains, and with Him our souls, ever in search of God. As St. Paul says, "I reckon that the sufferings of this time are not worthy to be compared with the glory to come, that shall be revealed in us" (Rom. 8:18).

Sickness and lice

Early in November my feet suddenly began to swell up, and fluid began to collect around my eyes and in my cheeks.

"That's the way it starts. The beginning of the end," predicted the old hands of the camp.

I reported sick and was given three days' "rest cure." Several hundred crippled and sick prisoners were ordered into an unheated empty wooden hut, where we spent the day as best we could, lying or sitting on the dirty floor. There were not nearly enough dressings available, and the stench of the many putrefying wounds of the unfortunate men around me was almost unbearable. Nothing further was done for us.

Diarrhea undoubtedly took the highest toll of lives, and anyone who got it was virtually doomed. Hunger and thirst drove so many to resorting to all kinds of substitutes for food and to drinking the camp water, which was polluted by the cesspool. Prisoners died like flies, from hunger and from diarrhea. The sanitary conditions and the general hygiene in Gusen were a death sentence in themselves.

Christ in Dachau

The daily roll calls, every morning and evening, presented a terrible picture. It was the rule that those who had died during the night, or during the day, had to be carried out, as well as the sick and the dying. They would be there already, before the rest of us were marched on in our long columns. The whole square was often covered with corpses and the prostrate bodies of the dying. There they would lie on the concrete, whatever the weather, in cold and hunger and misery. It was very often their last hour.

The mornings were particularly hard for us priests. I often thought back to the mornings when I had celebrated Mass in a church bathed in warm candlelight or perhaps flooded with early sunshine. Now we were turned out before dawn into the cold, sinister darkness of the prison camp, weak from hunger and lack of sleep. It was a grim start to the new day.

Fr. Mayr and I used always to pray together as we made our way across to collect the small bowl of watery soup that was our breakfast. We would drink it standing in the roadway, for there were no such things as tables and chairs. Here we would confide our hopes and fears for the new day before being marched off for roll call. And then the daily grind of hard labor would start all over again. Only when dawn broke did our spirits rise and our hearts would sing with the rising sun a Te Deum to our Father in Heaven.

We were plagued by lice in the camp, and a vigorous daily delousing campaign was an absolute necessity. It is hard for civilized human beings to realize just what this meant. We often rid ourselves of more than one hundred lice each day — it was quite impossible to find them all. And this had to be done in the evening when we were dead tired after the day's work.

These lice not only robbed us of our blood — and, God knows, we had precious little to spare — but they caused constant irritation and countless tiny sores. We often wondered how we would ever endure the coming winter if something were not done to ease our plight. The fleas were legion too, and they seemed much bigger than any we had ever seen before. It was almost as though the lice and the fleas had their own part to play in the plan to torment us to death by slow degrees.

Thank God we priests were no longer in Gusen when the camp was finally deloused by the authorities soon after Christmas. The five thousand prisoners still in the camp were driven out stark naked onto the square. By about two o'clock in the afternoon, the process of delousing the huts and the prisoners was complete. One of them, E. Gostner, says, "In the kitchens, they reckoned 188 portions less than usual; 188 prisoners had paid for this delousing process with their lives. They were simply frozen to death."

Hunger

A physical torment infinitely worse than the lice was the unceasing hunger. Unless you have known what hunger in a concentration camp is like, you cannot know what real hunger means. We would find ourselves talking for hours on end about food and discussing cooking recipes. Our imaginations simply ran riot.

I often thought of the parable of the prodigal son. I even envied the son in the Gospel story. He could, after all, go home. He could beg for something to eat — a crust of bread, a bowl of soup. He could even help himself to the pig swill. We had no resource to such luxuries, for although the pigs and dogs and rabbits kept by the SS were well cared for, thousands of human beings were kept perpetually hungry, indeed were being deliberately starved to death. I remember one day, when the bins of scraps from the SS kitchens were being carried past, we caught glimpses of the remains of cucumber salad and potatoes — dream food for us. I thought nostalgically of my childhood days on my father's farm and the big pot in which the pigs' food was cooked. I would have given anything to be able to fill my own tin plate with that homely mixture of greens and turnips and bran!

One day, a Polish prisoner made me a present of a dirty bit of raw turnip. Another time, I was given some carrots. The stalks of cabbages, sometimes found in the field, were priceless treasures. I once got hold of a whole raw cabbage by a bribe, and we divided it reverently between us: delicious raw cabbage leaves! Never had we eaten anything so exquisite in our lives!

The evening, when we came back from work, was the happiest time of the day. We were doled out a few ounces of bread, a cup of ersatz coffee, and a slice of horsemeat sausage. Occasionally, we might get two or three potatoes. Our midday meal invariably consisted of some kind of thick soup, mostly of the kind we called "blockade breaker," usually made from turnips. No homemade delicacy of prewar days had ever tasted as good as this soup. But there was never enough. This "meal" was, in fact, no more than a sort of snack that served only to make us all the more conscious of our ever-present hunger.

We had to wash our own plates afterward, and the water shortage was often so acute that we had to use the dirty water of our neighbors. We were still so hungry after our soup that we would willingly have walked a mile for a single potato.

The misery of our situation was characterized by a very vivid dream I had one night. I was sitting at home with my father, telling him about Gusen. All of a sudden, I cried out in anguish, "Oh, Father, if you only knew what it was like, you would die!" At this point, I awoke. My heart was pounding, and alone in the darkness I wept bitterly.

Not long after I had this dream, I collapsed during the morning roll call. My strength was exhausted. The man next to me got hold of a Polish priest. A few minutes later, he was with me, holding me in his arms. I was already unconscious. "You were as white as a sheet, and your face was bathed in sweat," he told me afterward. When our physical strength is exhausted, our spiritual strength begins to fail too.

Joy in the midst of suffering

But despite all the hardship and suffering it brought me, Gusen also brought me joy, the special kind of joy that comes through suffering. *Superabundo gaudio prae omni tribulatione nostra.* We, too, soon learned the truth of St. Paul's words, "I overflow for joy in the midst of our tribulation" (see 2 Cor. 7:4).

I knew the value of suffering, and this knowledge was of inestimable value to me. I had three years' hard training in the Jesuit novitiate behind me, but three months in Gusen were worth far more, as I used to tell myself in those dark days. Only in the school of the greatest suffering can we really experience what we have only learned in theory before. By this, I mean the sort of prayer that pierces the soul like a sword, the sort of faith in God that forges the soul on God's own hand, the final giving of one's whole being to God, an unconditional surrender, a blind submission to the divine will.

Sometimes after supper, I used to walk through the camp, arm in arm with our good friend and comrade Dr. Stepan. I remember once suddenly bursting out laughing for sheer joy. I was half shocked at the time by my own laughter in such a situation; it seemed almost grotesque. And yet it was my deep inner happiness that had made me laugh, the happiness that — thank God — never forsook me even during the worst days of tribulation and suffering. "Thou wilt always rejoice in the evening if thou spend the day profitably," as St. Thomas à Kempis declares in *The Imitation of Christ.*

I often thought back on the first Easter I had spent in the prison in Vienna. I had already spent some months in solitary confinement, yet never before in my life did I sing the Alleluia so often and with such deep joy as at Easter 1939. Happiness is never determined by outward things and circumstances — true happiness comes from within, from the harmony of the soul with God.

Thanksgiving

I never ceased to thank God for my suffering, and this, more than anything else, helped me to bear the cross of my imprisonment with fortitude. In the novitiate, we had frequently been urged to practice this act of faith in thanksgiving, and to this day, I have always found it of the greatest value, especially during the long years of internment in Gusen and Dachau.

I cannot sufficiently impress upon my readers how this can help them in their own particular troubles and afflictions. To thank God for the trials He sends us in His infinite love for us is by no means easy and requires practice, but in the end, it will be seen to be well worthwhile. Every new beginning is difficult, as we all know. We must begin with thanksgiving for the little crosses that we have to bear every day. In this way, we gradually proceed in prayer to the realization of the fact that every form of human suffering really comes from God in His goodness and wisdom. He sends us this suffering so as to prepare us for Heaven. For this very reason, our thanksgiving for suffering is not only the finest test of our faith but also our most powerful prayer to our Father in Heaven.

God, our Father, may chastise us in His loving wisdom, but if we believe in God and in His wisdom and love, how can we possibly fail in this act of thanksgiving? It represents our complete and unconditional surrender to God, who alone is all in all. It is our own free love, given in return for His divine love. Only in this act of thanksgiving can we really experience what St. Paul tells us when he says, "I overflow with joy in every tribulation."

Earthly suffering is sent to us that we may grow and mature in spirit. No harvest can be reaped without toil and sweat. Every farmer knows that his corn must have time to grow and ripen, and no farmer will curse and swear and grumble because he has to work so hard. He knows very well that his hard work means that his barns will be full when he has reaped his harvest. It is just the same with our suffering here on earth, for in the life to come, our earthly happiness will count for little. It will be our suffering that will count then, the hard days of tribulation and hardship that will be our righteous pride, our joy — and our glory. Days for spiritual growth, in readiness for the harvest of eternity.

And so I could find no hatred in my heart for our persecutors. "Whatever these men do to me," I told myself, "it doesn't matter. They'll have to answer for it some time, for no one can escape God's judgment. But that goes for me too. I'll have to answer for how I've borne this cross that God has placed on my shoulders here and now, through these men."

In this way, this time of suffering, terrible though it was, was immensely profitable. Nowhere else in the world, not even in the hardest school, could I have had such inestimable spiritual training as in this bitter school of the concentration camp. I would not have exchanged those five years for all the gold and treasure in the world. These words are especially addressed to those who have a heavy cross to bear. Thanksgiving in suffering really does bring consolation.

I had penance enough to do anyway for my own sins. God knew why He had sent me to this school, the hardest and most valuable of my life. Only when we are forced to endure the most profound suffering and hardship do we learn how to catch hold of God's hand in our misery — we learn to pray.

Fr. Gruber

We priests who were interned in Gusen shall always be deeply grateful to the memory of Professor Johann Gruber, a fellow priest from Linz. He was one of the nursing orderlies in the sick bay from August 1940. It was a privileged position, and in consequence, his life was easier than ours, but he was unceasing in his efforts to help his fellow prisoners, particularly his fellow priests. He somehow managed to find medicines for dropsy, for diarrhea, for fevers and coughs. He had arrived with us from Dachau and remained on in Gusen after we left, a mercy for the thousands of unfortunate men whom he was still able to help but disastrous for his own person, for he was murdered in Gusen in May 1944.

A Polish prisoner called Kakowski, number 46,511, writes the following appreciation:

> The last of my good Austrian friends was Fr. Gruber from Linz. He was a small man, rather broadly built, somewhat impulsive and immensely energetic. He was by no means any longer young, yet he would think nothing of undertaking long walks on his errands of mercy during the brief recreation periods. He would make use of every minute of the morning break, at midday, and in the evening to comfort and care for his flock. I would often see him with his inevitable can of soup in all sorts of strange places in the camp. I never discovered when he himself found time to eat anything whatever. He was to be found everywhere. One sensed his presence everywhere. He had friends among every European nation represented at Gusen, for he spoke the international language of the heart, a language that everyone could understand. A small man with a great soul, he knew no fear and was constantly on the lookout for new ways of helping his fellows. He was not always successful and often had to endure hardship and degradation as a result of his efforts, but he never allowed himself to be discouraged or deflected from his purpose. He was beaten up on several occasions, but he soon forgot his own physical pain and humiliation in thinking up new ways in which he could care for us.

In the spring of 1944, he established a sort of secret news service, sending bulletins from the camp into the outside world. He was able to continue this for some time until a careless slip on the part of his contact man on the outside led to the discovery of the organization by the Gestapo. Camp commandant Seidler had him shut up naked for three days in the concrete bunker. Despite repeated treatments with cold water and beatings in his cell, he refused to take his own life. He fought back gallantly until his very last breath. He died a martyr's death not very long before the liberation. The commandant had him hanged, but his next of kin were informed that he had committed suicide.

A daring idea

The first of November drew near, and I began to pray especially for the Holy Souls. It was, after all, a fitting devotion for us in our own kind of Purgatory in

Christ in Dachau

Gusen. Like the Holy Souls, we, too, were helpless and yet at the same time in the grace of God.

I began two novenas, making use of every minute of the time spent at work. I prayed the Rosary every day, too, using my fingers in place of the beads I no longer possessed.

The morning I began my third novena, it chanced that the camp commandant came to inspect the punishment squad on the square. He walked down the rows of prisoners and picked out several who apparently took his fancy at that moment and gave orders for their discharge from the punishment squad. He paused for a moment when he came to me, and I heard the clerk tell him who I was. "Fr. Lenz, sentenced on orders from Dachau to twelve months' hard labor." In this way, I first heard the details of my sentence. The commandant passed on to the next man without a word.

A plan began slowly to develop in my mind. On December 3, I found an excuse to slip away from work and back to camp during the afternoon. I made use of this time to write a brief note addressed to the camp commandant in which I asked him to consider my release. I based my petition on the grounds of my father's illness and old age, adding that he was a veteran of the First World War. I also submitted that Fr. Mayr and I should be dispensed from the black patch denoting criminals and, in Gusen, painted on our uniforms with a brush. I handed the application over to the senior prisoner of the block with the request that it be transmitted through the SS office to the commandant. My heart was beating fast as I made my way back to work.

That same evening, at roll call, my name and number were called out. Fortunately, the commandant himself was not there, and I had to answer to his deputy.

In my excitement, I forgot the regulation military salute and bowed to him as I had been accustomed to do in the old days. This was my undoing. I was rewarded by having my ears boxed. My petition for discharge from the camp was categorically dismissed, as I had feared it would be. As I turned to go back to the others, I once again forgot to click my heels. I got my face slapped.

The whole camp had witnessed my disgrace. I could not have had better publicity had I wanted it. Soon everyone was talking about my letter, and everyone predicted my public execution or at least the "twenty-five" and arrest in the bunker as punishment for writing letters without permission. But I went on praying.

Next day, the deputy camp commandant called me out again at roll call. This time, Fr. Mayr was called out with me. Five other "holy souls" were also released from the purgatory of the punishment squad. The others simply could not believe their ears. Everyone said it was a miracle, even the unbelievers who were not generally disposed to believe in such things. Here was proof indeed of the power of prayer! My heart overflowed in joyous thanksgiving to God and His saints — and to the Holy Souls.

Goodbye to Gusen

December 6, 1940, and First Friday. It was a real winter's day, but, working away in the quarry, we were impervious to the cold, for we had heard that the commandant had received orders from Berlin to send all priests back to Dachau for discharge! The rumor was verified at midday when we priests received the old command "Fall out!" Our joy knew no bounds that afternoon as we were issued civilian clothing — a sure sign that we would soon be free again. Or so we thought.

We had to undergo a final "medical examination" in the sick bay at the hands of an untrained prisoner-orderly. One of these "good Samaritans" suddenly fell upon an old Polish priest in a towering rage. "You!" he snarled at him. "So you're just a simple peasant, eh? I'll teach you, you swine, you dog, you priest!" And he set upon the unfortunate man with kicks and blows. It appeared that this Polish priest had been admitted to the sick bay only a few weeks before, and in order to save his life, he had told the dreaded orderly, who was known for his hatred of all priests, that he was a peasant.

There were several priests and theology students who had been afraid to admit that they belonged to the clergy and had thus been entered in the camp records as laymen. They now remained behind at Gusen, and almost all of them died.

We were joined next morning by several priests from Mauthausen, and at seven o'clock that evening, we were marched to the station, an hour's march, with a heavy pack.

A Pole, Fr. Z., was also among our priest contingent. During the train journey, one of the SS guards got hold of him and pushed him into the lavatory. We never knew what happened to him, but when we arrived at Dachau, his body was simply thrown out onto the platform like a log of wood. R.I.P.

Christ in Dachau

As we drew into Salzburg — this time not in cattle trucks — we saw the Church of Maria Plain through the window of our carriage. We decided then and there to make a joint pilgrimage to this shrine as soon as we were released. Had we but known it, it was to be years before we could realize this plan. But God's providence did, in fact, bring me to Maria Plain on the feast of the Assumption 1945. I said Mass there in thanksgiving for my survival and in intercession for Austria, the Austria that I was then seeing for the first time since my bitter ordeal in Gusen.

6

Back in Dachau

The Priests' Concentration Camp

In December 1940, orders were issued from Berlin to the commandants of the many concentration camps scattered over Hitler's Third Reich to transfer all priest prisoners to Dachau, where a "concentration camp within a concentration camp" was to provide for the internment of these offenders against the Nazi regime.

This order was the result of prolonged negotiations between the German hierarchy and the Gestapo authorities in Berlin, a great diplomatic victory, due in no small measure to the universal regard and esteem felt for the Holy Father, Pope Pius XII. Unable to secure our release, the bishops, headed by Bishop Wienken of Berlin, finally succeeded in achieving certain improvements in the conditions under which the clergy were to be interned. They had submitted a four-point petition, and although all similar petitions had hitherto been disregarded by the Nazi overlords, this time they were successful, at least in three of the four points submitted.

1. Priests were to have a chapel and be permitted to assist at Mass. They were furthermore to be issued with breviaries.
2. Priests were to be housed together in separate priests' blocks.
3. Priests were to be used for the lighter forms of work, so as to conserve their strength and allow more time for spiritual and intellectual work.

The fourth point, Christian burial for priests (bodies of concentration camp prisoners were normally cremated) was refused. All the same, Bishop Wienken had every reason to thank God for his success. And so had we priests. The

Christ in Dachau

German bishops had been untiring in their efforts on our behalf, and we knew that we owed Bishop Wienken and the Holy Father a debt of gratitude.

And so, though we were not to be set free, as we had fondly imagined on our journey from Mauthausen to Dachau, we did find considerable improvements awaiting us on arrival, and in this way, life was made much easier. It was, in fact, to be years before we would be free men again; in the meantime, we were to learn many new lessons in the hard school of the concentration camp. Now, however, we were at least together, and this in itself was a tremendous advantage viewed against our experience in the past few months in the punishment squads.

As a result of the new ruling from Berlin, Dachau was to become the largest and, at the same time, the most rigorous enclosed order in the world, for in due course, some 2,600 priests of the Catholic Church from 136 dioceses and 24 nations came to form this great religious community. In this way, Dachau was to become a real spiritual center, a "powerhouse of prayer" in the midst of Hell itself. Surely this was a miracle, a triumph for the Church of Christ behind barbed wire!

We knew that day we returned to Dachau that among the priests now concentrated in the camp, we should meet many whose names were almost legendary, men who had stood in open opposition to the Nazi regime, fearlessly facing imprisonment, hunger, and threats of death for the truth of their Faith in opposition to Hitler's pseudo-religion. These were the true heroes, the true followers of Christ, whose influence on the people was very naturally feared by "the others." We looked forward to meeting these men, to exchanging ideas and experiences, and all of us knew that we had much to learn from one another. So, although we were still not free, we resolved to face whatever lay ahead of us with gratitude, in patience, and in the knowledge that God was always beside us.

A priest community at last!

We arrived back in Dachau on Sunday, December 8, 1940, the feast of the Immaculate Conception. We arrived in the afternoon, but despite our intense hunger, it was evening before we were given anything to eat — our first meal in two days! We were issued new clothing, and I was given a new number — 22,031. We were then sent across to Block 30, the new priests' block. Although, according to the new regulations, we were segregated in a block of our own, there was no ruling about the block personnel, and our block capo, Sepp W., was an atheist of the very worst type. Conditions in Dachau were admittedly better than those in Gusen, but all the same, we were still half starved, and there were lice in Dachau too, despite the almost fanatical cult of order and cleanliness (all propaganda and eyewash for possible visitors) pursued by the SS authorities.

We found many Polish priests waiting for us in the block and countless others soon came to join us. Seven priests had arrived from Buchenwald the previous day. Those from Sachsenhausen arrived on December 14. On December 12, the last priests of the Dachau punishment squad were discharged and came to join us. I happened to be in the hut when they arrived. We had never seen each other, but we were brothers bound in sympathy by our common experiences. I knew only too well what they had had to endure; I knew, too, what it meant to them as priests to have to wear the prison uniform with the ignominious black patch of the convict. I seized a breadknife and ripped the offending patches off their clothing. Their haggard grey faces broke into smiles, and we all felt a great deal better.

One of the new arrivals, Fr. Richard Schneider, was a dying man when he arrived at Dachau. He was a priest well known for his dauntless courage, but even he did not want to go to the infirmary. He knew very well that priests were never accorded a warm welcome there. I knew that we would have to get him taken in all the same, for his hours on earth were numbered. I took him with me and used all my influence to get him admitted. He died within a few hours. He was only one of the many I was to take under my protection, and the nursing orderly in charge of the infirmary, an atheist with a bitter hatred of all priests, invariably greeted me derisively as "our good Samaritan." But I did not care. My job was to look after my fellow priests. It was difficult enough to gain admittance at all to the infirmary in those days. "You'll not be admitted unless you're dying" was the grim rule. Those who had care of the sick at Dachau seemed not to know the meaning of the words *pity*, *humanity*, or *brotherly love*.

Christmas comes again

Christmas came. We still had no chapel and no Mass. The Very Reverend Stanislas Kubsky, the eldest priest, addressed us in our hut. Our fervent mutual wish as we greeted each other that Christmas morning was that this would be the last Christmas behind barbed wire.

Christ in Dachau

There was a special dish of stew on Christmas Day, but a whole bucket of it "disappeared," so there was barely enough to go around. Our block capo and his communist cronies certainly knew where it had gone. This was just another instance of the many ways they exploited us and generally made our lives as difficult and unpleasant as they could. We knew that it would have been useless to protest about the missing bucket of stew, for they would only have laughed at us. They were communists and atheists, and we were Catholic priests. It was part of their "religion," their sacred duty, as it were, to take it out on us in every way they could — and all the better if it were to their own advantage into the bargain.

We suffered most of all at that time from hunger. I had an unexpected bit of luck on New Year's Eve when I contrived to get hold of a dish of red cabbage. I shall never forget the faces of my priest comrades as I bore it triumphantly into the hut at suppertime.

Diary for 1940

In November 1945, I recovered the diary I had kept throughout the years I was interned. It had been smuggled out of the camp in a vegetable cart and handed over to the safekeeping of a community of nuns in Freising, near Munich. The following extract, which is a brief survey of 1940, may serve to give a clearer picture of this highly eventful year.

February 11	My case submitted to the Supreme Court in Leipzig.
March 2	Msgr. Enzmann, my cellmate, discharged as not guilty after 19 months' imprisonment!
April 10	I am moved down to share Cell E 122 with Fr. Pauk.
May 3	My case considered by Supreme Court in Leipzig.
May 6	Verdict of not guilty confirmed. Released from jail.
May 18	Rearrested en route to the frontier.
May 20	Back in the Metropole (6½ weeks' underground arrest).

July 6	Transferred again to prison in the Rossauer Lände.
July 19	Forced to countersign second order for my protective arrest as a political prisoner.
August 5	Feast of Our Lady of the Snows: Priests in Sachsenhausen assist at Mass for first time in new chapel.
August 9	I arrive in Dachau.
August 10	Sent to punishment squad.
August 16–17	Sent to Mauthausen-Gusen with transport of 1,000 men.
September 10	Sent to punishment squad in Gusen.
November 17	Breviaries and rosaries restored to priests in Buchenwald. Priests withdrawn from hard-labor squads.
December 7	Priests from Buchenwald arrive in Dachau.
December 8	150 priests from Gusen and Mauthausen arrive in Dachau.
December 12	Priests from Dachau punishment squad and other blocks transferred to new priests' block, number 30.
December 15	Priests from Sachsenhausen arrive in Dachau, bringing two field Mass kits.

Hard work

January 2, 1941, the feast of the Most Holy Name of Jesus, was a hard day indeed for us. There had been a heavy fall of snow on New Year's Day, and we priests were gotten up in the early hours and turned out before it was light to clear the roadway with snow shovels and handcarts. It was terribly hard work on an empty stomach from five o'clock in the morning until midday, perpetually exposed to an icy northeast wind. What was more, we had virtually no winter clothing. The priests were always detailed for the worst jobs. Our "comrades" saw to it that our existence was made as hard as possible, and our Christian charity was often tried to the utmost.

As has been mentioned, the camp authorities set great store by the outward appearance of their "model concentration camp," and the SS men who inspected the dormitories every day demanded the highest standards of neatness and order. Bed making to comply with these demands was an art that many of the priests simply could not master, even with the best will in the world. Fr. Georg Schelling had been interned since 1938 and was therefore an old hand at camp life and a past master at bed making. In order to save us from the unending bullying, reprimands, and punishments to which so many of his comrades had had to submit as a result of their inability to comply with the SS regulations, "our Georg" volunteered as dormitory capo. This noble offer involved him in hours of selfless hard work in the intense cold, often with nothing to eat, until everything was spick-and-span for the daily SS inspection.

Rumors

Rumors reached us at the beginning of March that crates of breviaries had arrived, but it was another two months before they actually reached us. What a day that was! In 1941, we had time to spare for our breviaries. Things were to change in 1942.

In those days, most of us lived on rumors, even if we did not really believe them. Rumors brought us hope, and hope was all we had. We heard, for instance, that large batches of prisoners were to be released — on January 2, on January 16, on January 25, on February 2 … Prisoners from Buchenwald brought similar rumors: A high-ranking SS man had been heard to say … A Gestapo man had said … But the dates came and went, and nothing came of it. Such rumors were typical of camp life, and many prisoners lived on them from week to week, from month to month, cherishing the desperate hope that freedom would come, if not this time, then next time. But for some, these rumors were a sort of slow poison, for they were unable to bear the inevitable disillusionment. All the same, I must admit that I clutched at such rumors myself whenever I could, and I saw no reason why I should not hand them on. What harm could there be in handing on hope? Our situation was desperate enough, as we all knew, but we still hoped for freedom one day — if it was God's will.

We optimists were right in the end. The day of liberation did come, but not until 1945.

A great event — Christ in Dachau!

January 15, 1941. I was on my way back to our block that afternoon when I caught sight of a whole crowd of prisoners, many of whom I recognized as priests, collected outside Block 26.

A Polish lay brother called out to me as I hurried across to see what was causing the commotion.

"We're to have a chapel in Block 26!" he told me excitedly, his face shining.

I felt sure this was just another camp rumor, but I was wrong. I could see that they were already carrying away sections of the partitions that had divided the dormitory from the so-called living room. I, too, set to work, lending a hand where I could. I learned that Himmler was due to visit us within the next few days and expected to find the chapel finished — in accordance with orders from Berlin. I could scarcely believe my ears. A similar order must indeed have been received already in August 1940, for in Sachsenhausen, they had their chapel that summer; in Dachau, however, they had kept us in the punishment squad until December and waited until the last moment before they complied with the order for the furnishing of a chapel.

But now Himmler was to come on a tour of inspection of this "model" camp, and the SS authorities had detailed Capo H. to see that the chapel was completed as quickly as possible. And so work on Block 26 proceeded day and night, with Capo H. strutting up and down, bellowing directives, bullying, cursing, and swearing.

It had created no small sensation as the green glass windows painted with red crosses were carried across the barrack square, through the length of the camp and down the road to Block 26. The red Nazi flags hung limply on the camp buildings and Christ's red crosses blazed in the winter sunshine. Christ's Cross had triumphed in the hell created by the Nazi swastika!

It was ironic that precisely this man had been chosen as foreman of the working party for the chapel. He was a dangerous atheist with an unspeakable contempt for us priests. He was solely concerned with completing his unwelcome task as quickly as possible, viewing it as a waste of his valuable time. But he was efficient and a good enough organizer, and the chapel was finished by the evening of January 20.

"There you are," he announced irritably. "As far as I am concerned, you can get on with it and hold your fine Mass!"

He was only too glad that his task was complete. He had obeyed orders and provided us with a chapel and furnished it as best he could. This was true enough, but the man was an atheist and had no experience as a sacristan in his work for his Nazi masters. The chapel might well be finished in his eyes, but we had no bread and no wine. The essential offerings for the unbloody sacrifice were lacking and we could not "hold our Mass."

But by the morning of January 22, the hosts and the wine had been obtained, and we assembled for the first time in our new chapel. It was an unforgettable occasion for all of us. It was five o'clock in the morning, and outside was the darkness and misery of the camp. Inside, in the chapel, however, we had forgotten our misery in the joyful anticipation of the Holy Sacrifice of the Mass, of which we had been deprived so long. The priests stood there in their prison clothes, their faces drawn and haggard from hunger and lack of sleep but radiant with a new inner joy. We were weary, half starved, and lousy, but it would have been hard to find a happier group of men that winter's morning.

Our camp chaplain, the Polish priest Fr. Paul Prabutzki, was the celebrant. Each of us had taken one of the small hosts from the plate near the door of the chapel as we came in, and as the celebrant consecrated the host at the altar, the hosts that lay in the palms of our own priestly hands were consecrated simultaneously. We received Holy Communion together with him, from our own hands, hands consecrated as paten at our ordination.

Christus vincit! Christ conquers! This wonderful hymn of the Church of Christ resounded for the first time in our sanctuary that morning. Our hunger and every physical hardship were forgotten in the joyful realization that Christ Himself was here with us in the Blessed Sacrament. Christ Himself, our Lord, our God, was with us there in Dachau, fellow prisoner with us behind barbed wire. Hell might rage outside, but Satan and his followers could not prevail against us. God often chooses the strangest instruments for His work.

Through these godless men, He had manifested Himself in the chapel they had furnished for Him in a hut in their prison camp. Christ was in Dachau! Christ was victorious indeed!

The fact that we were given a chapel at that time, when not only the camp commandant but also his SS henchmen and the majority of the prisoner-capos were actively hostile to religion and filled with a bitter hatred of us Catholic priests, was nothing short of a miracle. Such an innovation would perhaps have been more understandable later on under Commandant Weiss and Camp Director von Redwitz, but God takes no account of outward circumstances, and He chose that very time to proclaim His victory in the midst of the hell of Dachau.

Christus vincit! Christus regnat! Christus imperat! These words are engraved on the granite obelisk in the great square of St. Peter's in Rome. They were true for us priests in Dachau. Christ the Victor gave us new strength with His strength. He Himself was our victory.

The gates of Hell ...

The new chapel was to bring us new suffering, new enemies, new hardships, and new penalties. Jealous of our sanctuary, our enemies thought up other ways of getting even with us. As a countermeasure, our communist "comrades" wanted to set up a party political-instruction center in the camp, but they had no success with the Nazi authorities. Christ had won His victory, but one godless ideology continued to fight against the other behind the barbed wire of Dachau.

They did what they could to prevent us from getting to Mass in the morning. Many of us were detailed for work in the canteen, which meant that we either missed Mass altogether or came too late.

The SS presented a real problem, too, for we never knew when they would come bursting into the chapel in the middle of Mass. They would often push their way rudely up to the altar and stand there, lolling against the wall with their caps on their heads, watching the celebrant, half curious, half cynical. They would usually turn away in boredom after a few moments and clatter out, satisfied at having interrupted our devotions, but there were times when they ordered us at pistol point to clear out, crying: "That's enough hocus-pocus for today!" The celebrant was very often forced to interrupt his Mass, and we would be hurried out of the chapel.

Christ in Dachau

An incident described by Fr. Seitz serves to show what these SS men were like. One of them pushed his way up to the altar one day just after the Consecration. His cap was still on his head, and a cigarette was hanging from the corner of his mouth. The man seized the Sacred Host from the priest's hands and threw it on the floor. "If that's your God," he cried, "then let Him help you if He can!"

He did help us. He helped us all the time, night and day. Every page of this book testifies to God's grace. Looking back today to those years in Dachau, we still cannot thank God sufficiently for His merciful providence. He helped us just as He rewarded our oppressors — according to the deserts of each. Whenever we recited the Litany of the Saints together, we would repeat the words "That Thou wouldst vouchsafe to humble the enemies of Mother Church" three times over. And God heard our prayer.

"Thou hast prepared a table before me, against them that afflict me" (Ps. 22[23]:5)

We had the greatest difficulty in obtaining enough hosts for Holy Communion that first year. It seemed as though the devil was conspiring with the unbelievers in a pact against us. As our first reserves began to run low, we found it impossible to obtain supplies through the offices of the camp administration. We had as yet no "underground" channel at our disposal, and in any case, this would have been highly dangerous. For this reason, it was not always possible for us to receive Holy Communion every morning. As it was, we often had to break the small hosts into tiny fragments, which we divided among us, and sometimes we had even to resort to our camp ration of black bread.

Christus vincit! From that first day, on January 22, 1941, right up to the end of May 1945, Christ was present in Dachau in the form of the Blessed Sacrament, night and day without a break, and the camp authorities never knew it. Our Lord was kept hidden, and in spite of all danger, the Blessed Sacrament was never violated.

They even came searching the chapel for arms and, on one occasion, for a clandestine transmitter. They came tramping into our sanctuary with their jackboots and truncheons, but their godless hands never opened the tabernacle in all those four years. It was indeed a miracle, a miracle of Christ in Dachau.

Fr. Steinkelderer had been interned in Sachsenhausen. The following account is taken from his manuscript describing his experiences there. It gives a vivid picture of what priests interned in the prison camps of the Third Reich had to endure. But it also testifies to the victory of Christ the Arch Priest.

Our situation in Sachsenhausen grew steadily worse from month to month. There were already several hundred of us in the camp, herded together first in two and then in one single hut. Our first block capo had been diabolical enough, but he seemed almost an angel to us in comparison with the criminal from the Berlin underworld with twenty previous convictions who later succeeded him. Our misery at that time was indescribable. We were quite helpless, exposed to the blackmailing methods of this dreadful man and the power he had over us. He even cheated us out of our miserable rations. The man was definitely antisocial, opposed to us in every way. We had to sleep on the bare floor at night, and there was only room for us all if we lay on our sides, packed together like sardines.

In spite of our protests, the sick were made to sleep out in the lavatories, so as not to disturb his night's rest. We took it in turns to stay up with them during the night and gave what consolation we could to the dying. There were many who died, for starvation brought a strange sickness of its own. At that time, we priests were not admitted to the infirmary. We were simply used as beasts of burden for every sort of unpleasant work. We grew more and more despondent, for each of us knew in his own heart just about how long his strength would last out. We prayed silently for the strength to meet death worthily.

This was our situation on August 5, 1940, a day that none of us will ever forget. We could scarcely believe our ears when we heard orders to move over to three huts that had been requisitioned as our new quarters. An even greater surprise was the order for twenty priests to start work on Block 57, which was to be converted into a chapel. We learned that a Mass kit could be collected from the commandant's office. "From tomorrow, Mass is to be celebrated in the chapel, attended by all priests." This was the camp commandant's surprising order!

We could hardly believe it. We thought the authorities must be playing one of their tasteless jokes on us. But we had no time for further thought. I volunteered at once for the work. Joy gave us new strength, and we set to work at full speed. We had hardly been working half an hour before a crowd of SS men armed with sticks and drawn pistols burst into the room and began to abuse us in the vilest language imaginable. They drove us out by the doors and through the windows. But they drifted off before very long, and we set to work again. The chapel was soon ready. The scene created by the SS men seemed like the raging of the devil in the Gospel before he was forced to retreat at God's word.

Almost a thousand priests were assembled around the altar the next morning. It would be quite impossible to describe our joy and our gratitude at being able once more to assist at Mass, at being able to have Our Lord and God present with us behind the barbed wire of the prison camp. We had to get up earlier so as not to be late for work. Because of the blackout (we were not far from Berlin), the chapel was lit by two candles only.

To save time, we received Holy Communion in a way reminiscent of Mass in the catacombs of the early Christians. Each of us took a host from a plate near the door and held it in the palm of his hand. The priest at the altar consecrated our hosts together with his own, and at Holy Communion, we received the Body of Our Lord from our own hands.

In this way, Christ gave us visible proof of His word, "Behold, I am with you all days, even to the consummation of the world" (Matt. 28:20). In this way, God manifested Himself in this stronghold of atheism where the end of the Church and of Christianity was predicted nearly every day. We knew that the Holy Father and our bishops had once again interceded on our behalf in Berlin, but we knew, too, that only God in His love and providence could have overcome the obstacles that, in the eyes of the world, seemed insuperable. We in Sachsenhausen never learned how all this was made possible. For us, it was simply a miracle.

Our camp chaplain

January 20, 1941. I well remember how I stole away from our hut that evening, across to the new chapel in Block 26. I wanted to have a look at it for myself. As I tentatively tried the door, it was opened from the inside, and I found myself face-to-face with a tall, broadly built man with a pair of eyes as clear and candid as a child's. He smiled at me slowly, told me he was the camp chaplain, and, opening the door wider, he proudly showed me the chapel.

I was to see much of him later, and I learned to love this great man who had the courage of a lion if need be, especially in his dealings with the dreaded capos Z. and H.

Fr. Paul Prabutzki was born on September 3, 1893, in Iwiczno in Poland. During the first war, he had served as a captain in the German Army. He was ordained a priest in 1923 and soon gained a reputation for his pastoral work. When war broke out in 1939, he became a military chaplain in Poland. He was arrested in January 1940 and was sent to a concentration camp at Stutthof, near Danzig. In April 1941, he was transferred to Sachsenhausen and was appointed camp chaplain there on August 5. Together with the other priests from Sachsenhausen, he joined us in Dachau on December 15, 1941, and when the chapel was opened in Dachau, he was appointed our chaplain. He was sent to work on the plantation in September 1941 and died of starvation in August the following year.

We all loved and esteemed this great man for his honesty, his simplicity, and his courage. He was a great Pole but was in no sense a narrow nationalist. We had all hoped that he might have received a bishop's miter in Poland after the war. Instead, he was to die of hunger in a German concentration camp.

But the tragedy did not end there. Only two months before his own death, his brother Alois died of starvation, and at the beginning of August, his younger brother Boleslaus met his end on an "invalid transport." Three brothers, three priests, murdered within two months at Dachau.

A plan for the future

January 6, 1941, the feast of the Epiphany. A plan began slowly to take shape in my mind, a plan that occupied me all through those years in Dachau. I had no idea at that time whether I would be able to realize this plan, but it undoubtedly helped to carry me over the worst of those years, and I offered up my sufferings to this end. "If only half the plan succeeds," I used to tell myself, "then all this will not have been in vain."

I visualized a great international press campaign for God. The unbelievers could and did use the press to further their own ends, so I reasoned. Why should it not be possible to launch a similar campaign and win the world for God? My mind was seldom free from new ideas in this connection; I planned out details and sought ways to overcome obstacles.

I foresaw a monthly paper with a world circulation. It was to contain news and notes of God's Church, stories and accounts to rouse the enthusiasm of readers and win them to work, each in his own way, toward spreading His kingdom here on earth. It was a great scheme, a worldwide scheme, and I knew it would cost a lot of money. But I went on praying, and I knew that, if it were His will, God would help me.

On my release, I set about the realization of the plan, and I put the money I had received as compensation for the years in Dachau into this scheme. Several unexpected benefactors came to my aid too, but we never had enough. By 1960, only a small fraction of my original plan had materialized.

At that moment in 1941, however, the ultimate realization of the scheme did not seem so vitally important. Everything lay in God's hands, and at that time, the idea served to give me new strength, to fire me with a new enthusiasm for God and His kingdom. And so I followed patiently and faithfully in the steps of Our Lord on the Way of the Cross of the prison camp. There were many of us priests in Dachau who found strength and consolation in plans for the future, for what they would be able to do for Him when they were free again. In Dachau, they were serving their apprenticeship, as it were. Whether or not these plans of ours materialized afterward is relatively unimportant. Our prayers offered in this intention brought us nearer and nearer to God.

Hard times

As though the winter were not hard enough, what with the intense cold, the endless snow shoveling, and the lice, we now began to be plagued by the itch. The infection spread rapidly, and soon the authorities had to set up a special isolation hut.

Dachau was supposed to be a model camp, and the Nazi administration attributed the itch to lack of hygiene on the part of the prisoners themselves. Uncleanliness! They viewed the itch as a slur on the camp hygiene. We had brought this skin infection upon ourselves by our own personal habits, so they told us, and we would have to take the consequences. We had only ourselves to blame.

The camp authorities had always been very particular about order and cleanliness on the surface. The floors of the huts shone so that one hardly dared to set foot inside, and there were rows of meticulously neat beds. But all this was just an excuse to make our lives harder. The visitors who inspected our huts did not know that the palliasses were lousy. And although we were made to strip to the waist to wash every morning, we were rarely issued with a change of underwear. In our cramped quarters, tormented by incessant hunger and by lice, we were exposed to every infection. But the SS saw things differently.

And so the skin infection spread, much to the fury of the camp authorities and to our own intense misery.

An SS officer who came to inspect our hut one day lost his temper at the sight of the priests he found there, many of whom had caught this infection.

"We're going to stamp out this itch, or stamp all of you out!" he declared, red with rage. "One or the other has to disappear!" He began to examine us there and then, one after the other.

He found several new cases among us, and these unfortunates were taken away for "treatment." We had brought this infection on ourselves by our own dirty habits, they told us. We would have to pay the penalty.

Over in the isolation hut, prisoners were herded into the washrooms, and there a powerful jet of ice-cold water was played upon the most sensitive parts of their poor, half-starved bodies. They were then taken off for a "hunger cure," lying on palliasses on the floor. They were allowed no blankets and no underwear. It was a strange cure indeed, and small wonder that many did not survive it. The death rate among the Polish priests was particularly high. I myself spent nearly a week in this "itch ward,'" and I shall never forget the indescribable stench in that room, nor the groans from my unfortunate companions lying on the floor all around me.

Exceptions to the rule

Not all the atheist prisoners were corrupt or hardened cases. Some of them were genuinely good comrades and shared what they could with us without discrimination. Such an exception to the general rule was Capo Pfeifer from Mainz, in charge of the working party engaged in the disinfection of prison clothing. He often gave me a can of soup left over from his own rations during those hungry days.

Even among the SS, there were some good, warmhearted men, some of them practicing Catholics. In this connection, I particularly remember the guards in charge of the punishment block in Gusen. Another Gusen SS man once came to me to ask what he should do about his obligation to attend Mass on Sunday. The SS officer in charge of the plantation at Dachau was another good man and a Catholic, and there were devout Catholics among the civilian employees in the camp.

But such men were exceptions. There was no doubt about it. The camp SS and the tough communist and atheist prisoners conspired to make our life a hell.

Early in March 1941, many of us priests were detailed for work on the plantation. Once more, I found myself handling a wheelbarrow, but this time with earth and dung. We were compelled to work on Sundays. I particularly remember one Sunday afternoon. It was a clear day with a sharp northeast wind, and we had been issued no warm clothing. I thought I would surely die of pneumonia. And all the time, the SS men, muffled in thick overcoats, would be checking us through field glasses. We were thus in constant danger of being reported for every trivial transgression, never able to relax for a moment.

Such a report almost certainly meant the "twenty-five" or the dreaded punishment of "hanging." Father B., a good priest from the Rhineland, knew only too well what this meant. He had borrowed a second pullover from one of the other prisoners as an extra protection against the icy wind. This was strictly forbidden. The SS heard about it, and the unfortunate priest was given the "twenty-five," as a result of which he spent three months in the infirmary. The punishment left him with a deep scar, the size of a child's fist. Another priest, Fr. Alois Sindler, was punished for some equally trivial offense by being hung up by his arms for a whole hour. I shall not easily forget the sight of him as he dragged himself back to our hut afterward. It took a great deal of massaging to get him to rights again.

There was no class distinction in Dachau. Former ministers of state and common workmen addressed each other in the familiar Du. We all wore much the same clothes and were all equally poor. The "reds" (political prisoners) and the "greens" (criminals) were an exception, of course, for there was constant friction here. Black patches marked the punishment squad, yellow with a red triangle making a star was for Jews, violet for Jehovah's Witnesses (among the first to be put behind wire in the Third Reich), blue for emigrants, and pink for homosexuals.

When all was said and done, the only difference between any of us was our religious outlook. Our various patches were the outward signs of the categories in which our Nazi jailers had placed us. But it was our inner selves that counted in the eyes of God. We found ourselves in all kinds of situations during those years in Dachau. Many of us went through severe crises, not only physical but also spiritual, and it often happened that we were able to help our comrades in their hour of need. Dachau was to teach us many a hard lesson, for nowhere can the difference between human beings and inhuman beasts be so marked as in the communal life of a concentration camp. But God never deserted those who remained faithful to Him, and with His help, we were often able to bring others nearer to Him.

Spring 1941

The spring of 1941 brought several innovations but still no sign of our release.

On March 24, we were inspected by officers of the Wehrmacht, and I was passed as fit for service. I was glad to see the noticeable difference between these army officers and those of the camp SS. It is important to discriminate here between the Nazis and those who were drafted into the German Army and served without accepting the Hitler ideology. Fortunately, the Hitler salute was forbidden for us prisoners at Dachau — we were not considered worthy! In this way, I escaped from ever having to say "Heil Hitler!" Things were not so easy for those outside who did not share the Nazi outlook.

On March 25, a new decree came from Berlin. Priests were now exempt from work in the various heavy-labor commandos. We were still, however, employed as "porters" from the canteen. Our block had recently been segregated from the rest of the camp by a barbed-wire fence with a gate — in the same way as the punishment block. There were rumors that we were to receive better rations, and this was indeed the case on several occasions.

Easter came, and our little chapel resounded with our Alleluia! as we praised the risen Christ for His victory over sin and death.

Christ in Dachau

April 20, Hitler's birthday. But once again, the day passed without the hoped-for amnesty. *Pardon* was a word unknown in the Nazi vocabulary, so it seemed, like *humility*, *truth*, and *love*.

At first, we found ourselves with a good deal of free time, and as yet we had no breviaries. The SS had, moreover, given strict orders that the chapel was to be kept locked during the day. We all felt the need of prayer, however, so I founded a Rosary confraternity. Each of us said the Rosary privately every day, most of us using our fingers in lieu of beads, but this communal prayer gave us all new strength and inspired us with a greater love of prayer and a renewed ardor in our devotions to Our Lady. We tried in every possible way to use the time to good advantage, for it was the sincere desire of all of us that this time in Dachau should be a time of spiritual fruitfulness that would bring us new and increased blessings in our work as priests in the future.

May came, and Fr. Moosbauer organized a choir for the hymns to Our Lady. Many of us thought back nostalgically to May devotions in the old days at home. But we gained special permission for May devotions each evening in our chapel in Dachau. We owed a special debt of gratitude to Our Lady. Through Mary to Jesus. Through Mary to Christ — in Dachau.

Grey monotony

Sometimes the grey monotony of the camp seemed more than we could bear. We felt as though we had been damned to the special torments of this kind of hell. Hunger and disease, sheer desperation, and hopelessness could gradually reduce the strongest characters to pitiable morons, devoid of all willpower. At first, these prisoners would live on hope, from week to week and from month to month, and then as their strength began to fail, their hope began to fail too. They had nothing left, and death was waiting for them just around the corner. Bitter and disillusioned now, many of these men had been highly respected citizens outside. Now, in the concentration camp, reduced to a number and robbed of the last vestiges of human esteem, they would often resort to stealing from their comrades, and their greed and envy would drive them to take part in brawls over an extra ladle of soup. They had lost all self-respect and self-confidence — because they had lost God. God was not part of their lives. They just let themselves go, a prey to hunger and desperation, until death came.

We priests had known routine in the old days too, of course, the daily round, the various duties that had to be accomplished, often tedious, often monotonous. But it had been quite different. One had had one's home, even if it were only a room, and had been able to furnish it more or less according to one's own taste. Hunger had been unknown, and one's family and friends had been near at hand. One had oneself been esteemed as a human being, and there had been varied work offering scope for personal development and rewarding contact with others. There had been enough money for a civilized existence with books and music. One had known what one was working for and what life really meant. Everything had seemed so sure: one's sense of purpose, one's whole attitude to creation, and one's hopes for eternity...

And then, all of a sudden, we had been snatched out of all this and transferred to a concentration camp. We were deprived of our freedom, surely the dearest prize of every man; deprived, too, of every right, reduced to a number, to the status of slaves. Stripped of every trace of human dignity, we found ourselves helplessly exposed to the brutality of our oppressors. Nor did we know how long it would last. The convict serving a prison sentence can count the days, crossing them off the calendar. For us, however, the weeks, the months, and the years passed, and there seemed to be no hope that our ordeal would ever end. The rumors that had given us hope to cling to in the early days gradually ceased. They had brought us only disillusionment.

As Colonel Adam writes:

> The methods used by the SS in dealing with the prisoners, indeed, their very manner and attitude as such — even in normal everyday contact — made the camp into a sort of mixture between a barracks, a prison, and a madhouse. Their purpose was to reduce us to mental and spiritual wrecks by keeping us in a state of perpetual uncertainty. They forced us into a joyless existence, and hard labor and constant fear were designed to make an end of us.

In May 1946, the "Camp of Horror" was exposed to the whole world in photographs, in books, and in the press. Anton von Mörl, who saw the documentary film, writes, "I saw the film in company with several former comrades from the camp. We all thought afterward that the camp was much worse in reality." Yet for us who spent years in Dachau, the horror was not something we encountered every day — or perhaps we no longer saw it as such?

Human beings can accustom themselves to almost anything if need be. It is simply a question of time. Every concentration camp was different. Each had its own administration and its own development and history, often dependent on the commandant, the SS officers, and the camp personnel, and these changed, in some cases quite frequently. Some of us had a harder time than others, and there were some good comrades who were lucky enough to have good jobs in the camp and were left in peace and got enough to eat — even when times were hard.

"To break a man spiritually, you must first break him physically." These were the words of a Nazi official commenting upon his own methods.

Despite the grim situation, there were relatively few cases of suicide in the camps. This may seem strange in light of the terrible revelations of the first postwar years and considering the large numbers of unfortunate "morons" who, for the most part, had quite lost all sense of religious feeling. But these men had long since been robbed of the last of their willpower and most of them were so crushed and broken as to be incapable of this crime.

"Fundamentally, the concentration camps aimed to make an end of all opponents of the Nazi regime and of all 'useless' people," writes Adam. This was true particularly in the case of the "morons." They were incessantly deprived of their rights as human beings and half starved, and when their last spiritual and physical resources were finally exhausted, they ended as invalids in the incredible squalor and misery of the huts reserved for such cases. There they just vegetated amid the dirt and vermin until death came.

Once the spirit was broken, the vital resistance of the body was lost, and it only remained for sickness and disease to take the final toll. Diarrhea, pneumonia, tuberculosis … Although millions were murdered in the Nazi camps, many more were the victims of the grey, monotonous everyday existence, deprived of every natural joy and stimulus. The fact that Europe turned away from Christ and no longer practiced His teachings led to the catastrophe of the Third Reich. It was this same denial of God's providence on the part of many of the prisoners in the grey everyday existence of the Nazi camps that helped to bring death to many.

These human wrecks had dreamed of their freedom up to the very end — and we along with them. We would be there "until the end of the war," we were told by the Gestapo. But although the Nazi officials still envisaged the end of the war as a victory for Hitler, we knew better. And we knew, too, that in the event of the defeat that we felt must come, the camp SS would almost certainly kill us all before committing suicide themselves. Now and again, we overheard conversations between the guards that left no room for doubt about their intentions. And so, for us, there appeared to be no way out.

There was one way, only one, out of our desperate situation, and that was to place all our confidence in God and to trust in His providence and mercy. And it was quite true that every one of us in Dachau who believed in God was, in fact, brought nearer to Him. This was the salvation — for body and soul — for thousands in all the various camps throughout the Third Reich. The story of Hitler's concentration camps is more than part of the history of this infamous era; it is the triumphant testimony of the power of the spirit over the flesh, of the soul over the body, of the power of faith in God — in every situation in life.

It would be wrong to exaggerate one way or the other. Faith can by no means be regarded as a sort of life-insurance policy that can be calculated in figures; there were many good Christians who lost their lives in the camps. But they all died in faith and hope; only their bodies were broken — their souls returned victorious to their Creator.

On the other hand, countless unbelievers and active opponents of Christ and His Church survived the horror of the camps unscathed. Here we can only declare, as so often in life, that God's ways are often beyond our human comprehension. Perhaps we shall learn the answer to such apparent riddles in eternity. Ever since the beginning of time, good men have died while evildoers have survived triumphant. Why? God in His wisdom knows. Let us rather fix our eyes steadfastly on Christ in the promise of life everlasting.

As for the godless among us, camp life, with all it entailed, served only to make them more disillusioned, hard, and bitter. They, too, had their dreams and plans for the future — fantastic and evil plans of their own. But while they were interned, they were ruthless in their sole concern to make their own existence as tolerable as possible, naturally at the expense of their unfortunate comrades.

Christ in Dachau

A temporary improvement

Our existence as priests was undoubtedly very much better than that of the other prisoners, for we did have our chapel, and Christ in the Eucharist was present daily as our fellow captive. Had we not had this consolation, many of us might have ended as broken in spirit as in body.

"I am the bread of life," said our Lord (John 6:35). Every day we could receive this Bread of Life in Holy Communion. "And where I am, there also shall my minister be" (see John 12:26).

Our common need in Dachau seemed to draw us closer together as followers of Christ. Priest and layman found consolation together in prayer, the prayer that saved us from spiritual ruin, the terrible despondency that so often led to physical ruin. As in every situation in life, we knew we must not allow ourselves to become obsessed by our misery and troubles. The only thing to do was to forget ourselves and seek God's protection and mercy. Only thus could we save our souls — and our bodies — in our perilous situation.

In His infinite providence and wisdom, God cared for us, His priests, in a thousand ways. He was to ask much of us later on, but first of all, He showed us that He alone was almighty, even in Dachau behind the "gates of Hell."

Toward the end of March 1941, various improvements were introduced that served to make life more tolerable for us. Such innovations were not to last very long, but they did at least help us to regain something of our strength. It seemed as though we were being allowed this period of comparative ease for some specific purpose.

First of all, they enclosed our block with a fence with a gate — for our protection. Shortly afterward, we were withdrawn from the various working parties, and at last there was a little more meat and fat to be found in our midday stew. At Easter, we even received cocoa, beer, and wine, but we knew that much of these supplementary rations were stolen before they reached us, and by fellow prisoners at that. The wine and beer had been sent to us by unknown benefactors.

Needless to say, all these improvements served only to increase the hatred of the unbelievers. Full of envy and bitterness, they took every opportunity to take it out on us. Most of the capos and the communist prison "bosses" had better food than we had anyway, for despite all the improvements, we still never had enough to eat. But there was more behind their hatred than just envy or jealousy. They were simply unable to bear the thought of the power behind the Catholic Church.

But it was sleep more than anything else that helped us gradually to recover our physical strength. We were allowed to lie down for two hours in the morning and in the afternoon.

That summer, we were lent a harmonium by the parish priest of Dachau town. It was a good instrument, and we were deeply grateful for it. The priest, Fr. Pfanzelt, was untiring in his efforts to ease our lot in the camp, and in recognition of his good work on our behalf, the Holy Father raised him to the rank of domestic prelate in 1957, the year of his golden jubilee as a priest. This fine man died suddenly on September 8, 1958.

7

Trials and Tribulations

Some queer reasons

Sooner or later during our internment, we were all asked the same question, though in different ways. "Why were you arrested, Father?" or "What happened that they sent you to Dachau?" our fellow Christians would ask us almost shyly. But the unbelievers could never hide their curiosity and contempt. The disparaging tone and mockery of their questions revealed this only too well. "What brought you here anyway, eh?" or "A priest in the jug! I'll bet you weren't arrested for nothing!" We took this sort of thing for granted; it was just part of the Way of the Cross that we had to follow in the steps of our Master. We knew we could not expect those prisoners who had deliberately shut God out of their lives to understand what had brought us to Dachau. Mixed up with the real criminals, with the toughs and rowdies, the gypsies, the Jews, and countless others who were regarded as a public menace and the scum of society, were also Catholic clergy and Catholic laymen whose outlook and activities were not to the taste of the Nazi overlords.

The reasons for our arrest were, for the most part, trivial. The Gestapo was always on the lookout for offenders, and the slightest lapse sufficed to put a priest behind the barbed wire of Dachau. "They watched Him"; "they consulted together that by subtlety they might apprehend Him" (Luke 14:1; see Matt. 26:4). Plain speaking in defense of Christian truths during the religious instruction of children was enough; an unwary word in a sermon that could be twisted into an indictment … The cases were legion.

Christ in Dachau

"Love your enemies," Fr. Josef Hornauer had told a class of schoolchildren in 1939. One of the children repeated his words to her Nazi parents, and Fr. Hornauer found himself in Dachau.

Another priest, who died of starvation in Dachau in 1942, had been arrested simply for fulfilling his duty as a priest of the Church. In a mixed marriage, he had insisted upon the promise in writing by the Protestant bridegroom that the children would be brought up as Catholics. The groom denounced him to the Gestapo.

"This war will end just like the First World War. It will be followed by the same period of hunger and misery." Our good Fr. Rohrmoser had spoken these words one day in 1939 while visiting a sick parishioner. They were enough to seal his fate. This good old man was particularly loved and esteemed by the priests' community in Dachau, and we all felt his internment to be especially unjust.

Bishop Galen of Munster was renowned for his dauntless courage in opposing the Nazi ideology, and he was both feared and hated by his enemies. His pastoral letters were fearlessly outspoken. But while the Nazis never dared lay hands on the "Lion of Munster" himself, more than a dozen priests of his diocese were sent to Dachau on one occasion for having read aloud the bishop's condemnation of the mass murder of the insane and the sick by the Nazi authorities.

Two old priests, Fr. Schulz and Fr. Zilliken, were also among those who died of starvation in Dachau in 1942. They had failed to give the Hitler salute when Hermann Göring came into a restaurant where they were having supper. They spent three years in the camp before they died.

"It is inner courage that really counts. Nobility of soul is worth far more than medals and decorations." These words in a sermon brought Fr. Konrad Tragesser to Dachau where he, too, died.

Another priest ended in Dachau because he warned one of his parishioners against joining the SS. There were plenty of spies and betrayers in the Third Reich.

In Salzburg, a priest said Mass for the repose of the soul of a communist who had been executed by the Nazis. The man had made his peace with God and had died a Catholic. Fr. Dürnberger was sent to Dachau.

The reasons were indeed grotesque: hearing the confessions of Polish prisoners; writing letters to parishioners at the front; giving cigarettes to deported workers — works of Christian charity but crimes in the eyes of those who seemed to have reversed the Ten Commandments and the precepts of the Sermon on the Mount and turned all good to evil.

There were certainly some priests who had been arrested on indictable charges. Priests are human beings, and every one of us recites the Confiteor daily at the foot of the altar. But the Nazis viewed sin in a different light. One of their acknowledged "prophets," Bergmann, declared that "the greatest sin is to believe in sin."

Our enemies made use of every slightest transgression by a priest to further their own ends. Fines and penalties bore no relation whatsoever to the triviality of the offense. Many offenses were against the labyrinthine laws governing public speech, a maze of traps for the priest in the pulpit, and arrests were frequent. The Gestapo was never unduly concerned about truth or justice, for they were out to get their man, and in their eyes, the end justified the means. Many a priest was falsely denounced to the Gestapo; libel and falsehood of all kinds were used, if need be, to place a dangerous opponent of Hitler's new religion behind barbed wire. It was a logical enough development that such methods should have been used to lay hands upon the priests of Christ's Church upon earth, for Christ Himself had been branded a political criminal in very much the same sort of circumstances and had been "legally" sentenced to death.

In time, interest in the "crimes" committed by our comrades in the camp virtually ceased, for it was taken for granted that we were all there due to some abuse of justice. We, the innocent, were at the mercy of the guilty in this totalitarian state ruled by Adolf Hitler in which human rights and the respect of human dignity were unknown.

Priests as workers

Characteristic of the Third Reich was the emphasis put upon work and productivity. The whole system was based from the start upon materialism. It was therefore logical that we priests should be expected to bear our share of the burden of work, and the authorities had no compunction about using us in every possible way. True, our situation was alleviated — for a time at least — by the diplomatic victory of our bishops, but by and large, we were not spared.

At first, it had been the unwritten law that all priests were detailed for hard labor in the punishment squad. The Berlin regulations changed this, but as the war continued, and so work for Hitler's victory assumed ever-increasing importance, priests were once again taken for the harder kinds of labor. After the end of April 1942, most of the priests in Dachau were made to work on the plantation. There were some five hundred to seven hundred of us working in the various sections, in the tea and herb gardens, vegetable gardens, in the six great glasshouses and the nurseries, as well as in the fields and in the special research and training section. The civilian steward in charge of the farm stock also made use of priest workers in all weather and in all conditions, right up to 1944.

There were also priests working in the carpenter's shop and various other workshops and in the office of the SS paymaster. Fr. Adolf Staudacher was in charge of this clerical department for almost a year, with a staff of 120 fellow priests.

Some of the working parties were employed outside the camp itself. It gave us a certain sense of freedom to leave the barbed wire behind us, but it was only an illusion, for the SS guards never left us, and from the perimeter watchtowers, machine guns kept us always covered.

The working parties, or commandos — to give them their camp name — on duty inside the camp were used for all kinds of work under the direction of the camp SS personnel. There were commandos for keeping the camp and the buildings clean, for work in the canteen, in the clothing store, in the library, for work as block clerks, for repairing straw mattresses, and so on.

On the whole, we were glad of this work, for at least it introduced an element of variety into the grey monotony of everyday life, as well as a certain order into our seemingly pointless existence. Although we always had the unhappy feeling that our work was aiding and abetting the enemy to organize his concentration camp, we knew, too, that in maintaining order and cleanliness, as far as was possible, we were also serving our fellow prisoners and protecting our own interests.

For us priests, however, our work served to further another and perhaps even more important objective. Many of the prisoners in the camp viewed priests as a sort of race apart. In their eyes, we had always had a soft life in comparison with the working man. It was obvious they had never realized what lay behind the exterior; they could not be expected to appreciate that the fact that we were not engaged in manual labor did not mean that we were "soft" in our work in the world. They had no idea what the constant nervous strain, the spiritual and physical discipline, and the daily grind of a normal priest's life really involved. In Dachau, however, our working-class prisoners saw us working alongside them, often engaged in really hard labor. We shared the same living conditions as these men and, like them, often had to work on an empty stomach. It was our aim as servants of God to set about everything we did in the camp with a light heart and in the spirit of Christian patience. They saw us bear our burdens as servants of Christ. We did everything we could to abolish old prejudices and mistaken ideas, and our work served to bring us closer to the other prisoners who, in turn, learned to see their priests with new eyes. Through our work, we were often also spared the taunts and active hostility of our atheist comrades. They could see for themselves that our situation was really no different from their own and that we were prepared to work with them. Our misery we had in common, and here, too, we were to draw closer, learning to know and understand one another better.

Last but not least, our work also afforded us the chance to gain a more intimate knowledge of the SS — their mentality, their system, their methods, and so on.

But for all the opportunities it gave us priests for indirect pastoral activities, work in the concentration camp, indeed all work within the Nazi system, was organized in the purely materialistic spirit typical of the Hitler regime — human dignity and human rights being sacrificed. God had not willed this attitude toward labor in His creation. The words of Pius XII, in his Christmas message in 1942, are significant in this connection:

> He who would have the Star of Peace shine out and stand over society should give to work the place assigned to it by God from the beginning.

I was myself by no means an industrious prisoner, at least not in the sense of the word as used by the camp authorities, for I counted it a sin to work for the interests of the SS. We had, as it were, fallen among thieves, and it was clear that we had no other choice but to serve them, but I took good care that such work was never more than the minimum demanded in order to preserve my own life and that of my companions.

Even in Dachau, news reached us of the Austrian resistance movement, and this spirit of resistance had indeed been active in the camp itself ever since

Christ in Dachau

1933. With the arrival of many of Austria's Catholic leaders in 1938, this spirit gained a new impetus. There were, of course, always some who were only too ready to toe the line and who went out of their way to serve the Nazi authorities for selfish motives. The elite among the prisoners, however, made a real effort to use their time and energy to the best advantage, seeking the protection and guidance of God in their endeavor to prepare themselves spiritually for the work of reconstruction later on.

I, too, did my best to make good use of my time — but not for the SS. I once set down my fundamental principles for daily life in the camp. Heaven knows what would have happened to me if the SS guards had found this paper.

For us priests, our life in the camp should be governed by the following:
1. Prayer and development of the spiritual life.
2. Intellectual study — as far as this is possible.
3. Work in the camp in the service of fellow prisoners.
4. Work in the camp that furthers respect and honor for the priesthood (e.g., good example).
5. Physical exercise in the interests of health.
6. It is wrong to undertake more work in the camp than is demanded by the reasons above.
7. It is wrong, especially for priests, to undertake more work than necessary and so neglect our spiritual life, intellectual study, or health.
   Dachau Concentration Camp, May 1944

A dreaded task

"Come on! Out you get, you lazy black dogs! Damn you all!" The stream of invective was accompanied by shrill whistles from the road outside our hut. The dreaded capos and block personnel were after the food carriers. Every day, three times a day, the ritual was invariable. Food carrying was a dreaded chore in the camp and the exclusive privilege of us priests. Even during the time we were exempt from other forms of hard work, food carrying had been reserved for the "black dogs." This went on until after the end of 1942, when, thank God, the metal buckets containing our food were delivered by truck. The job involved carrying more than five hundred great metal buckets from the kitchens to the huts. It took two men to carry one of these containers, for they held about thirteen gallons. In the morning, it was a black brew of ersatz coffee; at midday, stew; and in the evening, soup or tea. Each bucket weighed about 160 pounds when full and had to be carried by thin iron handles, which cut into our hands. Bucket partners were often unequal in height or strength, adding to the danger of spilling, particularly on the icy kitchen steps. Spilling might mean double misfortune, for in addition to the loss of the already meager rations, there was the danger of burns and scalds. Often there were not enough prisoners to go around, so some unfortunates had to make the trip twice. Winter made it worse — first, because our clothes offered no protection and, second, because chilblains often added to the pain and discomfort of hands blistered from the day before. In our half-starved condition, we could barely stagger along with our heavy burden, and accidents were frequent — broken arms or legs, ruptures, strained hearts, not to mention the inevitable scalds and burns. It goes without saying that the capos and the block personnel took no part in such strenuous activities — except, of course, as overseers.

Standing

Roll call was another of our trials and tribulations.

"We're standing our way to Heaven," we used to remind each other ruefully. Unless you have been in a concentration camp yourself, you can hardly imagine what this was like. We were made to stand quite straight in parade formation on the concrete square, sometimes for more than an hour on end, regardless of the weather. In the blazing, merciless summer sun, in torrential rain, in the icy northeast wind, in fog, and in blizzards.

We may have smiled when we talked about "standing our way to Heaven," but, in fact, it was true, for roll call in Dachau was a very real form of martyrdom, and it was possible to endure it only if it were accepted as an offering for the love of God. God is love, and love makes everything possible. Roll call in Dachau was thus another means of drawing closer to Christ. It was easy enough to pick out the prisoners who accepted the ordeal in this spirit. Their heads slightly bowed, their eyes half closed, their whole being was absorbed in prayer. There were hundreds, perhaps even thousands, of prisoners in Dachau who made use of this roll call as an interlude for prayer — three rosaries, perhaps, or the Litany of Our Lady, or morning or evening prayers. It was all possible. The difference between prisoners was nowhere else so evident. There were some who could never stop talking, some who just stood there staring vacantly in front of them, spitting now and then without the slightest consideration for their neighbors, there were the dirty-story tellers, and those who just gave vent to an incessant flow of vile language — though taking good care not to be overheard by the SS. The camp authorities sat comfortably behind the plate-glass windows of the administrative buildings and watched us through field glasses, and the worse the weather was, the longer they kept us standing there, swaying on our feet from utter exhaustion after the day's exertions on the evening roll call or, in the morning, filled with the nagging uncertainty about what new ordeal the day would bring. I often wonder how many hours we spent in Dachau standing our way to Heaven.

Things improved after 1942. The system was tightened up and changes were introduced, so that later on, it was usually possible to get through a roll call in fifteen minutes.

With all my heart, I used to pity those prisoners who could not pray in the apparent hopelessness and senselessness of our camp. Roll call taught us another lesson of prayer, being just one more of the things it was possible to endure for years on end in the spirit of devotion to Our Lord. If you could catch hold of God's hand in the darkness, you could begin to amass inestimable riches for eternity — and all through prayer.

Singing

After roll call, the command was given to form up in the various working parties. A sort of general shuffle then took place as the twenty thousand prisoners pushed and elbowed their way past one another, shouting and cursing, until they reached the point where their respective commandos were lined up. Each capo then checked the number of his party, for he had to tell the SS how many men he was taking off to work and that number had to check in in the evening. If they did not, the capo would be punished, and sometimes the whole party or even the whole camp. We were then marched off to work, SS guards accompanying any commandos employed outside the camp.

Of course we had to sing. Singing was all part of the Nazi idea of culture. Besides which, everyone outside the camp had to hear with what light hearts the prisoners from Dachau went marching off to work! The only thing that mattered to our SS masters was that we should sing loudly and in march time. So we blared and shouted our way to roll call, to the working sites, to punishment drill — and back. It was hard enough, as it was, to march properly in our hard wooden shoes, but the SS soon taught us the elements of Prussian drill — in their own inimitable way. I used to think I would go mad if I were forced to listen once more to those camp songs. After 1942, however, there were so many nationalities in the camp that it would have been impossible to go on singing those German marching songs. In any case, work was what counted then, and in the drive for more "work for victory," even the Nazi culture was forgotten. Armaments were far more important.

Christians who thought differently

"In my experience, the prisoners who denied God almost invariably lost every trace of self-respect and gave rein to everything base in their characters, whereas every contact with Christ served only to enrich and ennoble the prisoners who found their way to Him, even if they did not share our Catholic Faith." Anyone who has been in a prison camp will certainly agree with this opinion of a Catholic priest who spent seven years in a concentration camp. Their sufferings and privations served to bring many Lutherans, Calvinists, Anglicans, and others nearer to God.

Our relationship with our brothers in Christ, however, had certain aspects that presented their own peculiar difficulties, particularly for us Catholic priests. Our chapel in Dachau was a Catholic chapel and had been obtained for us with the greatest difficulty by the Catholic Church. We all knew this, and it was therefore only natural that we did not always welcome the use of our sanctuary by those who were, in our eyes, heretics — despite all the ties that bound us together in the love of Our Lord. For many of us, the use of our Catholic chapel by other denominations was something quite new and strange, and not altogether acceptable.

Our Lord was present there day and night in the tabernacle, and it was hard to witness the indifference, not to say irreverence, of those who did not recognize the Real Presence for all that they spoke of Christ. We could only think of the words in St. John's Gospel, "There has stood one in the midst of you, whom you know not." (John 1:26).

Nor could they understand our devotion to Mary, the Mother of God, Our Lady of Dachau.

Many of our Protestant friends and comrades called themselves "Evangelical" — followers of the Gospel. But surely, we argued to ourselves, we had the true Gospel of Christ?

For the most part, however, we Catholic priests were good friends with our fellow prisoners of other Christian denominations. There were many fine men among them, and many with true understanding and compassion for the misery, both spiritual and physical, of their unfortunate comrades. Many gave their lives for their religious convictions. We often profoundly regretted that they had not found their way to our Mother Church.

Believing Protestants, whatever their denomination, are, after all, our brothers and sisters in Christ. They, too, live in the Christian heritage; they, too, believe in Jesus Christ as the perfect Man and the Redeemer of mankind. But because they have cut themselves off from Mother Church, much of the Christian revelation has been lost to them.

I found myself wondering whether they would ever find their way back to the Church founded by Christ. The more I thought about the differences that kept us apart, the more I realized that faith, the true faith, is the greatest gift God can give us.

A Protestant theologian, Paul Schütz, declared in 1945, "Nothing can be harder for us, the heirs of the Reformation, than to have to admit that the schism has, in fact, served only to reverse the desired effect of our own Reformation." This is indeed true. The Reformation was to lead to a deformation — with the result that many fell away from Christ.

It was Cardinal von Galen who declared in Rome on February 20, 1946: "The Germans have been guilty of many crimes against their compatriots and against other nations. This is the result of the apostasy that has been poisoning the whole world now for centuries."

Two-thirds of Germany was Protestant when Hitler came to power. According to figures published in 1945, there were 17 German Protestant ministers interned in Dachau (and 33 of other nationalities). The Catholic third of Germany was represented by 190 Catholic priests. The figures are significant, for they reveal who was the true opponent, who provided the real challenge to "the gates of Hell."

Priests of God

"Is it really true, all that the newspapers say about the concentration camps?" Over and over again, people have asked me this question. It is not surprising, for those who lived through the Nazi era were naturally inclined to be a bit skeptical about newspapers. For years, they had been confronted by Nazi propaganda and lies. Many could simply not bring themselves to accept the facts; their own consciences gave them no peace, for the revelations were a terrible indictment of the Nazi regime, which they themselves had chosen to accept.

The accounts in the papers were certainly true, but they showed only one side of the horror, only half of the truth. The journalists could never have described the real misery, the spiritual suffering, the countless tragedies in the very depths of the souls of some of the prisoners.

The journalists and writers succeeded admirably in describing the background of our life in the concentration camp; they painted the background true to life in the appropriate garish colors, and they conveyed the horror atmosphere very well indeed. This was the scene in which we priests suddenly found ourselves. Everything was startlingly new for us. We had to sink or swim, right from the start, and it was by no means easy, particularly for those of us who were already old. For the younger champions of God's cause, things were infinitely easier, but two-thirds of the priests in Block 26 were over fifty, and a quarter were well over sixty. Yet in Dachau, just as everywhere else in this life, it was not age that really mattered but the inner, the spiritual, maturity — a fact demonstrated most patently by the noble and courageous attitude in the face of all his sufferings of an old Lithuanian priest, Fr. Stanislaus Pujdo, who was eighty-two.

A priest outstanding for the example he set us all was the saintly Benedictine Abbot Hondet, from the border country between France and Spain, who arrived in Dachau together with his prior toward the end of 1944. As number 137,737, he came to join the priests' community in Block 26. Abbot Hondet reminded us in many ways of our beloved martyr bishop, Dr. Michael Kozal from Poland, who had died in Dachau in January 1943. Like Bishop Kozal, the abbot from France refused, in true humility, any attempts on our part to alleviate his situation. Despite his physical weakness, he was filled with a spiritual fire that made him impervious to all outward things. This deep spirituality explained his complete lack of narrow nationalistic ideas. The man was supranational in everything he thought, said, and did.

People have often asked me how God could permit such injustice. How could God allow His own priests to endure such misery and suffering? Most of the people who asked me such questions had not taken the trouble to think clearly, but now and again, one even heard the question asked in Dachau among the priests. One glance at the Cross of Our Lord and Redeemer surely provides us all with the only true answer.

"The Cross is my book," the Capuchin saint Br. Konrad of Parzham so truly said in his simple peasant wisdom. We in Dachau heard these words for the first time in a talk given by one of the priests about St. Konrad. "The Cross is my book!" Many of us had grown old in the wisdom of books, but in the wisdom of the Cross, we still had much to learn. For the Cross provides the answer to everything. How could God have allowed His own Son . . . He not only allowed Him to die for us, but it was His active will that it should be so.

We were faced with many disillusionments on our Way of the Cross in Dachau, but perhaps the bitterest of these was the recognition that there were some among us who fell far short of the priest's ideal. No one would dare to deny that we are all human and that each of us is capable of falling, but all the same, the sight of a priest who had lacked the strength to resist the new temptations to which we were all exposed was something painful indeed. Tragic as such cases were, however, they served to make us realize our own weaknesses and to see that we could achieve nothing without God's help — a humbling but strength-giving recognition.

Life in Dachau demanded a high degree of patience and Christian charity. Unless you kept a very firm hold on God, you were in constant danger of falling. The sort of life that had been forced upon us presented new and inhuman temptations, and there were indeed some among us who fell victim to the spiritual and physical misery that often accompanied our situation. The incessant hunger was a terrible trial for both body and soul; the cramped quarters and nervous strain of the communal huts were almost intolerable — all this slowly broke their will and robbed them of their last spiritual resources.

Many of the priests were older men accustomed to authority. Transplanted to Dachau, they found themselves exposed to very real dangers of all kinds. It was sometimes too much to bear: the injustice of our imprisonment, which seemed interminable; the hopelessness of our situation; the constant petty irritations of community life; above all, the grey monotony of our everyday existence, which seemed so utterly futile. These were heavy spiritual burdens, and they proved too heavy for some. Tragic as this was, it was yet another lesson for us: we learned to draw nearer to God ourselves in the knowledge that we were all human. Just as Christ's Church is a divine institution in the hands of man, so God deliberately chose human instruments for His divine plan. We were the instruments, for all our weakness. "Satan hath desired to have you that he may sift you as wheat," said Christ to the first apostles, the first priests of the Church (Luke 22:31). The devil is indeed no respecter of persons.

The cross of nationalism

Not the least of our trials and tribulations in Dachau were those connected with the problems of nationality. Priests from more than twenty nations found themselves concentrated in the most cramped quarters — human beings, all of them, all different in temperament, in upbringing, in education, in susceptibilities and spiritual and intellectual gifts. It was inevitable that there should be differences. The peculiar obstacles and difficulties arising from such a situation must have been obvious from the outset to anyone with a little understanding of human nature. There were unfortunately some among us, however, who had no such understanding, and they were to make our Way of the Cross even more difficult inside the priests' block in Dachau.

Some of the peoples of Europe have strong nationalist tendencies. No matter how they might strive toward perfection in the eyes of God, the priests of these nations interned in Dachau could not and would not rid themselves of such inborn nationalistic prejudices and complexes. They identified themselves with their country and were incapable of thinking on a supranational plane, no matter how they might try. They were priests of the universal Church, filled with deep religious convictions, sons of God, but sons, too, of their own particular nations, with all their characteristic virtues — and weaknesses.

September 21, 1941. This was a dark day indeed, for orders came that the Polish priests were no longer to be allowed to use the chapel. Nothing we German-speaking priests could do, no intervention, no petition, could change this order, which came directly from Berlin. We were all incensed by the injustice of the ruling but were completely helpless to alter it. All we could do now was trust in God's providence and pray for help for our Polish comrades who, now more than ever, longed for Our Lord in the Blessed Sacrament in their spiritual desolation. We were, however, forbidden to allow anyone but the inmates of Block 26 into the chapel, and Block 26 was segregated from the rest of the camp by a fence.

It was a terribly difficult situation for us German priests, for, much as we longed to help the Polish priests, we knew that we would jeopardize the chapel for ourselves if we broke the rule. We all knew that it was vital that the chapel should remain in the camp. We knew that Christ in the Blessed Sacrament must be kept in Dachau, no matter how hard the sacrifice might be for our Polish friends. It was desperately hard for us to have to witness their misery, to have to deny them admittance to our sanctuary, but there was clearly no other course open to us in the circumstances. The SS were only waiting for an excuse to deprive us of our chapel, and we knew that failure on our part to comply with the new orders would immediately be classed as mutiny — with disastrous consequences. This delicate situation was further aggravated by the attitude of some of our German priests, for there were some who would turn away the Poles in a manner that served only to rouse resentment and old prejudices, thus widening the nationalistic breach. There were others, too, who went to the other extreme and, in their irresponsible open defiance of the new regulation, deliberately provoked punishment for the whole community.

As the months passed and more and more priests from other nations came to join us, it was inevitable that tension should increase. Most of these new priests came to Dachau with a quite understandable mistrust of anyone who spoke German. Germany had, after all, not only been responsible for their own arrest but had overrun their country and brought misery to thousands of their compatriots. It was certainly hard for them, in the circumstances, to view things in a truly Catholic perspective. Yet it was indeed our living Faith that enabled us to master the situation, for in our Faith we are all brothers, members of the universal Church, which is supranational. As Catholics, we all believe that suffering is the will of God. His purpose lies behind everything we are forced to endure in this world, for He alone is over everything, in everything. Thank God, there were many who saw things in this light. But there were some who thought quite differently, and they made our cross even harder to bear.

We were confined together for what seemed to us like an eternity, bearing the cross of our arrest together as best we could. For the majority of us, it really was the cross of our salvation, for it brought us nearer together, taught us mutual understanding, and broke down the senseless barriers of personal ambition and narrow nationalism. We learned to love and respect these men whose national character was often so different from our own. We knew that we were all God's children, and together we looked to Him for His protection.

Just because Dachau taught us so much here, it is our paramount duty as priests to preach the love of God. For the closer we come to know God's love, the more must we come to realize that there is no place for resentment or narrow nationalism. Christ's Church is Catholic, and no one who recognizes this can fall prey to false nationalist "ideals."

Our two bishops

There were only two bishops interned in Dachau, and neither was German. "Hitler had learned one lesson from the history of the Kulturkampf of the eighties and realized that the imprisonment of German bishops in the concentration camps of the Third Reich would be the first step toward a retreat" (Fr. Georg Schelling). Not even the great Bishop von Galen of Munster, who was feared and hated by the Nazis for his plain speaking, was arrested.

The first Dachau bishop was the gallant Dr. Kozal from Poland. "Bishop Kozal is a saint!" Anyone who had known him in the Dachau days could not but share this widespread opinion. Shortly after his consecration on August

13, 1939, he was arrested by the German SS and subjected to indescribable indignities. I shall have more to say about this heroic man later.

The second bishop was a Frenchman, Gabriel Piguet from Clermont-Ferrand, a kindly man who held his high office with simple dignity in the grey dreariness of camp life. Bishop Piguet was born in 1887, studied with the Jesuits in Villefranche and Rome, and served with the French Army during the First World War, in which he was wounded and several times decorated. He was consecrated bishop in 1933. He was arrested in full regalia after a Pontifical High Mass on Whitsunday 1944. His crime? Sending one of his priests to hear the confessions of a group of resistance men. He was sent to work in the quarries of the notorious camp at Natzweiler in Alsace. When he arrived in Dachau on September 7, 1944, he was a physical wreck and spent several weeks in the camp infirmary before joining us in Block 26. As number 103,001 he shared our life in the camp and was always the best and most loyal of comrades. We did what we could to protect him from the taunts and active hostility of the atheist prisoners and to spare him, as best we could, the hunger that so plagued us at that time. The bishop was nearly always to be found among his flock of French priests, and he spent as much time as he could with the young theology students.

By May 14, 1945, he was back in his diocese, and in September of that year, he wrote to Cardinal Faulhaber in Munich expressing his appreciation and gratitude for the help and comradeship of the German priests with whom he had been interned at Dachau.

The Nazis had succeeded in interning two Catholic bishops. For them, this was only the beginning. Their aim was to destroy the Catholic Church, for they rightly recognized it as their one real opponent. In their pride and vainglory, they thought lightly to destroy the divine institution of Christ Himself, an institution that had successfully withstood similar barbarous attacks upon it for almost two thousand years.

In his book *Cross and Swastika*, the German bishop Johannes Neuhäusler refers to a statement made by an SS official in charge of political prisoners at Sachsenhausen: "We shall destroy the Church once and for all. Christianity and the Catholic Church in Germany must be stamped out for good! We have a plan to this end, a plan carefully worked out down to the very last detail. This time we shall succeed. The Church must be destroyed."

The only logical answer to the problems of mankind is Catholic Christianity. This and this alone provides a complete answer, whereas Marxism and all the other "isms" can give only partial answers to these problems.

— Tom Keep, former communist president of a trade union
in England who became a Catholic in 1955

8

Calvary

Persecution

There was no place for God in the Nazi ideology, and it was logical that there should be no place for God in the hell of their concentration camp. The Nazi hatred of Catholic priests was intense, and anyone who stood out in defense of Christian values was liable to be subjected to all kinds of ill-treatment. The following accounts of their personal experiences by priests interned in Nazi prison camps prove the truth of this:

Dachau: "On Christmas Eve 1938, a university professor from Vienna who was a recent convert came over to my bed and asked me to say the Rosary with him. It was already late, and we sat there in the dark, praying together in whispers. We were halfway through when the SS guards arrived. It was forbidden to pray or indulge in any religious activities, and a fellow prisoner had reported us to the authorities. I was beaten up for the second time and sent to the dreaded bunker for two days on bread and water."

Dachau: "Some petty offense had sufficed for the order for 'punishment drill' for the whole block. The prisoners were ordered to lie prone on the ground, whereupon the guards armed with truncheons proceeded to drive the priests over the helpless bodies of their unfortunate comrades."

Sachsenhausen: "Father Würl, a priest from the Austrian Tyrol, was made to stand in a half-frozen puddle of water as a 'punishment.' He once moved his feet to prevent them from freezing, whereupon the

SS man made him lie in the puddle, holding his head down with his jackboot while he finished smoking his cigarette. No wonder Fr. Würl was branded for the rest of his life with a frostbitten nose. No sooner had he been allowed to get up than his tormentor ordered him to sing a parody of a well-known hymn. Würl refused, and to our surprise and relief, the SS man went off and left his victim in peace."

Dachau, 1938: "Two great water butts stood outside the kitchens. One of the SS men picked out a Jew and a Catholic priest and ordered them to blaspheme against God. When they refused, he spat at them and, seizing hold of them, ducked them alternately in the water until they were both exhausted and died."

Dachau: "A young priest had been ordered to work on a barbed wire fence. The sentry ordered him to plait a crown of thorns out of the barbed wire and then pressed it on the priest's head until it was a mass of wounds."

It was curious how we were subjected to the worst treatment on Sundays and feast days, particularly feasts of Our Lady — as though our enemies recognized the power of our mighty mediator against the forces of evil.

The punishment squad was a sort of hard-labor camp within the camp. As Fr. Schelling writes, "It was a terrible system of punishment. We were completely isolated from the rest of the camp, kept on hunger rations all the time, and forbidden to read or smoke. The working tempo was unbelievable. And all this even in peacetime."

Up to 1940, all the priests sent to Dachau were automatically sent to the punishment squad. Those who arrived later were spared some of the worst experiences of camp life.

Fr. Kleinbruckner was sixty-two when he was sent to Dachau. A good country priest from Upper Austria, he had been arrested as "a fanatical opponent of the National Socialist regime." He, too, was sent to the punishment squad.

"For several weeks I was made to eat off the floor," he recounts. "The usual form of address was 'Swine!,' 'Dog!,' 'Bastard!,' etc. On one occasion, I had not made my bed in accordance with the strict regulations. For punishment, I was given ten weeks extra-hard labor (two hours of extra work after the evening roll call every day)."

Modern martyrs

Toward the end of September 1939, Dachau concentration camp was temporarily closed. The authorities announced that it was to be used during the winter as a training center for SS troops, and three fortnightly courses were planned. The prisoners were transferred to other camps and were supposed to come back in the spring. Thus, the authorities were able to announce that Dachau was no longer a concentration camp, and they hoped that thereby it might lose something of the notoriety it had been gaining over the years. The camp was reopened in March 1940, the prisoners having been sent in the meantime to Mauthausen, Flossenbürg, and Buchenwald, camps at that time almost worse than Dachau itself. There were as yet relatively few priests in Dachau, but for these, the transfer to new camps was the start of another Way of the Cross, a way that often ended on Calvary. Life in a new and unfamiliar camp exposed them at once to new dangers and unexpected hazards.

Fr. Otto Neururer was the parish priest of Götzens, a village not far from Innsbruck in the Austrian Tyrol. He was the youngest of the twelve children of a poor peasant from the Pitztal. As Fr. Georg Schelling writes, "This simple man impressed everyone who came into contact with him." A small, thin man with an open face and a pair of keen, intelligent eyes, he was no match for his godless companions. He had been sent to Dachau for "hindering an Aryan marriage": he had used all his influence to dissuade a young peasant girl in his parish from marrying a man well over *sixty* with a bad reputation. The man had denounced him to the Gestapo, and within a month, on March 4, 1939, he found himself in Dachau, whence he was later transferred to Buchenwald. On May 28, 1940, with another priest prisoner, Fr. Spannlang, a great giant of a man who had been a parish priest in Upper Austria, he was ordered to report to the commandant. Both hoped desperately that they were to be discharged, but instead they were escorted to the bunker. At evening roll call on May 30, Neururer was reported dead. On June 4, Fr. Spannlang followed him. Both priests had been brutally murdered in the bunker. They had been betrayed by fellow prisoners who, acting as SS spies, had come to ask for secret religious instruction. Overjoyed at the prospect of being able to do some priestly work again, Fr. Neururer had agreed — but in Buchenwald, religious practices of any kind were punishable with death. Some lay prisoners who professed to have inside information said they had been crucified head downward.

Fr. Alfred Berchtold, however, who was in Buchenwald at the time and is an absolutely reliable source, told me that Fr. Neururer was hanged head downward for thirty-six hours until he was dead. "The whole thing was done with the greatest care," declared Fr. Berchtold, who had spoken with a warder present at the time. The actual murderers were two SS men.

"They wrapped his feet in sheepskin so that the chains they hanged him by should leave no marks on the skin," the warder told Fr. Berchtold. "Neururer made no protest whatever. When they strung him up, he groaned once or twice, and then I saw his lips moving as if in prayer. The SS men stayed there some time, laughing and jeering at their victim. When it was all over — and it took thirty-six hours — the warder showed me the sheepskins and the chains and explained how they had been used. He threatened to denounce me to the authorities if I dared mention as much as a word about the true cause of Neururer's death in the camp. He said it was the only way he could save his own skin. I promised to hold my tongue until the Nazi era had passed."

Fr. Neururer had been a good priest and was universally loved and esteemed by his flock. The camp authorities informed his clerical superiors that he had died on May 30, 1940, as the result of a cerebral hemorrhage, and the urn containing his ashes was later returned to his parish of Götzens.

As is the custom in Austria and Germany, a detailed announcement of his death appeared in the newspapers.

Msgr. Carl Lampert, the pro-vicar of Innsbruck, was responsible for the text of the announcement:

> God in His infinite love has called our dearly beloved parish priest Fr. Otto Neururer home to Him. Fr. Neururer died far away from his home and parish in Weimar-Buchenwald. We all knew Fr. Neururer to be an exemplary priest who served his parish with selfless devotion. His life among us and his death will never be forgotten. The date of the funeral will be announced later. — The Parishioners of Götzens, May 31, 1940

This announcement was later to cost Msgr. Lampert his own life.

Fr. Johann Schroffner, a strongly built, plainspoken man, was another of those sent from Dachau to Buchenwald. He, too, had been a parish priest in the mountains of the Tyrol and had been arrested for his outspoken comments about the Führer. He was also sent to the bunker, where he spent the whole of the terribly cold winter of 1939–1940. Dr. Roman H. from Vienna, who was one of the few to survive this ordeal, told me what it was like when I saw him in May 1940.

"I attribute my survival to a miracle," he declared. "We had nothing but thin summer clothing, and at night, our bed was a board without a single blanket. Only by keeping on the move the whole time could we stop ourselves from freezing. At night, the barred window would be opened, and if the guard found it shut again when he came round at midnight, he would set about the unfortunate priest with a dog whip."

Treatment in the bunkers of all Hitler's concentration camps was more or less the same, and the following account by Fr. Georg Schelling of the bunker in Dachau serves to give a universal picture of the sort of conditions prisoners had to endure. "I shall never forget the terrible cries and groans, the moanings and rattling of chains. Outside in the courtyard, they would carry out their punishments, beatings, and the terrible 'hangings.' We never knew when the door might be thrown open and we ourselves dragged out and subjected to the same procedure."

On Easter morning 1940, Fr. Schroffner caught sight of a Polish priest, Fr. Schulcz, for a brief moment. Both raised a hand reverently in a mutual Easter blessing. They paid bitterly for this consolation in the hour of their own Calvary, for they were both beaten almost to death and kept without food for several days.

A couple of days afterward, the terrible Martin S. brought a plate of food to Fr. Schulcz's cell. Half starved, the Polish priest began to eat ravenously, but five minutes later, his neighbor, Dr. Roman H., heard him beating desperately against the wall with his hands and then the sound of his body falling lifeless to the floor of the cell.

A few hours later, S. came in his felt-soled slippers to drag away the body of his poisoned victim.

Fr. Schroffner followed a few days later, this time from an injection given by the camp physician, Dr. W., who, with S., was responsible for the murder of countless helpless prisoners. "Some twelve priests were murdered in the bunker that terrible winter," writes Dr. Roman H. "They never appeared in the camp at all. They were simply sent to the bunker on arrival — and ended in the crematorium."

Dr. Roman H. was shortly afterward promoted to the office of bunker clerk, and in this capacity, he naturally saw most of what went on behind the scenes in this dreadful place. "The worst time was during the spring of 1940," he told me when I saw him in Vienna in 1946. "The cries and groans of the maltreated prisoners could be heard all the time, day and night. That alone was enough to drive one crazy! I saw the naked corpse of my good friend Fr. Schroffner lying in the passage afterward. Never shall I forget the sight of this skeleton, all that remained of a gallant man. May he rest in peace!"

Murderers

Murderers in the concentration camps were legion. Martin S., perhaps the most terrible of all the criminals employed by the Nazis, was virtually illiterate. A man completely without morals of any kind, strong and muscular, he seemed to be a "born murderer," and Buchenwald provided him with all the scope he wanted. Variety was the spice of life to him, and he was soon a past master in the different ways of killing off his victims — strangling, poison, cold douches, beating up — it was all grist to his mill. He took a bestial personal pleasure in his work, a really terrible man.

In 1942, he was transferred to a tank division for active service, but he soon found his way back to Buchenwald, for he not only felt more at home working in the concentration camp, but he was also found incapable of passing the necessary intelligence tests for the army. In the fall of 1943, he had to face an SS military tribunal, for he had been "working" in the bunker with too much initiative — even for the SS.

In 1957, he was once again charged in the German courts with having committed hundreds of murders and causing countless serious injuries.

Dr. H. was another cold-blooded murderer who worked in Buchenwald and thought nothing of killing off a hundred prisoners in a week. Dr. E. Kogon, who was a prisoner at Buchenwald at that time, describes how the doctor would stroll out of his operating theater, smoking a cigarette and whistling "The End of a Perfect Day" after having killed up to twenty prisoners by injecting them with Evipan-Natrium.

Dr. W. had other methods. He would visit his victim in his cell and inquire in a most friendly way about his health. "I'll just give you something for your nerves," he would say, producing a syringe. Phenol. Five minutes later, the corpse would be dragged out into the passage.

Dr. Roman H. described the weekly bath: "We were held under the shower and then not allowed to dry ourselves but made to put on our clothes and then stand out in the cold for an hour without moving. Sometimes the temperature was negative four Fahrenheit. Only an iron will and violent physical exercises in our cells kept us alive. There were many who died of pneumonia."

Pastor Schneider, a Protestant minister interned in Buchenwald, was a truly heroic martyr. "You're nothing but a mass murderer!" he had shouted at the camp commandant. "May God be your judge!" On another occasion, he had called out of the bunker window during roll call, moved by the sight of his pitiable comrades. "Christ said, 'I am the Resurrection and the Life,'" he started, but he got no further, for the SS guards had already arrived to beat him up. He, too, died that summer of 1939, and when his body was carried out of the bunker, it was one mass of wounds and bruises.

"Staged" suicides were a favorite form of murder. Dr. W. was only too willing to sign the death certificate with an understanding smile.

I asked my friend Dr. Roman H. whether he knew if priests had been crucified in Buchenwald. "I cannot say for certain," he replied. "All I can say is that there were some things I could never discover. S. set about his work in secret. He was modest about his achievements for the Third Reich. The pleasure he himself got out of his bestial work was enough for him."

Msgr. Carl Lampert

One of the most outstanding priests who came to Dachau was Dr. Carl Lampert, the pro-vicar of Innsbruck and the senior Austrian priest in the camp. He was to spend several years in camp and prison before being executed at Halle in northern Germany in 1944.

"Carl Lampert was loved and esteemed everywhere he went. His life was characterized by his natural warmth and gaiety and absolute goodness. He had the gift of inspiring all those with whom he came into contact with the fire of his own youthful enthusiasm." These words from a fellow prisoner are a fitting tribute to this born leader and great priest. The words that he himself wrote just before his death are typical of his whole life: "The hardest thing of all is that so many people are being made to suffer on my account — and all I ever wanted was to bring joy to others."

Anyone who shared imprisonment with Lampert in Dachau could testify to the truth of this. He was the best of comrades, radiating warmth, patience and goodness, strength and Christian forgiveness.

The Nazis had long been looking for a pretext to arrest Msgr. Lampert, who was a thorn in their side. The text of his announcement of Fr. Neururer's death gave them what they wanted, for the wording was interpreted as "inciting the people." The Gestapo was determined to get its man, and it set out to prepare a trap, using a trumped-up accusation of treasonable activities supported by spies and false witnesses. Msgr. Lampert's arrest and subsequent imprisonment in Dachau were a grotesque abuse of justice.

He arrived in Dachau in August 1940 already condemned to death. Still wearing his priest's soutane, he was harnessed to the great roller used for road making. This was an occupation reserved almost exclusively for the Austrian prisoners. Lampert made no protest but submitted to the treatment with patience and dignity. He had no illusions as to what was in store for him in Dachau and was determined to bear witness to God and the Church. It was not long before he was transferred to the punishment squad in Sachsenhausen.

On November 19, 1940, Lampert found himself one of a group of men from the labor squad engaged in transporting sand in iron carts. Fr. Karl Schmidt from Bavaria and a Czech priest, Fr. Franz Stverak, were also among the workers. All three gave each other absolution on the way to work, for they knew that that day could well be their last on earth.

Shortly after the midday break, Fr. Stverak was brought into the infirmary. He had been shot through the lung and had lost both thumbs. One of the SS guards had found the unfortunate priest lying half dead in one of the camp refuse bins. "What! The dog's still alive!" had been the only comment. But the doctor in the infirmary saw for himself that Fr. Stverak could not have been shot while attempting to escape. He saw, too, that his body was one mass of wounds, welts, and bruises. As a result of the doctor's report, all three priests were at last withdrawn from the punishment squad.

On December 15, 1940, all the priests from Sachsenhausen were transferred to Dachau in accordance with the new ruling from Berlin. Msgr. Lampert was among them. I well remember my first meeting with him the day he came to join us in Block 30.

Msgr. Lampert was discharged from Dachau on August 1, 1941, the feast of St. Peter in Chains. For all that we rejoiced with him for his freedom, we were saddened by the thought that we were to lose this wonderful priest and comrade.

His freedom proved to be short-lived. He was too trusting, and it was not long before the Gestapo found some new pitfalls for this unwary opponent of the Hitler regime. New spies and informers were found to denounce him, and a grotesque charge of high treason followed. He was rearrested. He knew that this time he would not be let out alive.

His martyrdom proper began after this second arrest in Stettin. He was brutally maltreated by the Gestapo in an attempt to make him renounce his Faith. They resorted to every form of physical and spiritual blackmail in their attempts to gain information about high clerical dignitaries whom they aimed to expose as being involved in their trumped-up charge of high treason.

The trial, which opened in December 1943, was a travesty of justice. The president of the court, an officer holding the rank of general, shot himself before the end of the proceedings, shocked and disgusted by the calumny and lies used against Msgr. Lampert and the two priests who appeared with him, Frs. Simoleit and Lorenz. The death sentence was passed on December 20, and Lampert's Calvary then began.

He spent the days in a dark isolation cell in physical and spiritual misery until he was transferred to the condemned cell, where he was handcuffed and made to lie on a bed made of sharp bricks. The electric light was never turned off, and he was perpetually watched through the grille.

When he was asked during an interrogation whether he thought *Mein Kampf* or the Bible of greater value, he replied, "*Mein Kampf* is the word of man and preaches the doctrine of hate; the Bible is the Word of God and preaches of love." It was an answer worthy of a martyr.

Christ in Dachau

Lampert's diary, his last letters, and his testament reveal the depth of his character and the nobility of his soul.

On November 1, 1944, he was able to celebrate Mass, like a priest in the catacombs. He must somehow have got around one of the warders with his goodness, which succeeded in winning almost all hearts.

"All Souls' Day," he wrote. "How wonderful to be able to say my three Masses again, even in this place, and to be able to offer my sacrifice with the Church Militant, a sacrifice of prayer and intercession for the Holy Souls! And how wonderful to be able to bring the Bread of Life to the hungry souls in this prison cell!"

November 3: "Another terrible morning. Once again, they came down the passage, picking out new victims. Many were shot at dawn this morning. I wondered whether it was to be my turn next."

He was executed on November 13, 1944. He wrote the following words two hours before he died:

> The hour has come at last. Though terrible for you and for all those I love here, it is the hour of my salvation. This is the last Station of the Cross. Darkness has gathered, but daybreak is not far off. O Lord, I place my trust in Thee. Alleluia! I can give you nothing but my brotherly love, a love that can never die. I will carry this love back to God, the source of all love, and there it will be purified and strengthened. Oh, how glad I am that this bitter ordeal has come to an end at last! I am going home now, thank God, but all the same, I shall always be with you.
>
> I have just said my last Mass and received Our Lord for the last time in the Blessed Sacrament. My heart overflows in praise and thanksgiving to Him. My blessing was given for the last time for all who are bound to me by the ties of blood, of religion, of love, and, above all, of suffering.
>
> *Nunc dimittis servum tuum ...* My soul doth magnify the Lord ...

So, with the Magnificat in his heart, Lampert went out to execution. He lived and suffered and died for God.

He wrote the following moving words to the Bishop of Innsbruck, Dr. Paulus Rusch:

> In less than an hour, I shall stand before my God, my Savior, and my Master. Pray for me, Paulus. *Kyrie eleison!* As for you, my dear friend,

here is my last blessing and thanks for your work for Our Lord. I wanted so much to work with you. How wonderful it will be to see Christ and His Mother. And we, too, shall meet again, dear friend. *Benedictus qui venit . . .*

A fitting testament

"This is my last will and testament," wrote Lampert in his beautiful, clear hand, "written of my own free will.

> I am prepared to give my life here on earth for God whenever and wherever He demands it of me. May He be a merciful judge of my immortal soul through the redemption won for us by His Son, Jesus Christ, Our Lord. With my last breath, I thank God from the bottom of my heart for all the gifts and goodness that I have received throughout my life from His fatherly hand, particularly for the inestimable gift of Catholic parents and a Catholic home, the right to be called a child of God, and the grace of my priestly vocation.
>
> It was my greatest happiness on earth to be a Christian and a priest — and my greatest sorrow to have failed so often out of human weakness. May God have mercy upon this miserable sinner. I trust in His mercy and in the promises of Christ, and I long with all my heart to enter His heavenly kingdom. This is my fervent hope and my humble prayer. I beg all those who in this life have in any way suffered injustice or pain at my hands to forgive me, as I forgive with all my heart every offense and humiliation committed against me.

He asked to be buried at his home in Göfis and solemnly protested against the cremation of his body.

He requested Masses for the repose of his soul to be said after his death, in Dornbirn, Rome, Innsbruck, and Stettin, in memory of his activity as a priest in those places, and he asked for alms to be distributed among the poor. He wrote:

> There are so many to whom I owe a debt of gratitude. I was never rich enough to repay them here on earth. May God allow me to help them in eternity — I should repay them in good measure. I give my blessing

in Our Lord to all those to whom I was bound in this life by the ties of blood, of suffering, of work, and of religion.

If they saw anything good in me, then I beg them to thank God with me; if they saw only human frailty, then may their strength atone for my weakness so that we may all rejoice together in the fulfilment of the promises of Our Lord Jesus Christ, to whom, with the Father and the Holy Ghost, be all praise and thanks and honor and glory forever and ever.

Carl Lampert

Stettin, April 8, 1943

On July 24, 1945, the old Roman town of Göfis was packed with those who had come from near and far for the solemn memorial service held for Msgr. Lampert. Bishop Tschann was the celebrant, assisted by twelve Polish priests who had been fellow prisoners. Hundreds of priests came, and representatives of the provincial government, as well as crowds of children dressed in white. A cross was erected in the cemetery and wreaths were laid in his honor — but the urn containing the ashes of this gallant priests who died a true martyr for his Faith had still not been received.

9

The Gates of Hell

One of the most urgent tasks that confront us is the detection and annihilation of all public and secret enemies of the Führer and of the National Socialist Movement.

— Himmler's 1934 New Year Message

I am not concerned with the exercise of justice but with annihilation and destruction.

— Goring, March 4, 1933

Still no release!

At the beginning of July 1941, new rumors that we were to be discharged began to go around. There was talk of the end of July, but the war with Russia changed the situation, and once again our hopes were dashed. We began to think we were being held as hostages, and it seemed as if we were doomed to remain in the prison camp until we died.

The new rumor predicting our release that summer had originated from an old doctor who had come to visit the camp. By a strange coincidence, he found in the infirmary an old Jesuit lay brother whom he had known years before at the Russian Imperial Court. The Jesuit, formerly a Polish count, had served with the doctor as an officer of the czar's staff.

Much as we longed for our personal freedom, we were really concerned with the freedom of the Church. Rosenberg had openly declared in Nuremberg in 1938 that "the worst enemy of National Socialism is the Catholic Church, and for this reason the Church shall be wiped out." And Hitler himself had proclaimed: "I shall crush the Catholic Church like a toad." Not that any of us seriously considered the likelihood of the total annihilation of the Church, for the words of its Founder served to reassure us. After all, Christ had Himself pronounced the words: "Thou art Peter; and upon this rock I will build my church, and the gates of hell shall not prevail against it" (Matt. 16:18). We knew quite well that the Church was in no real danger.

But we were concerned for the youth. We were all well aware that the youth of "Hitler's Greater Germany" were undergoing a systematic indoctrination in the godless Nazi ideology as propagated by the various national organizations such as the Hitler Youth and similar institutions. For us, this knowledge was even more tragic than the news that reached us of bombed cities or the casualty lists from the battlefields, for we knew only too well that if this were to continue much longer, a new godless generation would emerge, a generation with no respect for Christian teaching and morals. Baldur von Schirach, the head of the Hitler Youth organization, with five million of the youth of Germany under his leadership, later admitted his guilt at Nuremberg in May 1946. "Hitler and Himmler were the real murderers," he declared. "My own guilt lies in the fact that it was I who trained the German youth to believe in this man who permitted millions to be killed."

We made it a feature to pray for the youth of Germany every day, for on our youth the future depended. Christianity was at stake. We knew then what Dr. Tschurtschentaler, a leading Austrian statesman, was to declare in 1946 in regard to his country: "We not only want a freedom-loving and democratic Austria; we also want a Christian Austria, for, as Truman and Attlee both agree, Christianity is the principle by which the whole world should be governed."

Some respite

Toward the end of March 1941, things began to improve for us priests in Dachau. The winter had been long and bitter, and the respite was welcome. God, in His infinite wisdom, knew what lay ahead for us, and it was as though He was giving us this chance to catch our breath and gather strength for the trials that were to come. The spring and summer were to enable us to rest for a while on our Way of the Cross, a rest just before we came to Golgotha.

A new ruling permitted us to hear Mass after roll call; this meant we could concentrate upon the Holy Sacrifice in a calm, collected frame of mind and could also receive Holy Communion every day. Our huts were less overcrowded than they had been and were kept clean and tidy, and there was time now for prayer and study. We were able to read more, and we organized stimulating discussion groups. In this way, we developed into a closely knit priests' community, united in brotherly love by our common devotion to Christ.

Yet these months of comparative peace were only the calm before the storm. It was almost as though Our Lord were repeating to each of us the words He had used to His great apostle St. Paul: "For I will show him how great things he must suffer for my name's sake" (see Acts 9:16). A foretaste of these tests of endurance was the dreaded task of food carrying, which still remained our lot. Nor were we spared punishment drill, which often followed some trivial offense — it was enough to incur the wrath of one of the SS guards. The morning of May 21, 1941, brought a particularly unpleasant instance of what we had to endure "for His name's sake."

One of the SS men, known to be an out-and-out atheist with a bitter hatred of priests and everything concerned with religion, suddenly stormed into our hut and drove us out into the road with a tirade of the vilest abuse. Outside, we were all subjected to punishment drill, made to lie down and stand up to order, to roll and bend and jump until we were utterly exhausted. Our Polish comrades from Blocks 26 and 28 were also made to join us for this "morning exercise" — 370 priests, including Bishop Kozal, lying in the road while the SS man strode among the rows of prostrate bodies in his heavy jackboots, swinging his truncheon above our defenseless heads.

May passed, with May devotions every evening and Benediction of the Blessed Sacrament, and in June, we even began to plan "entertainment evenings" for Sunday nights. I was one of the instigators, together with a German priest, Fr. Seitz. We discovered quite a lot of talent in our ranks and several born comics.

We were very grateful for the opportunity to study and the chance to develop and deepen our religious life. We had not many books at our disposal, but there were many celebrated theologians among us who gave of their best in lectures on such subjects as the Liturgy, the Bible, questions of dogma, and various pastoral problems. Discussion groups were formed, and much fruitful work was accomplished. The winter of 1941 brought Advent and Christmas singing, "social evenings" with a religious slant, all designed to bind us more

Christ in Dachau

closely to one another in priestly brotherhood. We sought every means to encourage and stimulate one another, to comfort and strengthen one another on our common Way of the Cross behind the barbed wire of Dachau. In sorrow, in joy, and in death, we were traveling together the same hard road "for God and His kingdom."

1941: Year of Hope

January 2	Feast of the Holy Name of Jesus. Unforgettable hours of hard labor, shoveling snow in an icy snowstorm.
January 15	The chapel is furnished in Block 26.
January 21	Our first morning devotions.
January 22	Our first Holy Mass, celebrated by Fr. Paul Prabutzki, camp chaplain.
March 10	Priests' block (26, 28, and 30) isolated by wire fence with gate.
March 25	Priests withdrawn from hard-labor squads.
End of March	Rations begin to improve.
April 13	Easter Sunday.
May	Short May devotions each evening.
June	Evening devotions continued.
June 24	Our first monstrance completed by Fr. Karl Schmidt — black, in the form of a cross, with rays of yellow tin-plate salvaged from fish cans.

July	The chapel is redecorated.
August 15	Fr. Pfanzelt, parish priest of Dachau, lends us a harmonium. Bishop Kozal receives permission to celebrate a second Mass daily. The chapel is too small to accommodate the nine hundred priests already in Dachau. Second monstrance, carved in light-colored wood in the form of a sunburst, is completed by a Polish priest, Fr. Edmund Mikolajesak.
September 17	Fr. Josef Zilliken celebrates Mass on his seventieth birthday. The German Schubert Mass performed for the first time in Dachau.
September 19	All German-speaking priests transferred to Block 26; Poles moved to Blocks 28 and 30.
September 20	Fr. Franz Ohnmacht appointed camp chaplain in place of Fr. Prabutzki.
September 21	The Polish clergy forbidden to enter the chapel and once more detailed for work in various labor commandos.
September 25	Fr. Franz Wöss arrives in Dachau for the second time (first term: July 2–November 19, 1938). He remains until June 10, 1945.
October	Our first candlesticks, designed by Fr. Karl Schmidt, are completed.
October 7	Gehrke, a notorious atheist and bully, is put in charge of our block.

Christ in Dachau

Advent	A painting of Our Lady by the Austrian artist Maria Spötl is used to back our first Lady Altar.
Christmas	Our first Nativity picture, executed in colored chalks by Fr. Andritzki, from Dresden, completed.

"Destroy Poland!"

In November 1945, the Bavarian newspaper *Neue Zeitung* announced that secret letters written by Hitler had been found, one of which confirmed the Führer's declaration to his generals ten days before the invasion of Poland of his intention to use special SS troops in Poland for the purpose of "exterminating the Polish race."

Hitler's henchmen did their job well. They turned their attention first and foremost to the upper classes and the intellectuals, with the object of robbing Poland of her leaders. "Strike the shepherd, and the sheep shall be scattered" (Zech. 13:7). Polish priests were interned for the "crime" of being Polish intellectuals. The majority of the prisoners interned in Gusen were Polish priests and members of the professional classes, such as doctors, schoolteachers, and university professors. There were 1,780 Polish priests in Dachau, far more than any other nation, and of these, 738 secular and more than 100 regular clergy died; 583 secular and 247 regular priests, as well as 82 seminarians and 35 lay brothers, survived the ordeal.

We Austrians in Dachau felt a particular sympathy with our Polish friends. We were not only comrades in suffering but comrades also in our common Faith, and it was this that strengthened the bond between us and this Catholic Slav people. "If only we were where the Polish people stand today in their outlook and perception," said a prominent Austrian statesman in 1946. He had seen for himself the dauntless Catholic spirit of the Poles interned in Gusen and Dachau.

The following tribute to his Austrian comrades by a Polish prisoner in Dachau indicates the good feeling between us: "We Poles will always remember with gratitude the Austrian comrades who shared our suffering. We thank them for their warmhearted comradeship and for their spirit of self-sacrifice" (Rakowski).

Up to September 19, 1941, no distinction was made between us German-speaking priests and our Polish comrades. The sudden discrimination that then followed was made for political reasons. The Polish priests found themselves deprived overnight of the right to hear Mass in the chapel, a bitter ruling that was to be enforced up to the end of November 1944. In the fall of 1944, Fr. Theodore Korcz was put in charge of the Polish priests' block — the first time a priest had held this office — and it was he who succeeded in regaining the privilege for his compatriots.

The camp commandant gave permission for the Polish clergy to hear Mass once a week but had omitted to specify the day and the exact time. Needless to say, advantage was taken of this oversight, and they had their Mass every day. Fr. Georg Schelling had a hand in this, and the SS were too preoccupied with other problems at this juncture to bother very much about such niceties.

It was understandable that the godless ruling forbidding the Poles to enter the chapel was not strictly observed, but we had to take the greatest care. In due course, our Polish comrades began to celebrate Mass in secret, reminiscent of the catacomb Masses of the early Christians. Priests were detailed to keep watch against dangerous intruders while Mass was being celebrated behind the stove with a table for the altar. Leopold Arthofer writes, "The celebrant wore a stole that he had made himself over his striped prison jacket. The chalice was an ordinary glass tumbler, and a flat piece of metal served as paten. An aluminum cup did duty as ciborium, and over the 'altar' we had stuck a picture from an old calendar. In this way we offered the Holy Sacrifice of the Mass."

The spirit of the catacombs prevailed among these ruthlessly persecuted Polish priests. As Archbishop Josef Gawlina later declared to his compatriots, "Your hunger for the Bread of Life drove you to find new ways of bringing Our Lord in the Blessed Sacrament to your fellow prisoners.... You celebrated the Holy Mysteries in the quarries and on the plantation. You received Holy Communion on your knees while weeding the fields. You hid Jesus under your heavy loads and carried Him back to your hut, holding secret vigil through the night in adoration of God hidden in the Blessed Sacrament."

Not only the Polish priests took part in these clandestine activities. Lay prisoners were often present at these catacomb Masses, and never once were the priests betrayed. When the privilege of using the chapel was restored to the Poles in 1944, more than a thousand Polish lay prisoners were present at the Polish Christmas Mass. The other priests had gladly allowed them to take their place in the chapel.

The gallant Church of Poland suffered terrible things in Dachau, but there is no doubt that the 794 priests who survived the ordeal came out of the hell of the prison camp the richer for their trials. They were wiser and more mature. The hard school of endurance prepared them for the task of reconstruction in Poland. They set about their work in the Lord's ravaged vineyard with a renewed ardor and in the certain knowledge of God's blessing.

We may well ask how more than half of the Polish clergy interned in Dachau came to die. More than 80 priests died in 1941 as a result of the eight-day "hunger cure" imposed upon those who had the misfortune to catch the itch during that winter and spring.

On October 29, 1941, some 530 priests, most of them older men, arrived in Dachau from Poland. Although it was already bitterly cold, with early snow, there were no coats or caps available for issue to these new arrivals. They were made to work in all weather clad in thin summer clothing, their feet bare but for open wooden clogs. Only 8 of the 530 survived.

In February 1942, two groups of younger Polish priests were chosen for work as carpenters' and builders' apprentices. On November 10, 1942, Himmler came to visit the camp. Twenty of the priest apprentices, especially the fittest, were subsequently selected as human guinea pigs and were injected with serum. All developed the dreaded phlegmon, but eight survived thanks to the good offices of the chief nursing orderly, Heinrich Stöhr, a fine man and the best of comrades, who, at the risk of his life, injected them with an antiserum obtained through a priest prisoner with contacts in Leverkusen.

Similar experiments, this time with malaria, were carried out between July 1942 and May 1944 under the direction of Professor Klaus Schilling. Some 120 Polish priests, mostly the younger, fitter men, were forced to undergo these inhuman tests.

At morning roll call on that same terrible November 10, 1942, a group of Polish priests were selected for an "invalid transport." We knew and they knew that they would be sent to their death. A few days later, they had all been murdered, either by injections in the bunker in Dachau or in the gas chambers of Auschwitz and Niedernhart, near Linz. In many cases, the death certificate had been written out in advance. Heart failure and pneumonia were the usual "causes." A total of 304 Polish priests were exterminated in this way.

A bitter Holy Week

Holy Week of 1942 was a bitter week for the Polish priests in Dachau. Now and again, our clothes would be searched, together with our few poor belongings, in the hope that the SS would find an excuse to take it out of us. One day, eighty dollars was found tucked in between the pages of the breviary of one of the Polish priests. A lay compatriot had given him the money in the mistaken belief that it would be safe in his keeping. The priest himself was beaten to death, but the matter did not end there. The other Polish priests were made to relinquish their breviaries, their rosaries, and every religious object. Then began a Holy Week of suffering. Those who survived the ordeal will surely never forget it.

It began on Palm Sunday with the Polish priests' being ordered out of their huts and made to stand naked on the road outside while the guards searched their clothing and belongings in the hope of finding more dollars. Punishment drill followed every day, the usual routine of deep knee bends and other strenuous exercises to be performed by half-starved older men already worn out by a day's hard labor in rain and icy wind from six in the morning until seven at night, with only an hour's break at midday. It was too much. Eight priests collapsed and died during that terrible week. Even the tough capo in charge of the Polish priests' block felt impelled to inform his superiors that his men could not march another step. "If they can't march, let them roll on their stomachs," was the answer he received. And punishment drill continued.

The Pole's Creed

I believe in God, the Father Almighty,
Creator of Heaven and Earth.
I believe, though I am despised and humiliated.
I believe in Thee, living triune God.
I believe in Thee, Abba, my Father.
I believe, though no more than a number in this place;
Cut off from existence.

Christ in Dachau

I believe in Thee, my God —
Do Thou strengthen my belief.
I believe, O God, I believe!
Hungry and naked, I believe.
Exiled and in misery, I believe.
Torn from my home and from all that I love,
Not knowing what the future may bring,
Not sure that tomorrow will come,
My God, I believe in Thee.
My God and my Father,
Who rulest the whole world,
Free me from my imprisonment.
But if such be not Thy will,
If I must die,
Free, then, at least my country.
Free the peoples of the world from slavery,
Give us all peace —
That peace that the world cannot give.
I believe in Thee, the living God,
I believe in Thee, I hope in Thee, I love Thee. Amen.

Dante in Dachau

At the beginning of April 1942, I borrowed Dante's *Divine Comedy* from the camp library. I kept it two whole months, this masterpiece of literature, and made notes of the verses that impressed or pleased me most — in my breviary.

That Dante was to be found in that godless place was typical of the contrasts to be found in Dachau, where leading political figures and men prominent in the arts and sciences rubbed shoulders with uneducated proletarians, and high dignitaries of the law were "comrades" with every form of lawbreaker and professional criminal.

Richard Schmitz, a former vice-chancellor of Austria who was sent to Dachau in April 1938, was able to tell me something of the history of the camp library when I visited him in Vienna in July 1946. "It began in a small way," he told me. "We had to do without religious books for a long time." I myself knew from experience that there were thousands of prisoners who seized avidly upon religious books as soon as these were to be had. Up to September 1942, it had been possible to read these books in secret only, under penalty of severe punishment if discovered. In the spring of 1938, the Dachau library consisted of between two thousand and three thousand books, for the most part light fiction plundered from parish libraries, as was revealed by the censor's stamp, which often defaced page after page. By the spring of 1945, the library had grown to about eighteen thousand volumes. There were many educational and worthwhile books among them but also a good deal of trash, including pornography, misrepresented history, and books that were openly anti-Catholic. Unfortunately, not only the atheists read such works. Religious books, as such, were strictly forbidden and were weeded out of every new consignment. Only two books escaped this fate: an abridged *Divine Comedy*, with excellent religious commentary, and *Memoirs of a Country Pastor*, written by a Protestant. There was plenty of National Socialist literature, of course, but no one was interested in this.

In 1938, the books of general educational and cultural interest had been bought in the main by the political prisoners who were prepared to sacrifice what little money they possessed for books in order to be able to read and study. The arrival of the Austrian prisoners after the Anschluss of 1938 brought many new books to the library. "The new Austrian internees were mainly from the intellectual and professional classes with a real interest in books, whereas up till then, the majority of the German prisoners had been from the working classes," said Schmitz. When Dachau was temporarily closed in 1938, about a thousand of the inmates went to Flossenbürg, where there was no library. "The Austrians, more than anybody, saw to it that they were kept well supplied with good books," Schmitz told me,

> and when they were moved back to Dachau, these books were sent with them. In this way, the camp library gradually increased. Later, it was sometimes possible to smuggle in worthwhile books, for the SS were often too ignorant to distinguish between good and bad.
>
> As more and more non-Germans came to join our ranks after 1940, new books in several foreign languages were added. This accounted for the Russian books that the Russian prisoners of war found on their arrival in the camp in 1941.

Christ in Dachau

Needless to say, vacancies in the "library commando" responsible for keeping the books in order and maintaining the index were much-sought-after posts. They were filled, for the most part, by left-wing Germans. Dr. Viktor Matejka, from Vienna, was an exception. The late Dr. Kurt Schumacher, chairman of the German Socialist Party, was also employed in the library. He had lost his right arm in the First World War. In the early days of 1938, he would sometimes be harnessed to the enormous heavy roller used for road making, together with the most prominent Austrian political prisoners.

"Comrades"

September 1941, and we still found ourselves behind barbed wire, despite the various rumors of our release that summer. Our situation had improved somewhat in the last months, it was true, but the lot of our unfortunate Polish comrades grew steadily worse. Forbidden to enter our chapel, they were now used for every form of hard labor — carrying heavy buckets, shoveling snow, and so forth; and the dirtier and more degrading the work, the better.

The winter passed comparatively peaceably, although we were continually subjected to the tyranny of the two North German bullies who were the prisoner-bosses in charge of our block. They had no scruples about robbing us of our rations, and every evening, we had to watch them frying potatoes filched from our midday meal. It would have been useless to protest against this sort of thing, for these men were our bosses, and we would have gotten nothing but an extra ration of abuse, ending with blows or punishment drill. Or they would have reported us to the camp authorities for attempted mutiny.

There were many competent men in the priests' block who were born leaders and would have been ideally suited for the post of block senior, but instead, the SS chose to place the authority in the hands of unscrupulous atheist "comrades," for in their eyes, we, like the Jews, represented the scum of the camp.

True comrades

One morning in October 1941, a new prisoner came to join our ranks in Block 26. Fr. Reinhold Friedrichs had been the "propaganda chief" of Bishop Galen of Munster, renowned for his fearless stand against the Nazi regime. Fr. Friedrichs had come from Sachsenhausen, so Dachau had nothing new for him, yet his fine features reflected an inner sense of gaiety and a warmth that the environment of the prison camp could never dispel. It was not long before we all grew to love and admire this exceptional priest who was later to become the first priest block senior.

Mention must be made here of Dr. Josef Beran, today archbishop of Prague, who, for years, shared imprisonment with us in Dachau. He was the best of comrades. A man of the highest intelligence and broad outlook, unhampered by national prejudice, he was predestined for the high office he was later to hold as a prince of the Church.

The camp chaplain, Fr. Franz Ohnmacht, fell sick in November 1941, and our good comrade Fr. Georg Schelling took over his duties until February 1942. Fr. Ohnmacht was chaplain from September 1941 until March 1943, during the most difficult years, when the camp was under the command of SS men such as the notorious Egon Zill and Hofmann.

A new year begins

On January 7, 1942, Hofmann came to inspect the chapel. He began to rave like a madman when he saw that we had flowers on the altar and IHS sewn on the antependium. He turned on the unfortunate Georg Schelling, who had had to accompany him, hitting him over the head in his rage.

February 1942 saw the end of our better rations, and we were once more detailed for work in the various labor commandos. The hunger began anew, but our situation was still tolerable compared with that of our Polish comrades who had not even the solace of the chapel. For all our suffering, we German-speaking priests still had our sanctuary with Christ ever present in the Blessed Sacrament.

Another "invalid transport" of old and sick Polish priests was made up in May 1942. As already recounted, a total of 304 were exterminated in this way in the course of that year. According to the Nazi system, each concentration camp was virtually self-supporting, with an independent economy. It naturally lay in the interests of the camp SS to exploit their prisoners to the utmost, for any surplus went into their own pockets. Personal ambition for rapid promotion, the urge to wield power, and, in many cases, sheer sadism were further motives for the inhuman treatment of their slave laborers. In any case, anyone who could no longer work was considered deadweight, an unproductive consumer, to be disposed of quickly, cheaply, and, of course, secretly. The Poles were the favorite victims, but there were others, too, who were murdered in these "invalid transports." I particularly remember Fr. Bioly from Silesia, Fr. Karras from Vienna, Fr. Bernhard Heinzmann from Augsburg, and a Protestant minister, Pastor Sylten.

May 1942 brought news of the assassination of Reinhard Heydrich, the newly appointed Reichsprotektor of Bohemia and Moravia. After Hitler, Himmler, and [Ernst] Kaltenbrunner, Heydrich was one of the most brutal and dangerous of the party leaders. As a boy, he had always been at the top of his class in religion, but he had later substituted the Nazi ideology for his Catholic Faith, and he ended as the bitterest opponent of the Church.

After the war, secret documents were found in which Heydrich declared that he viewed the Catholic bishops as the most powerful enemies of Hitler's new world concept. Certainly he saw to it that as many priests as possible came behind barbed wire. Our arrest warrants all bore his signature. We knew that his hatred of the Church was bitter, and in his death, we saw evidence of God's justice.

We were simply not fit enough for May devotions in the evenings now that we were once more detailed for the various labor commandos. Worn out and hungry, all we could do was to try to sleep as much as possible so as to be able to get through the next day. So May devotions were held on Sunday afternoons. I shall always remember a sermon preached by Fr. Albert Eise, P.S.M., a great apostle of Our Lady. His theme was taken from St. Augustine's definition of love, *Inscriptio cordis in cor*, and he spoke of death — a priest's death under the protection of Mary.

A little religious picture still exists with his own *inscriptio cordis* dedicated to Mary and, underneath, the words of St. Teresa of Ávila:, "I am Thine alone, O God, born for Thee! What is Thy will for me? Send me riches or poverty, honor or degradation, liberty or shackles, consolation or suffering . . . What is Thy will for me?" He was to have his answer before long, for he died some months later, a cold and solitary death in Dachau concentration camp.

Death passes by

May 20, 1942. A wonderful early summer morning. I can still see that little group of men flanked on either side by SS guards in steel helmets and armed with rifles. We stood on the barrack square after roll call, waiting to march off to work on the plantation, and watched them march past on their way to the hill behind the crematorium, reserved for executions. They were themselves SS men, escorted to their death by their own comrades. It was all part of the day's routine. Some were marched off to work; others were marched off to death.

I could not rid myself of the thought of these unfortunate men who had, in all probability, long since broken off all contact with God. They were being escorted to their death at that moment, and there was no priest to help them at the end. In all likelihood, they did not even want a priest. All we could do was stand there and pray as they passed us by on that fine May morning.

If there were a greater number of prisoners for execution, the condemned men would be shot by a firing squad in a field used as a training ground by the SS. The field was near the plantation, and we often used to encounter the SS trucks loaded with victims on our way back from work in the evenings. Civilians, soldiers, prisoners of war — anyone who had displayed openly his opposition to the murderous Nazi regime.

One evening, a truck arrived from Stuttgart bringing nine members of one family, ranging in age from seventeen to sixty. They were all executed on the hill behind the crematorium. Their crime? They had given first aid to a severely wounded American airman whose plane had crashed during an air raid.

The wonderful sunny days of May 1942 were dark days indeed in Dachau. We priests witnessed the murder and terror wrought by these men who had turned into brutes because they had turned away from God, and we silently gave our blessing and absolution to their victims. We prayed with all our hearts that God might save their souls in their last hour.

I often thought in those days how hard it must be for some people to accept all this as God's justice, for it was often difficult enough to understand even for those who still held on to their faith. What about those who had lost God? How were they ever to find their way out of this labyrinth? How were they to find freedom? How were they ever to solve the endless riddle of life and of death? Surely, they must be driven to despair by the apparent senselessness of it all, by the absence of justice as seen with the eyes of the world. You had to cling to God in those days, for God's ways are not our ways, and only by trusting implicitly in His wisdom and providence can we hope to overcome such apparent obstacles to our faith. Viewed in the light of faith, such obstacles serve to lead us nearer to God the more incomprehensible and difficult they may seem.

The following reliable data concerning sixteen of the larger Nazi concentration camps during the first five months of 1942 are taken from Dr. Eugen Kogon's book *Der SS-Staat*:

1. 109,861 new prisoners registered.
2. Only 4,711 discharged in the same period.
3. 9,267 prisoners officially executed.
4. Approximately 28,000 intercamp transfers.
5. 70,610 deaths registered.

Starvation

We never knew when one of the bosses might turn up on a tour of inspection. Cupboards would be searched and our belongings examined. This could always end badly, for one never knew what they might find, and the most trivial fault could end in punishment drill for us all. I happened to be in Block 26 one day at the end of March 1942 when the deputy camp senior appeared to inspect our quarters. As soon as he caught sight of me, he began to drag me into a heated debate about God and the Church. It was not the first time we had crossed swords. He started to attack the Jesuits, laying all sorts of incredible charges at their door. At this, I banged my fist on the table. "Nonsense!" I shouted at him. "You don't know what you're talking about. I know the Jesuits better than you do — and the sort of rubbish their enemies go spreading around!" This proved to be the best answer I could have given him. We ended our controversy as good comrades. But you could never be sure how these anti-religious prisoner-bosses would react. My heated defense might well have ended quite differently.

Toward the end of April, they began to make use of us priests in Block 26 for all kinds of hard labor, particularly on the plantation. We were now sharing the same work, hunger, and privation as our Polish comrades. The Bavarian spring was cold and windy that year, and it was forbidden to turn out for work wearing an overcoat. So we worked on in wind and rain in our thin clothes without any form of protection, in constant danger of catching our death in the cold.

Our hunger was intense. I sometimes devoured raw turnips or carrots or even raw rhubarb if I had the good fortune to lay my hands on such a rare delicacy.

We had to take care not to be caught, of course. It was a frequent sight to see a priest kneeling for hours on end on the side of the road as penalty for having "stolen" a turnip.

Many of our comrades, especially among the Poles, died of starvation, among them Fr. Paul Prabutzki, that fine man who had been our first chaplain. We would ask ourselves when our own turn would come as we saw our friends and comrades dragging themselves around, already living corpses. It was easy to pick out the next victim; the symptoms were all too evident. There was no help for us. Our friends were powerless to aid us, and our enemies actively desired our death. We were driven in desperation to eating mice, earthworms, weeds, grass — anything we could lay our hands on.

Five hundred priests die of hunger

Many of us priests were employed in the herb gardens of the plantation, picking flowers. The flowers were in their prime, and Capo Walter Schneider was anxious not to lose a second of picking time. He ordered us to work on Sundays, not even allowing us time for Mass, and anyone who did not fill his quota was sent out for overtime. For the sick and the weak, this as good as meant death.

"Fr. Lenz, help me to collect more flowers, or I'll be sent out for overtime, and that will be my death!"

Fr. Bernhard Poether from Westphalia was a grand priest and a good friend and comrade. He was on the point of collapsing from sheer hunger, but he picked away in desperation. He knew that death was catching up with him. I did my best to help him, but it was too late. Two or three days later, he was dead. He had originally been in Sachsenhausen, sent there for caring for Polish prisoners, and had already spent four years in solitary confinement there in the dreaded bunker. He had been virtually starved, and his stomach and intestines were incapable of recovery. He arrived in Dachau a physical wreck, a walking skeleton suffering alternately from acute constipation and diarrhea.

Another young priest was suffering from "hunger dysentery," that characteristic sickness of the concentration camp. He, too, was expected to turn out for work, and on Sunday afternoon at that. I happened to be free that afternoon and begged him to allow me to take his place. Capo Schneider heard about this arrangement, and only the intervention of my good friend Toni Burger prevented him from reporting me. I well remember that Sunday afternoon in the merciless heat of the sun. It was a hard day, but a good day, a day of prayer and sacrifice — the Lord's Sabbath.

We turned our work for the camp authorities into service to God, for this was the best consolation in our hour of need. And so every day, as we picked our flowers in pairs, we used to say the Rosary together. The flowers were beautiful, their colors glowing in the sun, and we praised their Creator. It was a real joy to look at such beauty in contrast to the grey misery all around us. But we were terribly weak, and it was hard to stand or kneel all day in the heat.

Hunger took its highest toll in August 1942. Every evening when we came back from work, we would learn that two or three German-speaking priests had died during the day. As for the Polish priests, "most of our priests died of hunger," declared a prominent Polish priest later. Sixty German-speaking priests died, four of them from Austria. This brought the 1942 total up to four hundred — with 1941, five hundred — priests who died of starvation in Dachau.

Fr. Maximilian Kolbe

Of all the priests who died of hunger in Hitler's concentration camps, Fr. Maximilian Kolbe endured the most terrible death in the notorious Polish camp at Auschwitz, where more than one million victims of the Nazi persecution were murdered.

Raymund Kolbe was the son of a weaver from Lodz in Poland, where he was born in 1894. He joined the Friars Minor (Franciscans) and was known and esteemed as a deeply religious priest. He was gifted, a man of action who turned his love of work in God's cause to good account in his missionary activities, in his press apostolate, and in encouraging others to follow him in his devotion to Our Lady. He died a martyr, laying down his life in Christian brotherly love.

He was arrested and taken to Auschwitz on May 28, 1941. On June 30, one of his fellow prisoners escaped and was not found by the SS, whereupon the camp commandant chose ten other prisoners, completely at random, and ordered that they should die as hostages. Fr. Kolbe was not among those originally chosen, but he offered, of his own free will, to take the place of another Pole who was the father of six children.

The unfortunate hostages were stripped naked and thrown together into a cell in the notorious "death block." From then on, they were given nothing to eat or drink until they died. As is well known, thirst is an even greater torment than hunger for its victims, causing fever, delirium, and ultimate madness.

Fr. Kolbe led the pitiful group of prisoners in prayer and hymns until they could no longer speak. After fourteen days, only he was still alive, whereupon they killed him with an injection of carbolic acid. An eyewitness describes his face in death as "radiant like that of a saint."

The process for his beatification began on May 24, 1948. Countless prayers have already been answered.[5] During his lifetime, he was often heard to say with characteristic gaiety, "When I get to Heaven, I'm going to work with both hands."

Death Is Our Friend

The Savior is risen!
What have we to fear?
In death is no sting,
The Savior is risen!
O Victor, O King,
Look down on us here!

Father Superior Brunke, O.F.M., penned these words as an Easter greeting in 1942. I still have the slip of paper with his beautiful handwriting. He, too, died of hunger that year, on August 5. Two other priests from the Diocese of Fulda, Fr. K. Tragesser and Fr. G. A. Vogt, also died that year.

Death in the guise of a murderer had an easy time in Dachau, for hunger and sickness, not to mention the criminal element among both prisoners and SS, were willing accomplices and the prisoners died like flies.

Death became a sort of friend to us in Dachau. We thought about it almost all the time, for we were living in its shadow. Our thoughts soared upward toward God as the eagle soars toward the sun. The greater our misery and need, the stronger grew the urge to pray, and the nearer we drew to Christ.

There was nothing to cling to in the concentration camp, none of the things that otherwise make it so hard for us to leave the world. None of the things to which a dying man so often clings existed any longer for us. We had already lost

---

[5] Maximilian Kolbe was canonized by Pope John Paul II on October 10, 1982.
— Ed.

our freedom and had been robbed of our relations and friends, of our office and the regard of our fellow men. In most cases, we had lost our health, too, and so the shackles that bound us to the world fell away behind the barbed wire of the prison camp, and we were free to enter into the riches of God's kingdom.

We thus regarded death as our best comrade — for it was death who reached out for us in our misery to lead us on into life everlasting.

Priests died all around us, and they left us so peacefully, so easily, with such joy. They just slipped quietly out of our lives, home to God, their Creator. I remember one priest especially, though he was typical of countless others. For days, it had been clear that he was dying — it might be tomorrow, it might be the next day. He dragged himself into the chapel for the last time, motioning another priest to come with him. When he had received the Last Sacraments, he went across to the infirmary — to die.

During the summer of 1942, many of our community were no longer capable of standing or even of sitting upright during Mass. They just lay there, their eyes turned to the altar. I often thought of the accounts in the Gospels of the sick who lined the roadside as Our Lord passed by.

"I offer up my life for my sins and the sins of the world" were the last words of one of my priest comrades.

"I'll pray for you," I assured another as I accompanied him across to the infirmary. "I'll pray that you recover."

"No!" he answered. "Pray rather that God's divine will may be done in all things."

"For God and the workers!" were the dying words of the eminent French sociologist Fr. Victor Dillard, S.J.

Death was easy in Dachau, far easier than outside in the world. The priests who died there had reached the end of the Way of the Cross and entered into the kingdom of eternal light, where Christ was waiting with the crown of glory. We knew, too, that in these priests who had gone before us, we had gained new intermediaries before the throne of God. In their deaths, they had set us a new example of true Christian resignation to the will of God.

More than a thousand priests died in Dachau — in all truth, the greatest martyrdom of priests in the history of the Church. They gave their lives for Christ and His Mystical Body, the Church, in the defense of God's laws and of

His kingdom. As the Polish archbishop Gawlina declared: "They were martyrs killed in bitter hatred of Christ. But Christ Himself was ever present to make death easy for them."

Christ was the victor in Dachau.

Fr. Titus Brandsma

A modern martyr from Holland, Fr. Titus Brandsma, met his end in Dachau on July 26, 1942. We never had the privilege of knowing him, for he was sent straight to the infirmary on his arrival.

The process for the beatification of this great man has already been initiated as the result of the countless prayers that have been answered at his intercession.[6] He died a martyr for Catholic journalism, and the late Dutch cardinal Johannes de Jong, archbishop of Utrecht, paid tribute to the heroism of this Carmelite priest in defending the rights and obligations of the Catholic press in the face of Hitler's terror regime.

Fr. Brandsma was born in the province of Friesland on February 23, 1881. He was one of the founders of the Catholic university in Nijmegen and was himself professor of philosophy and Christian mysticism. He was rector of the university from 1932 to 1933. He soon became one of Holland's leading Catholic writers, wielding his pen in an active campaign against the godless spirit of the age. His name was high on the Nazi blacklist.

The Dutch bishops issued a pastoral letter directed against the godless Nazi racial doctrine, and Fr. Brandsma chose that decisive moment to launch an attack against the Nazi ideology. "We cannot tell," he wrote in a letter, "whether the authorities [the Gestapo] will take action. But if they do, then remember that God has the last word — and that He also rewards His faithful servants." This letter served to rally all Catholic pressmen to a unanimous campaign of opposition, but it finally cost its author his life. He had, in effect, signed his own death warrant. He was thrown into prison and interrogated by the Gestapo for hours on end. Tortured and mutilated, he arrived in Dachau already half dead. But even then, in all his misery, he never ceased to care for those around him and never lost the inner gaiety inspired by his love of Christ.

---

[6] Titus Brandsma was canonized by Pope Francis on May 15, 2022. — Ed.

Christ in Dachau

He set us a heroic example. He gave his life for God, and he has certainly received his reward in Heaven.

Msgr. Heinrich Feuerstein

Another dauntless opponent of the Nazis was Msgr. Heinrich Feuerstein, the parish priest of Donaueschingen, who gave his life in the defense of his Faith. Msgr. Feuerstein was loved and honored by all who knew him. He was not only a fine priest, a gifted preacher, and a selfless worker for his parishioners but also a talented musician and a recognized authority on art. His book on the medieval German master Matthias Grünewald has become a standard work. It was clear that a man of this caliber, so universally esteemed and never afraid of voicing his opinion in matters of truth and justice, was a real obstacle in the path of the Nazis. His sermon on New Year's Eve 1941 provided the Nazis with precisely the opportunity they were looking for. The man had too much influence for their liking.

He had prepared the sermon weeks before and knew quite well what the consequence would be as he mounted the pulpit on that decisive occasion. Friends who warned him not to say too much received the answer, "I'd rather be reproached for being unwise than for being cowardly" — a reply typical of many Dachau priests and inspired by a selfless courage prepared to sacrifice every personal interest for the sake of the truth.

Msgr. Feuerstein was taken to Constance jail in January 1942 and was sent to Dachau, already a sick man, the following July. Fr. Ferdinand Maurath told us afterward that Msgr. Feuerstein offered up his arrest and death for his parish in Donaueschingen. A few weeks in Dachau were enough to kill him.

I can still see this wonderful priest sitting in the corner of our room in Block 26. He was already dying, silently enduring the torments of hunger and sickness. By the time he was admitted to the infirmary, it was too late.

"The greater our own pain and sorrow, the closer is Jesus, the Man of Sorrows, with His peace and consolation. Our Lady, too, knows the meaning of suffering. She is the comforter of the afflicted, the healer of the sick. She will entreat her Son to grant us the grace of patience and resignation to God's will in our hour of need." These words were written by Msgr. Feuerstein during his imprisonment. He added the prayer, "Lord, Thy will be done, even if it is beyond my comprehension!"

His funeral on August 18, 1942, in Donaueschingen, was a veritable martyr's triumph. In point of fact, it was a funeral without a coffin or an urn. He had died in Dachau on August 2, and his body was cremated three days later, but it was more than a month before the urn arrived in his parish. Whether it contained the ashes of his mortal remains is doubtful. The Nazis had as little respect for the dead as they had for truth and loyalty to the living.

Only the Church stood squarely across the path of Hitler's campaign for suppressing truth. I never had any special interest in the Church before, but now I feel a great affection and admiration because the Church alone has had the courage and persistence to stand for intellectual truth and moral freedom. I am forced thus to confess that what I once despised I now praise unreservedly.[7]

— Albert Einstein

---

[7] "Religion: German Martyrs," *Time*, December 23, 1940, https://content.time .com/time/subscriber/article/0,33009,765103,00.html.

10

The Turning Point

Work

"Whenever need is greatest, God's help is nearest," says an old German proverb. We in Dachau were to see for ourselves the truth of this. It had been a terrible year, hundreds had died of hunger, and we priests had come to the end of our physical strength — only a relatively small percentage had managed to survive up to Easter 1943. And then came the turning point.

Camp Commandant P. was suddenly removed from his post. It seemed that he had been engaged in all sorts of profiteering activities on the side. Six months later, Hofmann, the camp director, also disappeared.

Back in 1938, Camp Commandant G. had openly declared to a batch of new arrivals the old Nazi principle on which the camp was run: "You've got only two things to do here," he told them. "First, to die like dogs, and second, to work until you do die." With the arrival of the new commandant Weiss and the new director von Redwitz in August 1942, a new era began for Dachau.

The old maxim was discarded overnight, not because the Nazi overlords were suddenly smitten with remorse for the previous treatment of inmates in their prison camps but because the situation had changed. Political events, the turn of the war, and, above all, the sheer need of as many workers as possible to speed up the production of armaments for Hitler's victory drove them to realize that it lay in their own interests to see that we slave workers were fit enough to contribute to their great drive for victory. A sort of party congress held on July 2 had decreed that the name "concentration camp" should be changed to "labor camp." Work was all-important at this juncture of the war, and it was this

Christ in Dachau

"gospel of work" that inspired the sudden switchover in the way things were done in Dachau. If we were to work for them, the camp authorities realized, we would have to be made fit. So they set about pepping us up. Since neither the state nor the camp economy was prepared to make any substantial increase in our rations, however, we were allowed to receive as many food parcels as we wished and were indeed encouraged to write home for them! Our families and friends were expected to contribute toward our support, for the end justified the means and, in the eyes of the Nazis, the end was victory. The terrible hunger period thus came to an end, and although, for some, the respite came too late, soon there were no more deaths from starvation.

We were still made to work twelve hours a day, but working conditions improved, and work was no longer the form of persecution it had been in the past when the capos and SS guards had seized every opportunity to make our lives a hell. Certain disciplinary measures, such as the "twenty-five" and "hanging," were abolished, at least temporarily, and we no longer lived in the constant dread of being punished for the slightest offense. The old camp commandant and his director had personally taken a bestial pleasure in punishment and had found no lack of sadists to carry out their orders. This sort of thing was stopped now. Discipline in the blocks was also somewhat relaxed, and we were no longer required to remove our shoes before treading on the shining waxed floors of our rooms. They no longer turned out the whole block for punishment drill for one badly made bed or untidy cupboard. They even organized sport facilities and a cinema for their workers' "free time."

Shortly after the end of 1942, the dreaded task of food carrying also came to an end. A working party of stalwart Russian prisoners took over the task of delivering the food — by truck.

In the autumn, the punishment squad was also disbanded. We priests had not been sent to this dreaded forced-labor gang since the ruling of December 1940, but we had suffered such terrible things there in the early days that we rejoiced with all our hearts for the prisoners now released from it. It was to be reintroduced at the end of 1943 but in a modified form with a less murderous working tempo.

Things had indeed changed! We priests who, up until then, had been regarded, in company with our comrades the Jews, as the scum of the place, were rehabilitated and found ourselves occupying many of the key positions in the camp, particularly in the infirmary, where we had unlimited opportunity to help the sick in body and soul.

Mail

Twice a month, we were allowed to write to a certain fixed address and were permitted to receive two letters or postcards. Any other letters were either returned to the senders or destroyed. It is impossible to describe what these greetings from home meant to us in the prison camp. For years, it had been drummed into us that we were "outcasts of decent society," "the scum of the earth." These letters from our families and friends reminded us that this was not true.

Since the summer of 1942, political prisoners had been allowed to write a brief letter each Monday to fathers or brothers serving in the armed forces. This was a valued privilege, particularly for us priests. Our thoughts were often with our good Catholic soldiers who had been forced into the Nazi war machine.

We had to be careful what we wrote in our letters, for even if the camp censor was not particularly bright, a certain camouflage was necessary, especially in requests for necessities (medicines, for example). News and certain questions had to be suitably "covered" and false names used in a sort of code. Our correspondents, too, resorted to all sorts of ruses, sending off their parcels from different post offices and often under different names. In this way, for example, Sr. Huberta, whose brother Fr. O. Hang had been interned with us but had been released at the beginning of December 1942, sent as many as seventy-five parcels, each weighing ten pounds, to different priests in Dachau.

Greetings from home! Despite all the precautions our correspondents had to take, their letters were invariably full of such love and esteem. And when the parcels began to arrive, we were often moved to tears by the proof of such selfless devotion. It seemed as though only the best was good enough for us. Yet we did not dare acknowledge receipt of these parcels for fear our friends might meet with reprisals.

We priests, particularly our Polish comrades, undoubtedly received the best food parcels in the camp. If our own families were too poor, our parishioners contributed, often with the widow's mite. Love, loyalty, faith, and a true spirit of sacrifice helped to make up these parcels.

Christ in Dachau

On rare occasions, we would receive an episcopal greeting. As Fr. Pies writes, "Many priests interned in the camp suffered acutely because they found so little understanding or help ... in their hour of need. When a letter did come expressing fatherly concern and sympathy, it was a real event." It was true that our priest friends would very likely have exposed themselves to arrest had they maintained any contact with us, but all the same, it was bitter. Year after year passed, and we remained behind bars or barbed wire. We had been jailed for our Faith, but outside life went on just the same without us.

In contrast, the loyalty and devotion of our families and friends, of parishioners and our sisters in religion was doubly touching. They prayed for us and cared for us and often sacrificed the best of their food for us. The rage and envy of our godless comrades knew no bounds. They threatened and bullied, but they still could not stop the flow of food parcels, for orders were orders, and this time the orders had come from Berlin.

I thank God to this day for the love and selfless devotion of these good people for the priests of Dachau. May their children and their children's children learn and profit from their example.

Feast of the Assumption 1942

"The prayers of my family and faithful friends at home implored God's protection and that of His most holy Mother for me. These were hard years indeed, hard years of suffering and of training. O my God, I thank Thee for it all! For all the sacrifice, for all the sorrow, for everything that was good in body and soul in these years!"

I found these words in the summer of 1945 in a secret diary kept by Fr. Alois Langhans. We had all of us prayed prayers like this in our time, for prayer was always our greatest source of strength and consolation. This was more than ever the case in the month of August 1942, when so many priests were dying of hunger. The feast of the Assumption came, and we began a novena to Our Lady, imploring her to help us in our hour of need. We begged her to save us or to allow us to die resigned to God's will. And Mary heard our prayer.

"Thy will be done!" We were ready to die if need be, but we still wanted to go on living; we wanted the chance to proclaim God's goodness to the world when these years of suffering were over.

Shortly afterward, Weiss and von Redwitz took over command. Unfortunately, they remained with us only one year. Nevertheless, they did succeed, to some extent, in breaking the sadistic rule of the SS and the corrupt power of the prisoner bosses, and even if things got worse again later, they were still never again as bad as they had been before August 1942.

On August 13, four German priests, Frs. Maring and Berndl, S.J., and Frs. Binder and Scheipers, were removed from the "invalid block" and thus saved from certain death. One of them had somehow managed to get in touch with his family, and in this way, the news that German priests were being killed by starvation and in the gas chambers reached Berlin, and the authorities there were at last obliged to intervene and put an end to such practices, if only to prevent the facts from becoming known abroad.

Another ruling from Berlin that August was that no German priest might in future be used for medical experiments, and a further order stipulated that we priests in Block 26 were to be "accorded normal treatment" in the infirmary. That such an order was necessary only served to show the kind of treatment we had been receiving before!

These were all proof positive of God's love for us. He had once again come to our aid, through the intercession of His Blessed Mother. Our way to Him — through Our Lady — lay in prayer. All through those years, it was prayer that saved us, not only in our physical but also in our spiritual need. We human beings are worth as much as our prayers are worth. This was perhaps the most profound lesson we learned from our experiences in Dachau. "Mary, came to our aid!"

Sister Pia

"The notorious Sister Pia," as I called her before the tribunal of the Dachau Trial (November 1945), was a well-known figure in the camp. A woman of between fifty and sixty, she had been decorated by Hitler with the Nazi "Order of Blood" and ranked with an SS general. She had once been a Catholic but had long ago left the Church and embraced a new faith — the godless creed of National Socialism.

She sometimes used to drive out from her villa to visit the prison camp, usually accompanied by the camp director. It was difficult to know what prompted the interest she showed in the prisoners. Was it just feminine softheartedness? Were these visits dictated by party political interest or a sort of hysteria, or were there other reasons? Some of the prisoners praised her efforts on their behalf; others just laughed at her.

I well remember the day she came to visit us priests in Block 26. It was early December 1942, and von Redwitz was with her. The visit was something of an event. She gave a "convert talk" in each room, fired with enthusiasm for Hitler, his party, and his concept for the world. She had once nursed Adolf Hitler through a serious illness — in the days when he was still unknown — and out of gratitude, he had raised her to the highest level of the party hierarchy. She seemed quite carried away by Himmler and what he had done for the German people, but she had clearly overlooked the human bloodshed caused by this German Robespierre who was to take his own life in 1945.

"I'll do what I can for you old jail-birds," she had promised the German communists who had been there for years. "But as for the others, they can die like dogs as far as I am concerned."

She made a similar remark in our block in regard to our Polish comrades. She probably thought she could win our confidence by this means, but at the same time, she had unwittingly revealed her true attitude toward the Church and God's priests.

She was indeed a strange and warped character. It is true that she did help some of the prisoners in the camp, and when she came to visit us, she brought us vestments and Mass vessels that she had obtained for us from Ettal Abbey. She also got the Sisters of Charity from a big Munich hospital to send each German priest in Dachau a parcel of Christmas cookies.

All the same, we got no pleasure out of her gifts, for we knew that they were given with the sole intention of winning us Catholic priests over to her own Nazi creed. She herself had lost the light of faith.

There were other women who shared the faith of Sister Pia, women who had lost their hold on God and substituted the myth of Adolf Hitler. But in the main, there were many more men.

A French periodical recently offered a prize for the best answer to the following question: Why are there more men in prison than women? The prize-winning answer was: Because there are more women in church than men.

Our Catholic nuns

No book concerned with our experiences in Dachau would be complete without a special mention of our Catholic sisters, for they played a highly important part in the lives of all those imprisoned for Christ's sake. Many of us priests had a sister or a near relative who was a nun, and we knew that their prayers were offered continuously for all of us. God alone knows what these prayers meant to us. The courageous attitude of these women in the face of Nazi oppression gave us new strength and courage. Their greetings and letters, and later their food parcels, assured us of their devotion.

Sister Pia was inspired by the pseudo-religion of the Nazi cult. Our Catholic sisters were inspired by the love of God.

The Nazis rightly recognized from the start that the convents of women religious were dangerous "cells of resistance" against their own godless ideology. They knew instinctively that these women who had no part with the world were quite prepared to die for their belief. They therefore set out systematically to undermine these centers of resistance, by tyranny, by threats, by false promises. But their efforts were unavailing. Our Catholic sisters risked their liberty and their lives over and over again in opposition.

The Nazis began with high hopes of "converting" our Catholic sisters, but the results were disappointing. "Eighty percent of Austria's teaching nuns will join our ranks," declared a cocksure Nazi leader in Salzburg in 1938. How wrong he was! Seven years later, the same man was obliged to admit that the Catholic teaching nuns were "after all, the best teaching material with the highest sense of duty."

The same was true of the nursing orders. Many doctors, themselves unbelievers, were so impressed by the quiet spirit of self-sacrifice and devotion that they protected them against the Nazi persecutors. Only true Christian charity could inspire such patience and gentleness. The Nazi nurses in the hospitals provided a sad contrast, but it was hardly surprising. They were only human, and their work presented them with all kinds of temptations. It is hard enough for the follower of Christ to strive for perfection; how much harder for those who have no Christian principles to arm them!

Our sisters never lost sight of their Faith, and in this lay their greatness. They followed with patience the Way of the Cross of Our Lord Jesus Christ, secure in the knowledge that He would be the victor, just as He was the victor on Calvary.

Christ in Dachau

"I've lived for Christ, and I'll die for Christ," declared Sr. Maria Restituta, a forty-nine-year old nursing nun from Vienna. These were her last words before her execution. She had already spent eight months in jail, having been arrested leaving the operating theater. One of the doctors had denounced her to the Gestapo for using "dangerous language." "I'm going home to Heaven," said this fearless opponent of Hitler's terror regime as they marched her out to be shot.

The nuns of the enclosed orders were no less heroic in their way, and their convents were real powerhouses of prayer. Here, too, the Nazis sought to induce the nuns to break away from the Church. In one community of contemplative nuns in the Tyrol, each sister, in turn, was interrogated by the Gestapo. Their efforts and their methods were ineffectual, for the sisters were unrelenting in their loyalty to God.

We priests in Dachau knew very well how vital it was that our Catholic sisters should return to the hospitals and schools when the Nazi terror came to an end. Many of the lay teachers had been carried away by the Hitler ideology. The training of the young must once more be placed in capable and responsible hands.

It was surprising what news from the outside world reached Dachau — and it was not always what we would have liked to hear either. Now and again, news reached us that a priest had turned apostate, a victim of the new pseudo-religion. More than ever, our thoughts turned to our Catholic nuns. We knew they were needed everywhere, more than ever before.

Our Catholic nuns! An army of millions spread over the whole earth, dedicated to the service of God and suffering humanity. The Nazis did their best to destroy the influence of the Catholic Church on the young — and the priests and nuns were very real obstacles to this course.

Dr. Felix Hurdes, in his valuable prison-camp book *Vater unser*,[8] relates the following significant anecdote:

> "You'll see," said an SS man to an Austrian nun after the Anschluss in 1938, "in ten years' time you'll be honoring Adolf Hitler on those altars where you now adore Christ."

---

[8] *Vater unser: Gedanken aus dem Konzentrationslager* [Our father: thoughts from the concentration camp] (Herder, 1950).

"If," retorted the nun, "Hitler is prepared to die on the cross for his people and then rise from the dead on the third day, I'll change my habit for a Nazi uniform then — but not before."

Priests in new jobs

The object of the sensational visit from Sister Pia and the camp director von Redwitz was clear enough: it was part of the Nazi propaganda campaign in the mistaken hope of winning us over to their cause. We had no illusions about the new interest displayed in us Catholic priests, but all the same, we noted the change of attitude with pleasure. Incredible though it was, the SS officer had addressed us as "comrades" — we the "black dogs," the "scum of the earth"! It was as though a light had begun to shine in our darkness. God had shown His face. The new attitude of the camp authorities was a triumph of the spiritual resistance of the priests' community in the face of the godlessness of many of our fellow prisoners.

The camp administration had at last come to realize an age-old truth: they had suddenly recognized that we priests really belonged to the most valuable section of every community. Far from being scum, we were, in fact, leaders and organizers. After all, most of us came from deeply religious families with the highest moral principles. Not only had we been well educated, but our training in the seminary had taught us discipline in the true sense, a training for use in the service of God. We were all accustomed to authority and responsibility and to dealing with people and human problems. At last, they had come to see that they could make very good use of us in running their camp!

Our comrade Karl Steiner was the first to put forward the names of two priests, Frs. Berchtold and Kiesel, for posts in the administration. The priests proved to be such a success that other priests began to be employed for such work. In due course, they were in demand to fill all the key positions — in the infirmary, the post office, the labor-control office, the SS paymaster's office, and so on. At long last, the authorities came to realize that we priests were not only capable helpers in these positions but also reliable characters.

Even the SS began to acknowledge our merits. As Catholic priests, we inspired confidence, for we were, after all, part of the indestructible Rock of Peter. They saw that they needed us in this camp, where corruption was rife and crime and scandals were everyday occurrences. For a whole year, only priests were employed in the "food parcel commando," and never once was there so much as a whisper of any irregularity in this section of the post office, which provided such opportunities for dishonesty.

Fr. Franz Geiger was capo of this group of workers from January 1943 until March 31, 1944, assisted by Fr. Friedrichs, Fr. Schelling, and Fr. Niedermoser. Some 245,000 parcels were handled during 1943, not counting smaller packets and Red Cross parcels. "Only a few months later," relates Fr. Geiger, "our successors were to be sent to the bunker for parcel stealing."

"Camp Commandant Weiss even wanted to arrange for priests from Dachau to be sent to Allach (a branch labor camp near Munich, a sub-camp of Dachau). They were foreseen for key positions as block personnel, etc." wrote Georg Schelling in 1945. "He had no one else who could keep the camp there in order for him. He knew very well that the priests were efficient and reliable, and in this case, their transfer to an external commando would have been a distinction. I had already prepared the list of names of those to be transferred to Allach (it was typical that this had to be done within an hour!). I then went to Redwitz to get his permission for a chapel in Allach and a room reserved for the sole use of priests. In the absence of Redwitz, the Rapportführer agreed to this request. Within half an hour, news came that the whole scheme had fallen through. As I later heard from Allach, Weiss had been unable to obtain permission from Berlin to send priests outside the camp."

Yet Another Christmas

Once again, Christmas came — Christmas 1942. We looked hopefully into the new year, confident that we would soon be free. At any rate, we had been, by the mercy of God, saved from starvation.

After evening roll call on Christmas Eve, we gathered in the chapel. Midnight Mass in Dachau! It was an unforgettable experience. Our priests' choir joined the angels in praising Almighty God, and at the end, everyone joined in the Christmas carol known all over the world: "Silent Night." Never before had we sung with such feeling this Christmas song of Christ the Savior.

"Christ the Savior is born!" The words took on a new meaning for us.

When we returned to our block after Mass, we found a heartwarming sight: the good things our families and friends had sent us in their Christmas food parcels set out among candles and sprigs of evergreen. It was an almost unbeliev-able sight. Who would ever have thought such a thing possible? Our thoughts turned instinctively to those who had gone on before us to the heavenly Father. Only a few months before, they had hungered with us, prayed with us, and worked with us. God had accepted their sacrifice, and we knew that they were our intermediaries at His throne.

Christmas 1942. It was almost like the end of a great passion. This terrible year had ended in the peace and joy of Christmas. The names of those who had died were solemnly read out on New Year's Eve, and prayers were said aloud for the repose of their souls. Yet even greater than our personal sorrow was our gratitude to God.

> Who then shall separate us from the love of Christ? Shall tribulation? Or distress? Or famine? Or nakedness? Or danger? Or persecution? Or the sword?
>
> (As it is written: For thy sake, we are put to death all the day long; we are accounted as sheep for the slaughter.)
>
> But in all these things we overcome, because of him that hath loved us. For I am sure that neither death, nor life, nor angels, nor principali-ties, nor powers, nor things present, nor things to come, nor might, nor height, nor depth, nor any other creature, shall be able to separate us from the love of God, which is in Christ Jesus our Lord. (Rom. 8:35–39)

1942: Hunger year

January	First venture of a sermon in the chapel. Block 26 once again a "labor block."
January 5	Camp Director Hofmann makes tour of inspection.
February 11	Our supplementary rations withdrawn.
Lent	Lenten sermons by Fr. Otto Pies, S.J., and liturgical lectures by Fr. Maurus Münch, O.S.B.

Christ in Dachau

End of March	Barrels of beetroot received. Communist block personnel defraud us of money.
April	A hard Holy Week for the Polish clergy. First large altar cross completed (cross by Fr. Karl Schmidt, figure by Fr. Johann Steinbock).
May	Sunday May devotions with address by Fr. Albert Eise, who died on September 3, 1942.
June–September	The worst hunger period. Sixty German and hundreds of Polish priests died.
July 8	Prisoner boss Richard S. ("the evil spirit of Block 26") removed from his post.
August 7–15	Communal novena to Our Lady for deliverance from hunger and death.
August 13	Dr. Kozal, today three years a bishop, came to join our "Paper Bag Commando" together with Frs. Knecht, Kolacek, and me. Weiss and von Redwitz take over the camp. The turning point for Block 26.
September 27–October 2	Novena to the Little Flower for our release. God willed it otherwise.
October	Food parcels begin to arrive.
November	Parcels officially allowed.
Beginning of December	Sister Pia and von Redwitz come to visit us in Block 26.
December	Beginning of typhoid epidemic. First two deaths.

Book 3

Dachau: Our Spiritual Sanctuary

I have loved, O Lord, the beauty of Thy house,
and the place where Thy glory dwelleth.

—Psalm 25:8

11

The Chapel

A humble beginning

Our chapel in Dachau was as poor and as bare as the stable in Bethlehem. But we would not have exchanged it for the richest of all the fine cathedrals in Christendom that morning of January 21, 1941, as we first set eyes upon the room in the hut in Dachau that was to be our sanctuary. It was a miracle to us that we should have been allowed to have a chapel in the concentration camp at all, and from the very first moment, we resolved to do everything in our power to transform this simple room into a chapel worthy of Our Lord, who was to dwell there in the Blessed Sacrament.

Many of us had already been interned for months, even years, and most of us had been through more than one prison camp — Buchenwald, Flossenbürg, Gusen, Sachsenhausen, Mauthausen . . . It seemed to us on that winter's morning that we had never seen such a beautiful room.

Bare as it was, the chapel had a wonderful atmosphere of peace and warmth. The camp authorities had taken down the partitions that had divided the hut into four small rooms, and the chapel was spacious enough, by camp standards. There were no pillars or beams to mar the clear lines. The sixteen big windows, eight on either side of the room, had been painted green with a pattern of red crosses. The idea behind this had been to prevent anyone outside from taking part in our services. In point of fact, it was a useless precaution, for they would have needed to reinforce the walls and provide us with double windows in order to prevent the sound of our prayers and our singing from reaching the world of the camp outside. All the same, the windows were highly decorative, and particularly in the daytime, the lighting effect inside the chapel was quite lovely. They had even gone so far as to paint the walls for us: a floral design executed in clear, fresh colors — no work of art, it was true, but it gave the room a fittingly festive character. The fact that it had decorated walls had made our chapel the most important room in the whole camp! The floor was of wood, laid like the deck of a ship, and we used to oil it from time to time and kept it polished regularly with heavy polishing blocks.

It was, however, the altar that meant the most to us. It had been months, even years, since any of us had assisted at Mass: now we were to be allowed to have Mass every day! A plain wooden barracks table did duty as an altar — without flowers, without a tabernacle. All we had that morning for the adornment of our chapel was the contents of the suitcase containing a field Mass kit that had been brought from Sachsenhausen by the priests who had joined us from there — a small cross and two metal candlesticks, two cruets, and three altar cards. There was one reversible chasuble available for the celebrant; it was white and red on one side and violet and black on the other, so that it could be used to suit every occasion. This was the chapel, with its primitive emergency furnishings, in which hundreds of imprisoned priests assembled that morning in January 1941 for the first Holy Mass in our sanctuary, right in the center of the hell of the concentration camp.

On January 21, 1945, a commemorative Mass was celebrated in the chapel in Dachau. Just behind the high altar, the first emergency altar had been set up again, furnished with our first cross and candlesticks. There were not many "old hands" still alive to assist at Mass that day, but for those of us who were still there, the sight of that barrack table roused many memories. For this had been our altar in the early days. This had been the table around which we had gathered in our darkest hours, offering up our sufferings — both physical and spiritual — every day anew as the celebrant offered the bread and wine. Here we renewed the sacrifice of our imprisonment and affirmed our readiness to make the last sacrifice of our lives for Christ, if it were His will. God alone knows what strength and consolation we derived from His Presence in the chapel in those days. He had accepted the last sacrifice from many, for more than one thousand priests died in Dachau from hunger, poison, and maltreatment. Their poor, tormented bodies were burned to ashes in the crematorium, and in many cases the ashes were used as fertilizers or simply thrown away. But we knew that their souls went straight to their heavenly Father and that their bodies will rise again in glory at the resurrection, in fulfillment of the promises of God.

It would be quite impossible to describe our feelings on the occasion of our first Mass in the new chapel in Dachau. Row upon row of priests in prison clothes, their heads shaved like convicts, their feet thrust into all kinds of primitive house shoes ... But their faces were radiant. For Christ had come to join us in our imprisonment — Christ the Crown of martyrs, Christ the Light of confessors, Christ the Joy of all His saints. He was with us in the midst of the suffering and death of the camp! Not only was He ever present in His divine grace, but He was also present now as God and man — in His Body and Blood in the Blessed Sacrament. He was to be present with us from now on, night and day, in the little Host housed in the tabernacle on our first altar. Christ in Dachau.

Three years later

Our chapel had begun as poor as the stable in Bethlehem, but it was not to remain like this. Within three years, we had furnishings and vestments that would have done credit to any parish church. It was not possible to obtain very much from outside by legitimate means, but we received many gifts from friends and benefactors in all kinds of ways, secretly, often hidden in carts and sacks from the plantation.

Many of the furnishings for the chapel were the work of craftsmen and tradesmen in the camp itself. What was more, astonishing though it may seem, it was not difficult to obtain the necessary materials. The camp was, after all, virtually a self-supporting unit, and the SS had plunder enough in their stores. With a little carefully planned "organization," it usually proved possible to obtain what we wanted. When the food parcels began to arrive after 1942, we priests would trade food or cigarettes for raw materials and would reward in the same way those who helped to beautify our sanctuary. There were many, of course, who wanted nothing for their services, but all the same, we could and would not accept these services without some form of material recompense. In this way, the furnishings for our chapel increased.

For almost a year, we employed a carpenter and joiner who used to come and work in the chapel every Saturday afternoon (later on, Saturday afternoons were free for some of the workers). The flowers and plants were the special care of a gardener from Innsbruck, and an electrician was available when necessary to install new lighting or to cope with repairs. Bricklayers, house painters, glaziers, tailors — they were all to be had with a little "organization."

We had two altars, the high altar and the altar to Our Lady, which stood to the left, in the corner. It had taken our carpenters hours of patient work to encase the two barrack tables that originally formed these altars. The fronts of both altars were, in due course, covered with silver-grey silk. After the day the camp director had lost his temper on the spot at the sight of the IHS on the antependium of the high altar in January 1942, new liturgical symbols were substituted, changeable according to the seasons of the Church year. Fr. Steinbock was adept at making these out of silver and gold foil.

As mentioned, there was no shortage of materials for our needs in Dachau. Strange though it may seem, things that had long become unobtainable in the austere world outside were still to be had — though at a price — in the concentration camp. Another paradox of Dachau! The SS had, after all, been feathering their own nests for years with the belongings of the dispossessed. Even in February 1945, virtually at the end of the war, we were still able to obtain the best-quality machine oil with which to polish our chapel floor. In all our "organizing," however, we still strictly observed the seventh commandment. But we felt that the exceptional circumstances fully justified a wider interpretation. As the war reached its final stages and even the most fanatical of the SS were forced to realize that Hitler's great victory was just another Nazi myth, they began frantically to load truck after truck with their precious booty, which they hoped to evacuate to a safer depot further south. But there was still so much left behind when the Americans arrived that the stores were thrown open to all and sundry. Much was deliberately destroyed by the prisoners themselves, and what remained after that was finally confiscated by the occupation troops.

We ourselves worked with our hands, and we organized helpers within the camp, but we also received valuable contributions toward our chapel furnishings from outside. The list of such donations at the end of this book testifies to the devotion of the friends of the priests of Dachau who, in turn, never forgot the warmhearted generosity of these benefactors in their prayers. Month by month, the precious store of our furnishings and vestments slowly increased.

Fr. Karl Schmidt made us our first tabernacle, with two adoring angels fashioned with the greatest difficulty out of the yellow tin of an old fish can. It was poor material, but it was made with loving and reverent hands. By 1943, this tabernacle was too small for our needs and was replaced at Easter 1944 with a proper two-door tabernacle made of reddish-brown pear wood, inlaid and finely polished. It, too, had two adoring angels and a sun, all cast in brass.

Behind the tabernacle rose a great oak cross, the gift of the men's sodality of the Münster School of Art. Two three-armed candelabra, lovely examples of the craftsmanship of our camp carvers, flanked the altar cross.

To the right of the altar, which was raised on a dais, stood the credence table, backed by a triptych with a picture of the Sacred Heart, a carved relief of St. Joseph, and a painting by Br. Konrad. During the last months of the war, this table was also frequently used as a third altar for Mass.

To the left of the high altar stood the raised lectern that served as our pulpit. Nearby was the harmonium, an excellent instrument with twelve registers; it had been lent to us by the parish priest of Dachau.

Half of the south wall was taken up by a shelf for shoes that reached to the level of the windows. Up to the end of 1942, we were not permitted to enter any of the block buildings in outdoor shoes, a ruling that also covered the chapel. The SS were very particular about the maintenance of outward order and cleanliness and were inordinately proud of their polished floors. Our footwear was less fine, but this escaped the eyes of admiring visitors. After 1942, when the new camp commandant put an end to this absurd rule, we used these shelves for storing breviaries and other religious books.

At the back of the room was a big brown tiled stove. It was very seldom used.

The chapel could accommodate eight hundred, but I have known congregations of more than a thousand prisoners. After the harsh ruling of September 1941 denying the Polish clergy further admittance to the chapel, the SS gave orders that the eight windows on the north side of the room should be painted milk white, in order — so they thought — to emphasize our complete segregation from the Polish Block 28.

That was our chapel. And Christ in the tabernacle was the shrine to which we made our pilgrimage in the midst of the perils of the camp. It was here that we gained new strength, not only for our own souls but also for our manifold works of charity and pastoral care. It was Christ who enabled us to overcome the envy and malice of our godless comrades.

That was our chapel, and we went on steadily adding to its treasures. Even the SS took a hand in this task, for the camp authorities had a special interest in the chapel, which was, after all, highly important to them for propagandist reasons. God often chooses the strangest instruments to carry out His will, and so in this way, the priests of Dachau soon had a room worthy of Him who had chosen to make His dwelling there. Our chapel soon became the "model exhibit" invariably shown to visitors to the camp. The SS overlords never failed to refer to this as proof of their "concern for the well-being of the interned German priests." The other side of the picture naturally remained hidden. But we were not greatly concerned with all this. The most important thing was that we had our chapel, fittingly furnished for the worship of God.

It was a holy place indeed. It would be impossible to describe what the chapel meant for us priests — indeed for the whole camp. Priests from more than twenty nations gathered under its roof and carried Christ to those who themselves could not enter. It was the powerhouse of prayer in the very center of hell, and many were the lost sheep who were helped back to the fold. It brought us consolation in time of tribulation and the perpetual assurance of God's love for us in the presence of His Son. It brought us Christ in Dachau.

Our Lady of Dachau

The marked devotion to Our Lady of the Catholic prisoners in Dachau was characteristic, and it was significant that the first communal act of worship in our new chapel was destined to take the form of devotions to Our Blessed Mother. We had assembled for Mass that morning, but the atheist "sacristan" appointed by the camp authorities had neglected to provide either hosts or altar wine. Fr. Prabutzki, our camp chaplain at that time, saw that it would be impossible to offer Mass and led the priest congregation in the Litany of Our Lady and in the singing of the Salve Regina. Devotions to Mary in this way preceded Mass in the chapel in Dachau. "To Jesus through Mary!"

Christ was ever present with us in the Blessed Sacrament, and Mary was ever present too, an unfailing mother to the priests of her Son, Jesus. She heard the countless Hail Marys said in her honor, she was present in every spiritual discussion, and she was remembered in the pictures and tokens that we had managed to smuggle through in our breviaries. She was ever present in the hope we all cherished that she would deliver us. With every Marian feast day of the Church, the hope of our deliverance grew. It was surely no mere coincidence that the terrible wave of deaths from hunger came to an end in August 1942 — on the feast of the Assumption.

"Our Lady of Dachau": this was her title from the very first day the statue arrived in Dachau at Easter 1943. It was indeed a miracle in itself that the statue of Our Lady could be borne in triumph through the length of the concentration camp to be placed in honor in the chapel. The Queen of Heaven in the hell of Dachau! It was a remarkable occasion indeed. The news spread like wildfire. I myself was in the infirmary at the time, recovering from my first bout of typhoid, but even there, I heard about the enthusiastic reception. Once back in the priests' block, it was not long before I, too, had joined the crowds of kneeling prisoners before Our Lady of Dachau.

The statue representing our Blessed Mother had been sent to us from Freudental by the superior of the Salvatorian Order there. Fr. Karl Schrammel and Fr. Ludwig Hiller, who were both Salvatorian fathers, were interned in the camp with us. About a year later, a reliquary containing fragments of the bones of St. Konrad of Parzham was placed at the foot of the statue. Our Lady Dachau was a most beautiful piece of carving, noble in every line, and the figure made a deep impression upon all who saw it. Fresh flowers from the plantation made a sweet-scented bower of Our Lady's altar. More than five hundred priests were workers in the gardens of the plantation, and they saw to it that the loveliest flowers were placed on the altar of Christ and His Holy Mother. Not all the power of our enemies could succeed in removing Our Lady from her chosen place. No matter how diverse in language, nationality, upbringing, or education they might be, the friends of God were unanimous in their praise of His Blessed Mother and in veneration of Our Lady of Dachau. Mary, the refuge of sinners and the comforter of the afflicted, was always ready to hear our prayers.

The Rosary was said often, not only in the chapel and in our own block but also at work, in secret. During the early years, we were often searched, and it was a punishable offense to be found in the possession of a rosary. Many had no rosaries at all, and I once exchanged bread for the services of a hungry prisoner who cleverly fashioned more than fifty rosaries from old china beads strung on wire that I had salvaged with the help of some prisoners employed on a cable-laying job. Prisoners working in the "Messerschmitt commando" used to make us rosary rings — metal rings with ten little cog-like points — "on the side." We were well aware of the danger involved, and we met with many obstacles, but nothing could deter us from proving our devotion to Mary.

In September 1945, the Eikeplatz — the great concrete square in the center of the camp, which had been named after a notorious Nazi atheist — was appropriately renamed Marien-Platz, or "Mary's Square." There were plans to erect a church on this site, a "church of reparation." Unfortunately, this plan has not yet materialized. An impressive ceremony took place in September 1955, when ex-Dachau priests met for the procession that marked the transfer of Our Lady of Dachau to the parish church of St. James in Dachau town. The statue of Our Lady was borne through the streets in a long procession headed by the late Msgr. Friedrich Pfanzelt, the parish priest, followed by His Eminence Cardinal Josef Wendel, archbishop of Munich. In his address, Msgr. Pfanzelt declared: "We feel sure that the Catholics of our parish will follow the devotion of the priests who were interned in Dachau concentration camp and make their way as pilgrims to Our Lady, whatever their need may be. And Our Lady will continue to bless and protect the people of our town."

We priests of Dachau know from personal experience how Mary triumphed over terror and hunger, over crime and godlessness, in the midst of blood and of tears. The Queen of Heaven was victorious and never failed to spread her mantle of protection over those who remained true to her Son. We call upon her in confidence and invite Catholics all over the world to join with us: "Our Lady of Dachau, Mother of grace, pray for us!"

Care of the chapel

As the store of our treasures for the chapel grew, it was obvious that someone would have to be found to take over the responsibility for their safe custody and supervise their care and use. The chapel had also to be kept clean and in order and the flowers and various altar furnishings changed according to the seasons of the Church year.

The Chapel

The chaplain naturally assumed first responsibility for all this, but the actual work of sacristan fell to Fr. Heinrich Steiner from Upper Austria, who was his able and untiring assistant. Year in and year out, Fr. Steiner worked selflessly to maintain the chapel in impeccable order. He had excellent taste, as was evident in his floral arrangements and the way he made use of the other ornaments. He was one of the tireless and much-valued workers in the gardens of the plantation. During the last year, he found another grand worker and fellow priest, Prince Alban Löbenstein, to help him in the chapel.

Transmitter and arms?

We always had to be prepared for visits from the gentlemen of the SS. They were likely to come barging into the chapel at any time and were capable of all kinds of irreverent behavior. The most extraordinary visit took place in the spring of 1944, however, when an SS officer suddenly appeared — to search the chapel for a radio transmitter and arms!

Facts about Dachau concentration camp had been constantly leaking out and reaching other countries abroad, much to the chagrin of the SS, who were quite unable to understand how such a thing was possible. They were quite convinced that a secret radio transmitter must be hidden somewhere in the camp — and why should those Catholic priests not have it tucked away somewhere in that chapel of theirs? Perhaps they were even hiding weapons? They considered us capable of anything — and they came to search our chapel.

The chaplain had been tipped about this visit beforehand. In any case, his conscience was quite clear, for it would never have occurred to us to make use of this holy place for anything but the worship of God. We were all indignant at the very idea. The Church of Christ had no need of arms to fight against the evil in the world.

The SS officer arrived in the afternoon; he was a notorious character in the camp, known and feared for his brutality. He was accompanied by an SS guard known, for some reason, as "Glass Claw." Fr. Schelling was standing in the doorway of the chapel as they arrived, and he conducted them inside. It goes without saying that they entered the holy place without the slightest sign of reverence — after all, they were not looking for Our Lord but for a radio transmitter and hidden arms.

Christ in Dachau

There was a little recess at the back of the chapel that we used for storage purposes. The men wrenched open this "confessional," as they called it, but were visibly disappointed by what they found there. They little realized that we had no need of confessionals, for all the penitents we had in the camp and all the confessions we heard!

To his horror, Fr. Schelling suddenly caught sight of a prisoner kneeling behind the big stove at the back of the chapel. The man was a Polish priest as the *P* on his red political prisoner's patch only too clearly revealed. The order banning all Poles from the chapel was still in force, and the situation was critical indeed for the unfortunate priest who had stolen into the chapel for a few minutes to pray. No one had known that he was there.

But in his ardor to carry out his orders for a thorough search of our chapel, the SS man apparently did not even notice the incriminating *P*. He took the Pole for a German priest and ordered him to assist in the search by lifting the coal box. As luck would have it, the man knew no German, but Fr. Schelling mercifully saved the situation by lifting the box himself. The SS men were far too absorbed in their task to give the matter another thought. They were not satisfied until they had examined every corner of the chapel, and their impatience grew the longer the unrewarding search continued. Fr. Schelling told us afterward that he had hardly been able to stop himself from laughing outright at the sight of their obvious disappointment. Satisfied at last that we had nothing to hide, they left with the grudging admission: "It seems you're not such a bad lot after all!"

The chapel in danger

There was, of course, always the danger that we might lose the chapel, for although it had a decided propaganda value for the camp authorities, they recognized at the same time that it was the stronghold of the Church in the camp, the same Church that Hitler had sworn to "crush like a toad." We all knew that a word from Berlin would have sufficed to deprive us of the chapel, and we were also well aware that our godless "comrades" were only too ready to denounce us to the camp authorities for the slightest transgression, which might well have been met with such a reprisal.

A critical situation developed in September 1944, as the overcrowding in the camp broke all records. In some of the huts 1,000 men were being accommodated in quarters intended for 250. Conditions in the invalids' block were particularly bad. Only Block 2 — the block reserved for the inspection of visitors — was an exception. The unscrupulous block personnel, the prisoner bosses about whom so much has already been written, also contrived to secure relatively good quarters for themselves at the expense of their unfortunate comrades.

Such overcrowded living conditions provided the authorities with just the chance they were looking for. They approached us with the demand that we should offer to relinquish the chapel of our own free will. It was a clever move, or so they thought, for only in this way could they get around the orders that had been issued from Berlin. The chaplain met the demand of the SS officer with the reply that he would like to submit his answer to the camp administration in writing. To his surprise, his request was granted.

Fr. Schelling set to work at once, together with several others, to draft an appropriate letter of protest stating the seven reasons for our refusal to give up the chapel. The document was read aloud to the community in the chapel that evening and met with unanimous approval. The text ran as follows:

1. We feel that we cannot possibly relinquish something that was secured for us by the German bishops after so many difficult and prolonged negotiations.
2. Other accommodations exist in the camp that could be made available — Block 29, for instance, which at present houses a private shoemaker's workshop.
3. We do not regard it as our function as prisoners to provide accommodation. This is the task of the administration authorities, above all by the erection of new buildings.
4. Some of our fellow prisoners have appealed to our Christian charity, an extraordinary appeal considering the interpretation of Christian charity by these same prisoners in the days when we priests ranked as the scum of the camp. We have by no means forgotten all this.
5. Our chapel would provide accommodation for 250 men at the most. It would thus be no real solution to this urgent problem, for within a fortnight, the situation would be as bad as ever.

6. Block 31 (the brothel) can scarcely be regarded as "essential for the war effort." If this were to be closed, valuable accommodation could be made available. Or is the Temple of Venus perhaps more important than the temple of God?

7. The danger of illicit mail is by no means negligible. I can offer no guarantee that the news that we have been deprived of our chapel will not very soon reach Berlin.

In the name of the priests of Block 26,
(signed) Georg Schelling, Chaplain

It was a fearless document, worthy of a priest, and it was delivered next morning to the appropriate SS office. The matter was never raised again. The storm was over, and our chapel had been saved.

Before the tabernacle

Christ in the Blessed Sacrament was the perpetual source of our spiritual and intellectual life in the concentration camp. The grace and blessings received will be revealed only in Heaven. The chapel became the place of pilgrimage for the whole priests' community, the center of unification for the many and varied national elements that made up the army of God's servants, the priests of the universal Church of Christ. National differences were forgotten; national chaos was ordered in the united adoration before Christ in the tabernacle.

We had orders that the chapel should be kept closed during the day, but the godless rule was not generally observed. Only if the atmosphere in the camp was particularly highly charged did we exercise special caution. We usually got wind of such events in sufficient time to take the necessary precautions, for we had all kinds of ways and means of securing such inside information.

Once the danger was past, it was not long before we would be back again in the chapel, kneeling before the tabernacle. Except during roll call, the chapel was practically never empty. Many of the priests had time to spare, for there were many who were ill or convalescent and many who were too old for further work. Some priests even succeeded in slipping away from work for short periods, although this was always risky, particularly as the war reached its climax and more and more controls were enforced upon the workers for Hitler's victory.

Somehow, however, we always found our way to Our Lord in the Blessed Sacrament sometime during the day, and it was often even possible to spend hours there in prayer, in silent meditation, and in spiritual reading.

In this way, we found the strength to face our situation. Our suffering was dedicated to Our Lord, and the apparent futility of our imprisonment gained a new meaning. The time of waiting was turned to good account. Such spiritual refreshment was highly necessary, not only for the good of our own souls but also in view of our unceasing pastoral work carried out in the most difficult circumstances in the camp. Every day we spent in the concentration camp was consecrated to God in prayer.

"Give us this day our daily bread!" Never before had the words had such meaning for us. In no great cathedral or fine parish church outside had we ever received the Bread of Life with such longing and devotion as in the little chapel in Dachau during those years of hunger.

"O God, my God, look upon me: why hast Thou forsaken me?" The words of Psalm 21 took on a new meaning for us in the midst of our own tribulation, and we began more deeply to understand Our Savior in His Passion and Agony.

We began to realize that our own suffering was serving to bring us nearer to Him. We could share His Passion with Him, close to Him all the time. And He shared His strength with us. The knowledge that He had chosen us as His witnesses made our burden easy to bear, for in the hell of Dachau, we were privileged to share His victory. God's ways for us are indeed often strange! It had been His will that we should come to Dachau, and it was in Dachau that all this was revealed to us. This was the miracle of Christ in Dachau!

In the tabernacle in the chapel, Bethlehem and Golgatha were wonderfully fused in the person of Our Lord, who shared our tribulation, fought our battle along with us, bore our burdens. We His priests knelt together with the shepherds and the angels at His crib, just as we stood together with Mary and John under His Cross. And our prayers for His faithful, for His Church, reached Him with a new fervor, a new urgency.

And so we knelt there in our striped prison clothes to adore Christ. No matter how poor our altar might be, we knew that the Savior of the world was present there day and night. No matter how bloody the Golgotha of Dachau might be, we knew that Christ was there, the fellow prisoner of those who were faithful to

Him. And we hoped that we would one day glorify God in an everlasting hymn of praise and thanksgiving in the place which He had gone on to prepare for us.

Only if we worship, love, and live according to God's divine commandments are we human beings and really free.

— Fr. Alfred Delp, S.J., ten days before his execution on February 2, 1945

12

Priests

United in Christ

"They were persevering in the doctrine of the apostles and in the communication of the breaking of bread, and in prayers.... The multitude of believers had but one heart and one soul" (Acts 2:42; 4:32). This testimony in the Acts of the Apostles to the wonderful communal spirit that characterized the early Christians might well have described the priest community in Dachau. Dr. Richard Schmitz, ex-vice-chancellor of Austria, was to pay tribute to this spirit later in the Vatican, and Dr. Fritz Schäffer — who later became minister-president of Bavaria — also told of what he had himself seen: "What I saw for myself of the spirit of the priest community in Dachau reminded me of accounts of the early Christians."

It was prayer, first and foremost, that accounted for this strong community spirit, a ceaseless wave of prayer imploring the help of God and His Blessed Mother. And just as we were united by prayer, we were united also by the eternal mystery of grace, the grace we obtained every day anew at Mass and, above all, in the miracle of the Eucharist. The priest community in Dachau was a eucharistic community.

Christ was the focal point of all our prayers and all our hopes as well as of our brotherly and pastoral love. We were cut off from the outside world, and as the months and the years passed, the prospects of our release grew more and more remote. Death was never far away. Only Christ remained, Christ in the daily Sacrifice of the Mass and in Communion. He was all in all to us: our bread, our light, and our strength. His own words took on a new significance for us: "I am the way, and the truth, and the life" (John 14:6). In this way, Christ became the unifying factor among priests so widely differing in nationality, upbringing, and temperament.

We set out consciously to deepen, strengthen, and defend this unity anew every day in our prayers and in our lives. We had plenty of opportunities of proving this intention. Our numbers increased, and clergy from many other nations came to join us in our already cramped quarters. Soon the chapel was not large enough to house the whole community all at once. The point came when we also had to eat in shifts, for there was not room for all of us to sit down together. So half the hut would wait out in the road while the other half was eating. Soon there were far too few straw sacks. Our "beds" were already tiered in three stories, with the old and the invalids down below. The sleeping quarters were so full that it was barely possible to find the door, and it soon needed real dexterity to reach one's bed at all. We were sleeping two to one straw sack before very long, and during the last six months, even five men to two sacks! All the same, newcomers were invariably given a warm welcome. St. Augustine's great words were fulfilled here: "Si angustiantur vasa carnis, dilatentur spatia caritatis" (*Sermo* 10).[9] It was quite true: the more confined our living quarters became, the more our Christian love expanded in God's grace. As Fr. Otto Pies truly says: "In spite of it all, our priest community still remained a miracle of the sacrament of prayer and of love in the midst of the diabolical world of the concentration camp; it was like the early Church in the pagan world of ancient Rome and Corinth." Such love, such Christian charity, could never have sprung from ourselves alone. Only the strength we received from God enabled us to apply this love unstintingly, despite all the trials and temptations to which we were subjected.

Christ in the Eucharist gave us strength. The Son of God — who is Himself love — gathered us every day around His table. We received everything from Him. Without Him, we would have been lost, unable to surmount the obstacles and the trials and tribulations that beset us on the Way of the Cross of the camp. The transplantation from the presbytery or the cloister to Block 26 was too sudden, too bewildering to be borne alone. Who knows what might have become of us in the camp, robbed of our freedom, faced with danger, hunger, fatigue, and fear? Not only the physical trials we had to bear, but also the very

[9] If the vessels of flesh are constricted, let room for charity be enlarged. — Ed.

real spiritual problems that are the lot of every priest but were accentuated in the atmosphere of the camp would almost certainly have sufficed to bring about our fall without the help of Christ in the Eucharist.

Una Sancta Ecclesia

"We're the largest religious community in the world," we used to remind ourselves, not without a certain pride. There were advantages to such a large community, for it was often possible for the individual to "go under cover" among so many: he was thus in many ways less exposed to the merciless persecution of his godless fellow prisoners. On the other hand, there was also the great disadvantage that the petty offenses or even the unfavorable characteristics of any one of us would often be attributed to the community as a whole. It lay in the nature of things that among so many, there was always someone or other who was the bête noire of the all-powerful prisoner bosses, and others who either deliberately or inadvertently provided the authorities with welcome occasion to wreak their vengeance on all of us priests.

We did our best to be good comrades, not only to each other, but also to the lay prisoners. This spirit of good comradeship formed the basis of all our pastoral activities in the camp. There were no class barriers in Dachau and no differences in clothing or in rations. We were all equal, all reduced to our prison numbers. Only the inner value of each individual as a human being counted. It goes without saying that we had more in common with our priest comrades and were especially bound to them by the ties of our common vocation and our brotherly love.

The concentration camp made new demands upon us. Age and duration of internment and, above all, physical condition were far more important than intellectual training. Academic degrees or clerical rank were unimportant when it came to bed making or dexterity in maneuvering wheelbarrows in the gravel pits. Tenacity was all important — tenacity and adaptability. High-ranking clerical dignitaries and simple lay brothers were equals, and no mention was to be found of their distinction in the lists of the camp authorities. The only exception we ourselves made to this rule was our Polish bishop Kozal. He was our bishop in chapel; otherwise, he was our fellow comrade, our fellow prisoner in Christ.

In the same way, the young seminarians and the lay brothers ranked equally as members of our priest community. The eighteen-year-old seminarian Jean

Christ in Dachau

Muller from France was the youngest prisoner among us. After the summer of 1944, the great majority of student priests in Block 26 came from France. Only with the greatest difficulty did Frs. Jost, Lanique, and Schelling succeed in obtaining permission from the camp administration for them to be sent to our block. We all knew of the shortage of priests in France, and as Schelling himself writes: "We felt a special responsibility for these young people; we knew it was up to us to save them if we could. In any case, it was an act of Christian charity and proved to be well worthwhile." Back in their native France after the war was over, many of these young men were to achieve their goal.

It was not always easy for the older priests to find understanding for this younger generation, nor were the young students always tolerant of the point of view of the older men. Language difficulties placed further obstacles in the way of mutual understanding. The Polish students were less of a problem in this respect, for most of them spoke at least a little German. Up to 1944, there were many more young Polish seminarians than French, and the Polish priests took them under their wing and cared for their spiritual and intellectual training as best they could in the circumstances.

There were a considerable number of lay brothers among the clergy interned in Dachau, and, true to their calling, they rendered many valuable services to us priests in the camp. One of our best comrades, for instance, was "our Franzl," a Capuchin brother from South Tyrol, universally known and loved for his unfailing good humor, deep piety, and untiring hard work in the service of others. *Lay brother* was a term unknown in the Nazi vocabulary, and prisoners were only assigned to the priests' block if they gave their calling as *Klosterbrüder* when they arrived in the camp. Anyone who called himself a lay brother was automatically sent to some other block.

Since there were priests from twenty nations among us, it was only natural that the peculiar problems arising from differing national outlooks should add to the trials of everyday life. On the other hand, we learned many new and valuable lessons in surmounting these difficulties and were to profit in a thousand ways in experience.

Distinguished priest prisoners

The Nazis were aiming to stifle the Church inside "Greater Germany," and this was why they interned us Catholic priests in their concentration camps.

Whenever possible, the party picked out the most influential men, but all the same, they had to be careful. They encountered difficulties here, for they could never go as far as they would have liked in their "suffocation policy"; the eyes of the world were upon them, and they could not afford to jeopardize the morale of the home front. They had to tread warily. All bullies are notoriously cowards at heart, for real courage is, after all, nothing more than the strength that comes from a clear conscience secure in the protection of the Almighty. All down the ages, those who have persecuted the followers of Christ have been marked by a certain cowardice, the fear of going too far. This time, too, the Church was to profit by this innate cowardice, for if it had not been for this characteristic fear of going too far, the Catholic Church would certainly have been robbed at the outset of all her bishops and leading clerics. As it was, a very considerable number of distinguished priests were sent to Dachau, men well known in their own countries as well as abroad. In the main, however, the Nazis reserved the greater majority for the great purge that was to come when Hitler's victory was finally achieved and public opinion was a factor that would no longer need to be considered. The arrests and imprisonment of the clergy before and during the war was only the prologue. The Nazis went as far as they dared.

The following list of some of the priests interned in Dachau serves to give a cross section of the types of men whom the Nazis considered better off behind barbed wire. Their influence was too dangerous, their speech too outspoken, their Christian example too "demoralizing." The names of these men serve to show the widely differing spheres of activity, intellectual interests, and practical experience of the priest prisoners among us. I have picked out only a few names, almost at random, for it would be quite impossible to include the hundreds of highly talented and scholarly men, quite apart from their spiritual qualities. Unfortunately, I have as yet no list of our gallant Polish comrades who formed the majority of the priests interned.

- Agnello von der Bosch, O.F.M. Founder and director of the Belgian association for the blind. Died in Dachau, March 9, 1945.
- Korbinian Aigner. Parish priest and fruit-growing authority in Bavaria.
- Jules Anneser. Founder and director of a large Catholic newspaper concern in Metz.
- Leopold Arthofer. Parish priest and poet.

- Josef Beran. Became archbishop of Prague.
- Titus Brandsma. Dutch Carmelite priest and journalist. Died as martyr in Dachau, July 26, 1942.
- Leo de Coninck, S.J. Professor at Louvain University.
- Victor Dillard, S.J. French professor of sociology. Died in Dachau, January 12, 1945.
- Josef Dupong. Professor and brother of the Luxembourg minister.
- Karel Fanfrdla, O.S.A. Deputy mayor of Brno, Czechoslovakia.
- Heinrich Feuerstein. Writer, scholar, and art authority. Died of starvation, August 2, 1942.
- Anton Fränznick. Parish priest well known for his special "Mission of the Blessed Sacrament." Died in Dachau in January 1943.
- Reinhold Friedrichs. Professor and chaplain to the police.
- Peter van Gestel, S.J. Rector and assistant-general for the German province of the Society of Jesus.
- Giuseppe Girotti. Celebrated Italian biblical scholar. Died of cancer in Dachau, April 2, 1945.
- Franz Goldschmitt. Parish priest and writer in Metz.
- Franz Sales Hess, O.S.B. Professor in Münsterschwarzach, Bavaria. Author of *Dachau Concentration Camp: A World without God.*
- Michael Höck. Rector of the priests' seminary in Freising near Munich.
- Coribian Hofmeister, O.S.B. Abbot of Metten, Bavaria.
- Jean-Gabriel Hondet. Abbot of Urt in southern France.
- Franz Hrasteli. Deacon, journalist, and director of a large printing concern in Slovenia.
- Nikolaus Jansen. Canon from Aachen.
- Joseph Kentenich, S.A.C. Founder of the "Schoenstatt Movement," celebrated for his retreats.
- Wilhelm Knegel. Missionary of the movement known as "The wandering Church."
- Carl Lampert. Pro-vicar in Innsbruck. Murdered in Torgau, November 10, 1944.
- Albert Maring, S.J. Scholar of natural history and journalist for *The Grail.*

- Johann Morell. Professor of biblical manuscripts in Czechoslovakia.
- Emil Muhler. Parish priest in Bavaria, well-known sociologist and public speaker.
- Maurus Münch, O.S.B. Liturgical scholar.
- Matthias Munda. Evangelical-Lutheran propst.[10] Lost his right arm in Dachau.
- Johannes Neuhäusler. Became auxiliary bishop of Munich. Author of *The Cross and the Swastika*.
- Berthold Niedermoser, O.Cist. Became abbot of Schlierbach.
- Martin Niemöller. Leading pastor of the German Protestant church.
- Otto Pies, S.J. Rector in Münster in Westphalia and author of several German prayer books.
- Rudolf Posch. Editor of a large Catholic newspaper in Bolzano.
- Joseph Regout, S.J. Professor of international law, son of a Dutch minister. Died of starvation in Dachau in 1942.
- Michel Riquet, S.J. Celebrated French theologian and preacher.
- Augustin Rösch, S.J. Former Jesuit provincial in Munich.
- Georg Schelling. Camp chaplain and former newspaper editor. Became a parish priest in Vorarlberg.
- Laurenz Schmedding. Professor in Westphalia and expert on Slav and Eastern liturgy.
- Karl Schrammel. Music critic and rector of the seminary in Freudental, Silesia. Murdered in Buchenwald.
- Josef Schulte, P.S.M. Provincial of the German Pallottine Fathers.
- Gregor Schwake, O.S.B. From Gerleve Abbey in Westphalia. Authority on choral music.
- Josef Sebela. Deputy mayor of Prague.
- Otakar Svec. Canon in Prague.
- Josef Teulings. Vicar-general and professor of theology in Holland.
- Carl Ulitzka. For his wide social, economic, and religious influence, he was known as "the uncrowned king of Silesia."

[10] The title *propst* is used by the Evangelical-Lutheran Church of Northern Germany for a pastor who is leader of a church district. — Ed.

Christy in Dachau

- Ernst Vykoukal. Abbot of Emmaus in Prague. Died of starvation in Dachau in 1942.

Loyalty

The priests of Dachau remained loyal to one another through thick and thin. They never lost sight of their priestly vocation. This firm adherence to their calling, to their responsibilities as priests, was something that the other prisoners in the camp were never able to understand. In the eyes of the godless "comrades," our office was something that had been forced upon us. As they saw things, we were absolved from our obligations now that we were interned, and since we were no longer subject to outside control, they saw us as "free to lead our own lives." They were quite incapable of appreciating the priest's life as a vocation, as something that in itself brings freedom — freedom in the fullest sense as sons and servants of God. For the atheist element among the inmates of Dachau, the concentration camp automatically freed us from what they saw as restrictions. There had been a few priests who had turned apostate "outside" — and thank God they were few. These had been received with open arms by the Nazi Party. The anti-Catholic prisoners might laugh derisively or shrug their shoulders in incomprehension of our attitude, but the priests of Dachau were of a different caliber.

The one single instance of a Dachau priest who had betrayed his calling back in 1938 had served only to strengthen the spirit of the priest community in the camp. Occasionally, very occasionally, there would be one man among us who — human as we all were — had simply not had the physical and spiritual strength to withstand the trials and temptations that were our daily lot. Tragic though this was, it served only to make us all the more aware of our own frailty and, at the same time, to increase our sense of responsibility for one another as members of Christ's Mystical Body. Never once would it have occurred to us to denounce a fellow priest to the authorities. There were betrayers enough among the others.

But just as there were some who were our sworn enemies, there were also others among the unbelievers who began for the first time to realize just what the Catholic priesthood meant. By their example in endurance, courage, and patience and, above all, by their love of God manifested in their love for their neighbor — no matter how hard this might be — the priests of Dachau achieved great things. If we could not bring these others to share our belief in God, at least some of them began to think differently. Maybe the priests were not such a bad lot after all.

In due course, some of us began to receive extraordinary "offers" from outside. The brother of one of the priests in Block 26, for example, had succeeded in intervening on his behalf with the Gestapo, who had declared themselves prepared to arrange for the priest's discharge on condition that he "resigned" from his priest's office. "I would rather die here in banishment in the name of God," the priest wrote back to his family. "Much as I long to be with you all, I could never do such a thing. Unworthy as I am, God has protected me here in the midst of such dangers that I could never desert Him now just for the sake of what seems like a worldly advantage. I could never betray my inner convictions." It was the only fitting priest's answer, and he gave it for thousands of others. God rewarded his loyalty, for he survived the ordeal of Dachau almost by a miracle and is back today working in his parish in Upper Austria.

"Offers" made on such conditions were rarely made officially. But when they were received, they were directed at all of us; of this we had been convinced from the beginning. Had we accepted, had we played the Nazi's game, we knew that we would have been released immediately. We longed so desperately for freedom that the temptation was sometimes great. But we knew what was at stake. "Among the 1,500 priests in the camp, only two accepted this offer; they were released — and they remained priests. All the others remained to suffer and very often to die as prisoners" (Fr. Otto Pies).

On the evening of October 16, 1944, an appeal was made to all Germans interned in the camp to volunteer for military service. The news was greeted with the greatest excitement by all the prisoners. Freedom seemed near at last. We were given two hours in which to consider the matter, and names were to be submitted to the political office.

Almost all the lay prisoners volunteered. Among those who were passed as fit were many of the camp bosses who were all assigned to the SS. In this way, we were ridded of some of our worst tormentors. As far as the priests were concerned, only about 250 of these were fit for military service, and of these only a handful volunteered at first — for service in the medical corps. We scented the

Christ in Dachau

danger that they would send us to the SS. Under the leadership of Fr. Georg Schelling, we decided that we should not volunteer on grounds of canon law. We agreed that if we were forced, we should apply for service without arms, in the medical or ambulance corps. We duly informed the camp authorities of our decision, after which they expressed no further interest in us for military service. It was obvious, however, that the prestige of the priest community had increased enormously in view of the united front presented in this decisive question.

It was only natural that Dachau and all it involved should have exercised a tremendous influence upon the characters of the priests interned there. The completely different circumstances of the camp, the new kind of existence, with its unique opportunities for getting to know and understand human nature, often brought out all kinds of latent qualities. For many of the priests, their true strength of character was revealed for the first time. Back home in their parishes and monasteries, they had never been confronted with problems and difficulties on quite the same scale. Now their hour had come, for camp life really served as a sort of high school for self-examination and self-development as well as providing a wonderful opportunity for observing human nature at close quarters. There can hardly be a priest who has survived internment in Dachau who has not profited in wisdom, humility, and understanding for his fellow human beings.

Life in a concentration camp is a perpetual battle for sheer existence. It was a ruthless battle, but it afforded many priests the chance to show just what true Christian charity really meant. In the face of greed, corruption, and brutality, the priests of Dachau were to achieve heroic things in their fearless demonstration of the nobility of Christian ideals applied every day in the hard life of the camp. There were no textbooks on moral theology and canon law in any of the concentration camps of the Third Reich, nor were we any longer under the jurisdiction of our bishops. We had to make decisions for ourselves, hard decisions that were often tests of heart as well as of spirit, and for each one of us, our conscience was our only guide.

It was a hard school — but the best school of all.

"I wish every priest could spend just one day in a concentration camp," declared Fr. Georg Schelling afterward. "Not seven long years, as I had! One single day would suffice to give every priest the best retreat of his life!"

Fr. Georg Schelling

Fr. Schelling knew what he was talking about, for he was a wise man. He himself had learned much from the seven years of which he speaks. "His wisdom, moderation, selfless goodness, and simplicity made him an outstanding personality," wrote a fellow prisoner afterward in praise of our camp chaplain. "Even in Block 26, there were few who realized to the full just what we owed to him. Only the 'old hands' could really appreciate the qualities of this man."

Fr. Schelling was born on September 26, 1906, near Bregenz in the Austrian Alpine province of Vorarlberg. He was ordained in 1930, and four years later, he took over the editorship of a Catholic newspaper. It was his work on this paper that brought about his arrest on March 21, 1938. On May 29, he found himself in Dachau. He spent forty-seven terrible days in the disciplinary bunker, after which they sent him to the punishment squad. In September, he was sent to Buchenwald. Back again in Dachau, he volunteered for the thankless task of dormitory capo in order to spare his comrades the difficult and unwonted task of bed making, which he saw was often the cause of severe punishment for the whole block — for the merciless SS guards attached immense importance to appearances and order in the prisoners' quarters. "Our Georg" had a varied career in Dachau. He was first put in charge of the tools used by one of the working "commandos"; later, he was responsible for looking after the rabbit hutches on the farm; and at the end of 1942, when priests began to be used for better jobs, he took over the new working party concerned with the receipt and distribution of food parcels. After Fr. Ohnmacht, our camp chaplain, was discharged on March 17, 1943, Fr. Schelling took over this office, combining these duties with those of the tedious and exacting work of block clerk for the priests' block. For eighteen months, he bore the double burden of these two jobs without once losing his patience and good humor.

Fr. Schelling saw quite clearly that he must retain these two posts at all costs if he were to help his comrades. He carried out his duties so efficiently that he was officially appointed a "privileged prisoner," a distinction that was to be of the greatest value to us all, for it afforded him an insight into much that went on behind the scenes, and he gradually established invaluable contacts with the SS administration. He made the widest possible use of these contacts to help his comrades. It became clear, however, that he needed some official recognition from the Church in order to establish his authority fully.

Christ in Dachau

Two Jesuit comrades, Fr. Pies and Fr. de Coninck, managed to contact the diocesan authorities in Munich through the good offices of Fr. Pfanzelt of Dachau parish, and it was not long before Cardinal Faulhaber appointed Fr. Schelling as dean of Dachau concentration camp.

A solemn ceremony in the camp chapel marked this appointment on October 15, 1944. The hardest months lay ahead for us. Fr. Schelling met each new situation with his usual calm and wisdom, inspiring us all to work together as a true spiritual community. He himself was discharged from Dachau on April 10, 1945, and he is now back in his parish in Austria.

Mass

The memorable first Mass offered in our chapel in Dachau on the morning of January 22, 1941, had not been the first Mass in the concentration camp. The good parish priest of Dachau town, Fr. Friedrich Pfanzelt, had offered Mass in the camp back in 1937.

"I knew there were Catholics among those interned," so he told me afterward. "And I knew that in their banishment they had, more than ever, need of Mass."

So he approached the camp authorities and was surprised by the cooperation of the camp SS, who unhesitatingly agreed to his suggestion to offer Mass for the Catholic internees. Little did he guess what was at the back of their minds.

When he arrived at the camp the following Sunday, he was greeted by the sound of a German dance tune popular at that time. "O You Dark Gypsy!" blared through the microphone across the parade ground where the prisoners had been lined up to await the arrival of the priest. Those who wished to attend Mass were ordered to fall out. About two hundred men assisted at Mass that morning in 1937. The SS had not reckoned with this attendance, and Fr. Pfanzelt continued to come to Dachau camp every Sunday for several months, much to the chagrin of the SS. Only after Whitsun 1937 did they discover an effective means of putting a stop once and for all to Mass in the concentration camp. They had lists compiled of all participants, and the next Sunday, these unfortunates were "sentenced" to work in the punishment squad for twelve consecutive Sundays as a penalty for having heard Mass.

When Fr. Pfanzelt appeared the next Sunday as usual, only two or three men dropped out of the ranks; the others were already hard at work in the dreaded gravel pits. The SS officer apologized with a cynical smile. "There you are, Father," he said. "You can see how things stand for yourself. They're a useless lot of rats. No one wants to come to Mass anymore. No point in your coming here again. A hopeless situation."

Fr. Pfanzelt saw how things were. He saw that it was useless to persist, for even if the SS sentry on duty at the gate had allowed him to enter the camp on the following Sunday (which was extremely unlikely), he would only have exposed his little flock to even greater dangers.

We priests soon heard about these attempts by Fr. Pfanzelt to establish regular Sunday Mass in Dachau in the early days, for there were many prisoners in the camp who had been interned since as far back as 1933.

"We grew wary as time went on," so they told us. "We made a special point of warning all the Catholics who arrived in Dachau after the first years. We made it clear that they would certainly be asked on their first Sunday whether they wished to attend Mass, and we told them not to go, for we knew from experience that the SS were only laying a trap for them. By reporting for Mass, they would, in fact, only be reporting for extra work on Sunday and for punishment drill!"

One Sunday in June 1938, the camp director announced at roll call that the authorities proposed to arrange for regular Mass for the Catholic prisoners — provided there was a sufficiently large number who wished to attend. Those who were interested were ordered to fall out. About a dozen prisoners, most of them gypsies, fell out of the ranks. Unfortunately, their comrades had neglected to warn them beforehand. Richard Schmitz, the former Austrian vice-chancellor, was another Catholic who wanted to join them, but fortunately, his neighbor succeeded in holding him back. A few minutes later, a group of tough SS guards armed with truncheons set upon the unfortunate gypsies and beat them up.

Sunday

After the chapel was established in the camp in 1941, only the priests of Block 26 who were not engaged in work at that time were allowed to attend Mass on Sundays. All other prisoners were strictly forbidden to enter the chapel. It was a bitter ruling, but all the same, there were still some who contrived to get around the order and managed to find their way into the chapel. It was dangerous, of course — for them as well as for us — but their longing for Christ in the Blessed Sacrament was so great that they were prepared to risk everything. Even if it was not often possible to hear Mass on Sundays, though, there were few Catholics in the camp who neglected their Easter duty.

When Fr. Georg Schelling was appointed camp chaplain in March 1943, he succeeded in effecting several far-reaching changes. The camp director, von Redwitz, decreed that Fr. Schelling alone as chaplain should in future be responsible for the administration of the chapel. Our communist comrades were thus deprived of any further interference in our affairs. Fr. Schelling also obtained permission for other priests from the community to celebrate Mass, and soon we were having several Masses on Sundays. In this way, some of us who had not been able to offer Mass for years now had the opportunity for which we had been praying for so long.

As the war reached its climax and more prisoners came to join us in Block 26, the chapel became as crowded and cramped as our living quarters. In addition to the Catholic priests from twenty nations, there were also ministers from many other religious denominations, and by 1944, the chapel could barely accommodate the vast congregations.

Sunday was a day of ceaseless activity in our chapel. The first Mass was at 4:30 a.m. After roll call came the half-hour sermon, followed by High Mass, at the end of which Fr. Schelling would address the priest community, informing us of ways and means by which we could give practical assistance to those in special need, indicating particular cases, pointing out dangers and suggesting ways of avoiding these, and exposing any abuses or slackness that might have crept into our community. He had a wonderful way of combining good counsel with humor, and he had no hesitation in stating his opinion, severely if need be.

Low Mass then followed for those who had been prevented by work or other duties from assisting at High Mass, after which the chapel would be quickly cleaned up and aired in readiness for the French Mass. Next came the service for the German Protestants, followed at noon by High Mass for the Poles (after they had once again received permission to use the chapel in November 1944). Two Low Masses for Block 26 were offered in the early afternoon, after which the chapel was free for the Italians, followed in turn by the Czechs. Choral Vespers were sung at 4:30, after which there was Benediction of the Blessed

Sacrament. A sung German Mass followed and then another Low Mass. The Dutch Calvinists had their service next, and then the Czech Protestants. There was just time to clean the chapel and for a last brief visit to Our Lord in the Blessed Sacrament before bed. Another Sunday was over in the concentration camp, a day of prayer and praise, of consecration and dedication, a day that was to give us new strength for the next week in prison and for our work as priests of Christ in Dachau.

Ordination behind barbed wire

Incredible though it seems, a priest was actually ordained in Dachau concentration camp. On December 17, 1944, our young comrade, the German deacon Karl Leisner, was ordained a priest of Christ by Bishop Gabriel Piguet in the chapel of a Nazi prison camp run by the SS. It really seemed nothing short of another miracle of Christ in Dachau!

Karl Leisner, who had had some lung trouble while at the seminary, was sent to St. Blasien in the Black Forest, on the recommendation of his bishop, for a few weeks' convalescence shortly before he was due for ordination in 1939. A few unguarded remarks about the Nazi regime had sufficed for his arrest and subsequent internment in Dachau. After five years in the concentration camp, he was dying of tuberculosis in the isolation block. He knew how things stood with him, and it was his dearest wish to be ordained a priest before the end came.

Fortunately, we had still a bishop in our community at that time (on January 22, 1945, the bishop was removed from our block and placed under special arrest with the other "distinguished prisoners"), and permission was duly obtained in all secrecy from the diocesan authorities in Munich and in Münster. It was also necessary to obtain certain items of the bishop's insignia from Munich, although much of the regalia was made "on the side" in the camp itself by the many fine craftsmen among the prisoners. The alb, the slippers, and the mitre, for instance, as well as the "gold" pectoral cross and crozier were actually made in Dachau.

It was a memorable occasion that winter Sunday morning, as the bishop made his way in slow procession from the hut across to the chapel. His episcopal vestments were worn over his striped prison uniform, and his miter covered his shaved head. Instead of some great cathedral, he was entering a humble chapel in a concentration camp. More than a thousand priests had crowded into the chapel for this unique ceremony. The choir provided music worthy of the occasion.

Nine days later, Fr. Leisner celebrated his first and only Mass. A dying man, he had achieved his goal on earth. Five days after the camp was liberated by the Americans, he was taken to the convent hospital in Planegg, near Munich, where he died that summer. The last comment in his diary might well have been written for all his priest comrades in Dachau: "Love — charity — atonement. O God, bless my enemies!" May his soul rest in peace.

A priest's prayer to Mary

Our Lady of Dachau! Much as we ourselves need your help and consolation in this place, we beg you to comfort all those others who so desperately need your aid.

In these dark days of war, millions are in constant danger, day and night — in danger of body and soul. Reveal yourself as their Mother, Holy Mary, and give them strength. Millions have lost all their earthly possessions and are wandering homeless among strangers, lonely and desolate. You, too, knew the meaning of banishment in Egypt — be their refuge and strength.

You stood beneath the Cross of your beloved Son: comfort the sick and the wounded. Console the prisoners, and be with all those in the hour of their death who must sacrifice their lives in this war.

So many churches have been closed or have been utterly destroyed. So many parishes have been left without priests, and everywhere the forces of evil are striving to overcome the Church established by your Son. Reveal yourself as His Mother, and save and defend His pastors and their flocks. Save the priests serving at the front or working in the hospitals in His Name.

Give strength to all candidates for the priesthood. Inspire priestly vocations, despite all the obstacles of this godless era, and never allow the flame of faith and of virtue to be extinguished. Let nothing destroy the loyalty of Catholics to Holy Church.

Bless and strengthen our bishops in their difficult office. Above all, protect and support our Holy Father, whose heart must be so heavy because he cannot make an end of all the misery in the world, alleviate the suffering of humanity, and bring about peace.

Our Lady of Dachau! Our families and our friends, our parishioners, and our fellow priests have been praying for so long for our release. Give them the assurance that we have your protection — in life and in death.

Our Lady of Dachau! Reveal yourself as Mother where the need is greatest. Amen.

— Msgr. Adam Ott, Dachau, 1943

13

Spiritual and Pastoral Work

Our priestly ideal

Our dean, Fr. Schelling, rightly recognized the vital importance of fostering the esteem of the other prisoners for the priests interned in Dachau. Not only was the prestige of the priest community, as such, as stake, but it was also obvious that only by winning the regard of our comrades as priests of Christ could we ever hope to win them for our Master. Respect, confidence, and trust were prerequisites for our pastoral work in the camp, a unique kind of pastoral work such as we had never known in our parishes at home.

"I saw three ways in which we could further this esteem for the priesthood," wrote Fr. Schelling afterward. "First of all, by our moral and religious example; secondly, by our practical application of Christian charity — among ourselves and among the other prisoners, no matter how hard this might be — and thirdly, by our industry and goodwill in our work, which contributed to the well-being of our fellow prisoners. It was up to us to adapt ourselves to camp conditions. There was no place for petty-mindedness, nor could we afford to be incompetent or demanding. We had to prove our worth, even at the risk of being stamped as proletarians."

This was very true, and all of us strived to the best of our ability to live according to these principles. It was far from easy for many of us, accustomed to life in a parish or religious community, to adjust ourselves to long hours of purely physical labor. But it was even more difficult to "keep our level" in the mass society in which we found ourselves. This had nothing to do with class distinction, as such, which was unimportant; the fact remained, however, that

Christ in Dachau

"stamped as proletarians" though we might be, we were nevertheless priests, and we knew that we must never lose sight of this for one moment. Our godless comrades were waiting like vultures to seize upon the slightest peccadillo, the most trivial remark, a chance slip … They were adept in making mountains out of molehills, and within a few hours, the whole camp would be humming with the latest "scandal" from the priests' block. We had to watch our step very carefully.

Work and study

Our life in the camp imposed a discipline upon us that, viewed in the right spirit, proved to be immensely beneficial to our development. Patience, tolerance, endurance, and understanding were strengthened and deepened by our contact with our fellow prisoners in such close quarters. Our work in the camp taught us other and no less valuable lessons. But we realized that we owed it to ourselves to devote as much time as possible to our spiritual development, for a certain intellectual and spiritual discipline was essential to counterbalance the effects of the abnormal life we were being forced to live.

Conditions in the camp changed throughout the years, depending on the development of the war, the political situation, and the attitude of the camp administration. We priests began as "the scum of society" in Dachau, but later, during the era when Weiss and von Redwitz were commandant and camp director, the authorities began to recognize some of our qualities, and priests were given some of the key positions in the camp. On the other hand, there were periods when we were employed for all the worst chores and assigned to the punishment squad, and later, as the drive for the German victory reached its peak, we were used for every form of work that contributed toward the war effort. There were, however, interludes in which we found ourselves with time to spare for reading, prayer, and meditation — brief, God-sent intervals in which to rest from the ceaseless round of labor. We made the best possible use of these periods of comparative calm for the spiritual training that we knew was vital for our priestly development. Priests were to be found in the chapel at all hours of the day. Indeed, the chapel was never empty, except during roll call. The Old and the New Testaments, as well as other spiritual books, were always available there. Above all, Christ was an ever-present source of strength in the Blessed Sacrament, and Our Lady of Dachau was ever ready to hear the prayers of those who asked for her intercession.

After 1940, we priests received permission to order books on condition that these were made over to the camp library. Many thousands of marks were spent on books by the priests of Dachau, and, as has already been recounted, the religious section of the library soon grew. Here again, the changing temper of the camp administration is evident, for despite the strict ban on all religious books and pamphlets during the early years, the very fact that, by the spring of 1945, there were some five hundred books listed in the catalogue of religious literature (a hundred of which were Bibles) reveals the increasing tolerance of the authorities here. After 1943, we priests finally succeeded in obtaining some of the jobs in the library that had hitherto been a strongly socialist, not to say anticlerical, bastion in the camp. A new field of pastoral activity was opened up for us priests as librarians. A real book apostolate began.

Books were indeed an unfailing source of consolation in the camp, and it was significant that it was, above all, the religious books that were most in demand. Readers had to put their names down for months in advance. We priests read as much and as widely as time and our physical strength permitted, and we used books to supplement the lectures and discussions that we arranged within the program we tried to lay down for our intellectual schooling. We had first-rate lecturers and teachers at our disposal. The extent to which we were able to carry out this tentative training plan naturally varied according to individual circumstances and the general "atmosphere" of the camp at the time, but a great deal of valuable spiritual and intellectual work was done all the same.

A feat of translation

A notable feat of pastoral work was achieved in the face of what seemed like insuperable obstacles by Fr. Hermann Dümig. He was moved by the physical and spiritual misery of the unfortunate Russian prisoners and resolved to do what he could to help them. He set about learning the rudiments of the Russian language in long hours of hard study with a Czech priest, Fr. Hoffmann, and an old Polish lawyer. Fr. Dümig sacrificed every minute of his free time to his work, and as soon as possible, he began translating extracts from the Bible, the most important prayers, and certain parts of the catechism, as well as the finest passages from *The Imitation of Christ*. He made fifteen manuscript copies in Russian, sitting on his straw pallet in the dormitory in bitter winter cold or in the heat of summer, always in danger of being surprised by the SS guards. It was hard and difficult work, and it cost him time and energy, not to mention the "wages" in the form of items from his own food parcels that he paid the helpers who kept him supplied with paper and bound his work for him when it was finished. At Fr. Dümig's request, another priest, Fr. Duschak, wrote a pamphlet — *Young Men and Young Women* — that was duplicated in six editions and circulated among the Russian prisoners. These works and the various other homemade catechisms that were later distributed among the Russians proved to be a tremendous help, and Fr. Dümig received countless rewarding tributes to his selfless task. "I learned so much from these books," declared one Russian prisoner, "that I intend to spend the rest of my life back in Russia in working for the Catholic Faith among my people!"

Writers, craftsmen, and musicians

Many of us priests in Dachau were writers, and there is no doubt whatever that the unique circumstances in which we found ourselves served to develop our gifts. Our faculties were stimulated; our understanding of human nature was deepened. Moreover, camp life provided us with a wealth of material. We sought to express our own desperate longing for freedom, our sense of frustration in our inability to work as priests in the world outside, and our own spiritual need in hymns and verse dedicated to God and to His Blessed Mother. Much of the work produced by the writer priests of Dachau was of high quality; some of it was subsequently published. Wide use was made of many of the hymns, songs, prayers, and other spiritual writings in the chapel in the priests' block.

The artists and craftsmen among the priests of Dachau also found many forms of expression, especially in the designing of altar furnishings, decorative panels, and religious symbols that were used in the chapel.

Special mention must be made here of the musical achievements of the priests of Dachau. Here Dom Gregor Schwake, O.S.B., from Westphalia, a recognized German plainchant authority, did magnificent work in organizing and training the Dachau priests' choir with the able assistance of Fr. Duschak from Dresden. Dom Gregor, who was also our organist at the chapel harmonium, composed the Dachau Mass, which was sung for the first time on Sunday, September 24, 1944, on the feast of Our Lady of Ransom. This Missa antiphonaria was written for a four-part choir alternating with the congregation. In this Mass, Dom Gregor made use of a brass quartet that resounded triumphantly throughout the camp.

As Fr. Otto Pies writes: "It was the choir that fused the priests from so many different European nations with their diverse languages, customs, and outward forms into a single unit with one prevailing style. The choir thus became a living symbol of our Una Sancta Ecclesia, a fitting expression of the one faith and one charity that bound us to one another."

Not only Gregorian chant and medieval church music was sung in the chapel in Dachau. There were several priest composers who produced some remarkable modern church music, and much valuable work was also done in the adaptation of the old traditional sacred music of the many different nations. In this connection, the Poles, who had suffered more than any of us in our imprisonment, produced new settings of some of the most lovely of their old Polish choral music in their darkest hour. Special mention must also be made here of a "Polish Credo" composed and set to words in an inspiring creed written for Dachau. The Czechs and the Slovenes, the Italians, the Dutch, and the French made notable contributions toward the church music in Dachau — at May devotions, at Christmas, and, above all, during Holy Week. The Passion of Our Lord was something that was brought ever nearer to all of us in our own suffering. We followed Him on His Way of the Cross with the wonderful prayers written for this devotion by Cardinal Faulhaber, while between the Stations the choir sang sacred motifs. The "Hymnus paschalis" written by Fr. Heinz Römer for the Easter of 1945 was a fitting tribute to Christ, the Victor of Dachau.

There was indeed no lack of spiritual and intellectual stimulus, and if one availed oneself of the many ways of counterbalancing the strange — and, for us as priests, abnormal — life we were forced to lead, there was little danger of growing slack.

And so we worked on ourselves, conscious that it was our duty to develop intellectually and spiritually and to profit by all that Dachau had to teach us. Christ was our ideal, and we knew that a tremendous task awaited us — if God willed us to come out of Dachau alive — in helping to rebuild a world shattered by war. We wanted to be prepared.

Christ in Dachau

A European parish

As for our pastoral work in the camp itself, this, too, was governed by the unique conditions. There were priests from almost all the nations of Europe in the religious community of Dachau, and there were prisoners from every nation of Europe among the lay internees. It would be logical to suppose that the priests of each nation were concerned solely with their own particular national flock, but in point of fact, this was by no means always the case. Of course, the Poles and the Czechs and the French and the others were glad of pastors of their own nation, but it was interesting to see that the activities of the priests of Dachau were not confined exclusively to their own nation. We were a European community, and the camp was a "European parish," in which all narrow thoughts of nationalism were overcome in the spirit of Christian charity. The following testimony written in 1947 by twelve Dutch and Belgian priests is significant: "It is only fitting to declare that it was, above all, the German and Austrian priests in Dachau who set us a wonderful example in their truly Catholic outlook, in their priestly discipline, and in their recognition of the supranational character of the Church."

The following statistics serve to give some idea of our European priests' community (counting date: February 15, 1945):

I. Religious Denominations

1. Roman Catholic: 1,412 (a total of 2,579 since 1933).
2. Non-Catholic: 141, including 109 Protestants, 22 Orthodox (Greeks, Russians, and Serbs), 5 Old Catholics, 3 representatives of the Bohemian-Moravian National Church, 2 Mohammedans.

II. Dioceses

France, 56; Germany, 22; Poland, 21; Italy, 12; Austria, 8; Holland, 5; Belgium, 5; Yugoslavia 2, Luxembourg, Romania, and Croatia, each 1.

III. Nations

Poland, 791; Germany and Austria, 325; France, 122; Czechoslovakia, 73; Holland, 38; Belgium, 34; Italy, 29; Yugoslavia, 19; German nationalities (from western Poland, lower Styria, etc.), 19; Luxembourg, 8; Hungary, 4; Lithuania, 4; Denmark, 3; Switzerland, 2; Greece, 2; Croatia, 2; 1 representative from each of the following nations: United States, England, Norway, Spain, Russia, Romania, and the Ukraine. A further 4 priests were stateless.

IV. Clerical dignitaries

1 bishop (in special custody); 1 bishop who died in January 1943; 2 abbots (1 in special custody); 6 canons (2 in special custody); 2 vicars-general.

From Block 26 alone: 2 archdeacons, 1 propst, 2 priors, 1 provincial, 15 deans. To these must be added 1 Orthodox archbishop and 1 archimandrite.

N.B. Another census registers 14 prelates and 15 university professors.

V. Secular clergy

246 parish priests, curates, and so forth; 52 professors, writers, and catechists; 100 chaplains.

VI. Regular clergy

26 Jesuits, 17 Benedictines, 11 Franciscans, 11 Pallottine Fathers, 9 Capuchins, 8 De La Salle Brothers, 6 Dominicans, 5 Redemptorists, 4 Cistercians, 4 Premonstratensians, 4 Missionaries of the Sacred Heart, 3 Augustinians, 3 Knights of the Holy Cross, 3 oblates, 2 Alexian Brothers, 2 Assumptionist Fathers, 2 Barnabite Fathers, 2 Salvatorians, 2 Trappists, 2 White Fathers, 1 representative each of the Africa Missionaries, the Fathers of St. Joseph of Calasanz, the Society of Christ the King, the German Knights (Ordo Teutonicus), Filius a Caritate, Sacred Heart Missionaries, Brothers of Mary, Oblates of the BVM, Oratorian Fathers, Picpus Fathers, Montfort Fathers, Society of St. Paul, and of a Ukrainian monks' order. A total of 40 orders and religious communities in Block 26, among them some 120 seminarians and lay brothers (70 of the latter from Poland).

Christ in Dachau

We German and Austrian priests thus found ourselves concerned with the welfare of prisoners from a dozen nations. We would, in any case, have found it difficult to confine ourselves to the German prisoners alone, for the majority of these were strongly communist or socialist in their outlook and actively hostile to the Church. Not that we were resigned to this state of affairs — on the contrary, we did what we could to change things — but there were so many prisoners in Dachau who had a very real need of pastoral care, Catholics who were in danger of losing their faith, men who had lost their way and needed our help to find it again. We knew that we owed our first duty to them, and we did our best to fulfill it in the extraordinary circumstances of the concentration camp. It was difficult and dangerous work, and once again, we looked back on the early Christians and the example of the first holy saints of the Church for inspiration and help in our own task.

Certainly, there were obstacles in our way as pastoral workers in Dachau concentration camp. We were up against the SS authorities, who viewed the Church with open hostility as the declared opponent of their own Nazi pseudo-religion; we were up against the enmity of our Communist and Left-wing comrades, who were often in a position to make our lives a hell and to torment any of our protégés; we were up against the very understandable fear of those who most needed our help: fear of reprisals, of losing their jobs in the camp, of the scorn of their fellow prisoners … We had to work in secret, in seemingly hopeless situations, often working against time, against hope. On the other hand, the unique conditions in the camp often provided us with wonderful opportunities and valuable means of camouflage for our priestly activities. In many ways, pastoral work was easier than it had sometimes been at home. There was, after all, no class distinction that made for easier contacts. Old-established barriers were broken down, and many of the prejudices against the priesthood and the priest's way of life had been done away with once and for all by our example in working alongside our lay comrades and sharing the same conditions. We all wore much the same sort of clothing, so that there was no visible distinction between us (a fact that could sometimes be most useful). Above all, in their need, their loneliness, and their fear, many of the prisoners were much more open to a word from a priestly comrade than they might have been in different circumstances. All the same, they did not all come to us. More and more, we realized that it was we who must go to them. Many did not dare to come to us in the priests' block, and many were too diffident. Some had stayed away from God for too long, and for all their desperation, they still hesitated to take the first step. And many more were too sick to come anyway, physical wrecks, worn out by the rigors of camp life; they were simply waiting for death to come and release them from their misery.

It was up to us to seek them out, our flock in the great European parish of the concentration camp. "House visits" were all important (another lesson for the future that I learned in Dachau!), but such visits were very unconventional, for we had to take the greatest care in everything we did.

Each one of us priests had not only himself to consider — this would have been the least consideration — but we knew that we must think of the community as a whole. We had also to protect those whom we wanted to help, above all from the reprisals or open scorn of their "comrades." In everything we did, however, we most certainly had the protection of Our Lady of Dachau and the holy guardian angels — otherwise, we could never have achieved half of what we did.

The physical need of many of our fellow prisoners was often very great, and a loaf of bread, even a cigarette, often helped to build a bridge back to Christ. Inevitably, there were some who took advantage of us in "converting" all too readily with an eye to acquiring even a little more food, but we usually saw through such ruses before very long. In any case, what we gave in God's name in Christian charity was certainly never lost. We soon saw that God would not help those to find the way to Him unless they really wanted to come. Now and again, the scales would fall from the eyes of one or another of our hardened atheist comrades, a genuine conversion in the spirit of St. Paul, but such cases were unfortunately rare.

It was strictly forbidden to hear confessions in the camp, and yet this was one of the chief forms of our pastoral activity! Prisoners would come to us on the building sites, in the gravel pits, on the plantation, in the workshops, on the road outside our huts in the evening. "Will you hear my confession, comrade?" Prisoners who had neglected their Easter duty for years would often come to us of their own accord, or we would find a way to reach them.

Never shall I forget the most terrible confession I have ever heard. To this day, I have no idea of the man's name. As I gave him a light for the cigarette I had offered him, I caught sight of the hopelessness, the sheer desperation, mirrored in his eyes. We started to talk. I can see his face before me today, shining with a new peace and serenity after he had received absolution. He received Holy Communion secretly from my hand the next day. For years, he had starved himself of the Bread of Life: now his life began anew.

We must have heard tens of thousands of confessions in Dachau, in the most unlikely places and in the most extraordinary circumstances.

In the same way, we brought Holy Communion to thousands in the camp. Sometimes it was not possible for us to bring it ourselves. We had to find a trusted comrade to deliver it for us, wrapped in a slip of white paper and enclosed in an empty Vaseline tin. Countless lay prisoners received the Host reverently from their own hand, in the darkness of the parade ground at roll call on a winter's morning, on working sites, in the infirmary. We managed to send Our Lord in the Eucharist to console prisoners in the transport block, in the cells in "Death Row," and even into the bunker. It was all a miracle, a miracle of Christ in Dachau.

A predicament

The Berlin regulation of 1941 had stated expressly that the chapel was reserved for the use of the priest community only. It was a strict ruling, and in breaking it, we knew we were risking losing the chapel altogether. We were, however, placed in an intolerable situation. It was bad enough to have to deny our Polish brethren the right to enter the chapel (until the ban was lifted later on), but it nearly broke our hearts to have to turn away the hundreds, indeed thousands, of Catholic prisoners who wanted to come to Mass. As Catholic priests, we were forced into the position of having to send away our comrades who had come to seek God!

Here again, we were governed by the attitude of the camp authorities at the time. If things were a little more relaxed, as they sometimes were, we would now and again allow a few trusted lay prisoners into the chapel. Everything depended on the current situation in the camp, and the atmosphere had to be sensed. It was always highly dangerous to attempt such "smugglings" if visitors were expected, for then the SS guards were always especially vigilant. We were, of course, always in danger of being betrayed by spies, and this made us selective. There were dangerous elements, too, among the motley crowd of our European parish.

The fact that our priests' block, and with it the chapel, was segregated from the rest of the camp by a fence with a gate made it more difficult than ever for lay prisoners to get into the chapel. It was a camp regulation that a priest should stand as "sentry" at the gate to guard against entry by unwarranted persons. It was thus the unpleasant task of these priests to turn away any unknown prisoners who sought admission. Many good men were certainly turned away at first, but "where there's a will, there's a way," and especially at Christmas and other great festivals of the Church, there were many who found a means of getting past all barriers.

It was another miracle that we were able to keep our chapel in the face of all dangers.

And so our pastoral work continued, quietly, unobtrusively, founded on works of Christian charity in the recognition of our responsibilities as priests, even if banished to Dachau.

Five Musical Programs

Advent devotions to Our Lady, December 8, 1944

1. Four-part choir: "Praise be forevermore" (Czech)
2. Motifs in honor of the Immaculate Conception (Polish)
3. Four-part choir: "Ave Maria" (Slovene)
4. Litany of St. Lawrence — sung in Latin, with Oration
5. The Angelus (Czech folk tune)
6. Chorale for the exposition of the Blessed Sacrament (Slovene choir)
7. Benediction of the Blessed Sacrament
8. "Omni die dic Mariae" (unison)

Choral music for devotions at the crib, December 26, 1944

1. "Transeamus," by Schnabel, Breslau
2. "Quem vidistis, pastores?" 3, Responses; 1, Nocturne, by Moosbauer
3. "Quem pastores" (fourteenth century, adapted by Moosbauer)
4. "Resonet in laudibus" (fourteenth century)
5. "O parvule dulcissime," text: Fr. de Coninck; music: Schölgen
6. "Adeste fideles," adapted by Ferdinand Habel, St. Stephen's Cathedral, Vienna

7. "Tantum ergo," by Hermann Spies, cathedral choirmaster, Salzburg
8. "In dulci jubilo," Dom Basilius Breitenbach, O.S.B., four-part setting, Capuchin friary, Feldkirch, 1885

International Christmas carols, December 28, 1944 Choirs

1. Italy: "Tu scendi dalle stelle," four parts, two verses
2. France:
    a) "Entre le boeuf et l'âne gris"
    b) "Les choeurs angéliques," four parts
3. Holland:
    a) "De Herderkens lagen by nachte"
    b) "O Kerstnacht, schoner dan de dagen"
4. Luxembourg: "En Engel koum no Bethlehem"
5. Poland:
    a) "Bog sie rodzi" (eighteenth-century carol)
    b) "Gdy Sliczna panna" — Mary's cradle song
6. Slovenia: "Gley zrezdice Bozje," four parts, two verses
7. Czech choir:
    a) "Chtíc, aby spal" — cradle song
    b) "Narodil se Kristus pán"
8. German choir:
    a) "Es ist ein' Ros' entsprungen," four parts
    b) "Still, still, still, weil's Kindlein schlafen will," four parts, Salzburg
    In fine omnes cantant:
    "Adeste, fideles"

Meditatio

De Passione Domini, sabbato die February 17, 1945

1. "O bone Jesu!" Giovanni Pierluigi da Palestrina (1526–1594, Rome)
2. "In Monte Oliveti," Giovanni Battista Martini (1706–1784, Bologna)
3. "Tristis est anima mea," Martini
4. "Vere languores," Antonio Lotti (1667–1740, Venice)
5. "O vos omnes," Tomás Luis de Victoria (1540–1630, Rome)
6. "Adoramus Te, Christe!" Palestrina

7. "Tantum ergo," Giulio Cesare Martinengo (d. 1613, Venice)
8. "Stabat mater," Claudio Casciolini (d. 1759)

Meditatio viae crucis

Secundum Em. D. Archiepiscopum Michaelem Card. v. Faulhaber
Inter stationes decantabuntur sequentia
Initio: "Popule meus" (Victoria)
Post 2. stationem: "Per signum crucis" (Francesco Durante)
Post 4. stationem: "Quis non posset contristari" (Casciolini)
Post 7. stationem: "Vere languores" (Lotti)
Post 12. stationem: "Tenebrae factae sunt" (Michael Haydn)
Post 14. stationem: "Ecce, quomodo moritur" (Jacob Handl)
Meditationes et cantilenae fient in Lingua Latina

14

Miscellaneous

Help from outside

Fr. Ferdinand Schönwälder, one of the Polish priests employed on the plantation, had a very important job. Officially, he sold flowers and seeds at his stall inside the gates of the camp — unofficially, he was our vital link with the outside world. Originally, it had been forbidden for camp prisoners to hold this particular job, but Hauptsturmführer Vogt, the SS official responsible for running the plantation "organized" things so that Fr. Schönwälder got the post. Vogt was always a good friend to us priests. He was a convinced Catholic and had found himself with the SS almost by chance, as it were. Although he wore their uniform, he shared none of their views, and he made every use he could of his position and authority to ease the lot of the prisoners working under him.

"For two years, Schönwälder risked his head for us," Fr. Otto Pies rightly declared. More than 440 pounds of medicines and drugs, more than 2,000 illicit letters and hundreds of food parcels reached the prisoners of Dachau through his hands. The Jesuits in Pullach, near Munich, a teaching order of nuns in Freising and in Dachau, drug stores and hospitals, and numerous families in the town of Dachau itself helped us with contributions of all kinds, ranging from altar wine to aspirin, from bread to glucose. All kinds of commissions were carried out through his good offices by the many courageous "agents" who risked so much to help us. Special mention must be made here of a little girl of ten called Christine from Dachau town. Every day, from October 1944 onward, either she or one of her family would come to "buy flowers" at Fr. Schönwälder's stall. Christine and her fifteen-year-old brother, Willi, were able to keep a secret.

Christ in Dachau

Another grand helper was "Mädi," a young woman who later became a nun. It was she who kept us in touch with the diocesan administration in Munich. These and many others willingly took this work upon themselves, fully aware of the danger involved, not only for themselves but also for their families. We owe much to these brave people. May God reward them.

The "Cathedral Chapter"

The oddly named working party the "Cathedral Chapter" was really the paper-bag commando set up by head capo Hans Gaster on the plantation. Gaster had himself worked alongside a large group of Austrian priests in the Dachau punishment squad back in 1938. Since those days, the good man had been promoted to the office of head capo on the plantation, and in this capacity, he seized the chance to provide his old priest comrades who had been through so much already with a relatively "protected" job. So he organized a working party, responsible to him alone, that was to provide the paper bags and other containers for the various needs of the camp. These ranged from packets for herbs, spices, pepper, and so forth to stout paper bags and sacks for seeds, potatoes, and many other things grown on the plantation.

At first, the working party was exclusively Austrian, but later, priests of other nationalities came to join it, the most distinguished of whom was the Polish bishop Michael Kozal, who came in 1942 together with several other priests, including me. By degrees, the working party developed into yet another unit typical of Una Sancta Ecclesia. Our job of sticking labels on paper bags was envied by some of our less fortunate comrades. Soon we were known throughout the camp as the "Cathedral Chapter."

Since we were all priests, it was natural that we should pray together. We would begin each day with the fine prayer of the Cure d'Ars to the Sacred Heart, dedicating everything we had and everything we did to Jesus and confiding ourselves to His providence. We would then add our own intentions, offering up all our worldly sufferings for the glory of God. The Rosary was another fitting devotion that we would say together as we sat around the table with our stacks of paper bags and pots of glue in front of us, always on the alert for the footsteps of the SS guards.

It was not very arduous work, though deft fingers were certainly an asset. Sometimes we had to "go slow" in order to justify our existence as a commando at all, but there were also periods when we had so much to do that we could well have done with twice the number of workers. It was only natural that we should sometimes differ in our opinions, for some of us were widely different in character and in temperament, but on the whole, we were the best of comrades. We were to lose three of our company — Fr. Gredler died in June 1942, Fr. Summereder was one of the typhus victims in February 1943, and in January 1943, we lost Bishop Kozal.

A saintly bishop

Bishop Kozal was a truly holy man; indeed, since his death, many have called upon his name, and countless prayers have been heard through his intercession. In April 1946, the Vatican officially announced that the first steps had been taken toward the process for his beatification, initiated by his compatriot Bishop Gawlina[11]. We priests of Dachau who lived and worked beside this martyr of the Polish church have a special interest in his cause.

Michael Kozal was born near Posen of peasant parents in 1893 and was ordained in 1918. In August 1939, he was appointed suffragan bishop of Włocławek. Only a few days after his first and only Pontifical High Mass, he was arrested by the Gestapo, and after months of the most brutal maltreatment, he finally arrived in Dachau on April 25, 1941.

I well remember how he stood beside the altar the morning after his arrival, a tall, thin figure in convict's clothing with wooden clogs, and gave each one of us his episcopal blessing.

"He was loved and esteemed by us all for his intelligence and wisdom, his unbreakable will and his idealism, his humility and his deep personal piety," wrote one of his fellow prisoners.

He had never been concerned with politics, but he was feared by the Nazis for his influence as a pillar of the Church in Poland. The Gestapo removed him from his office, and he was among the first of their victims in their ruthless drive to stamp out the Church in Poland. The SS in Dachau and their henchmen among the communist prisoners subjected him to almost intolerable indignities and ill-treatment, and there was very little we could do to protect

[11] Bishop Michael Kozal was beatified by Pope John Paul II on June 14, 1987. — Ed.

him. In any case, he had made it clear from the outset that he could accept no preferential treatment.

"I'm no better than anyone else," he had said firmly. "I'm only a number here too, and I'm determined to carry my cross along with the rest of you."

He was far from strong, and he had the greatest difficulty in coping with the dreaded task of food carrying. The SS made a special point of seeing that he was used for the hardest and most unpleasant forms of labor. But he submitted to the baiting of the unbelievers and the maltreatment of the SS with a dignity and humility worthy of his Master.

"I have the certain feeling that I shall not come out of Dachau alive," he said one day. "It is as though God had demanded my life as a sacrifice for the Church in Poland."

He proved to be right.

The enteric epidemic

"Typhus abdominalis" read the notice on the door of the big ward in the infirmary. On December 19, 1942, three cases of enteric occurred in the camp, but these were not reported. During the night of December 20, two of these unfortunates died. It was the beginning of an epidemic that was to cause the death of some 600 prisoners and 290 members of the SS.

On December 21, "precautionary measures" were taken. We were herded stark naked across to the washrooms for showers and back again to our huts. It was bitterly cold, and it was small wonder that many died of pneumonia. In the priests' block alone, there were seven deaths from typhoid, while countless others caught the disease and came through by the skin of their teeth. Among the most severe cases who survived — as though by a miracle — were Frs. Albinger, Brantzen, Burger, Just, and I. Many were to die later of exhaustion, indirect victims of the terrible fever.

On January 22, I somehow or other managed to get through my work for the day — 150 red-pepper bags. But I had reached the exhaustion point, and my temperature was already very high. I was admitted to the infirmary that evening. Bishop Kozal had been admitted just before me. He was to die four days later.

The burning thirst and the delirium were almost unbearable. Despite the fact that I was desperately ill, I nevertheless had to move four times from one ward to another. I finally ended up in Ward 7, a veritable den of thieves and murderers with nursing orderlies of the very worst type. The night orderly had a simple method of dealing with delirious patients who disturbed his night's rest: he would drag them, raving in their fever, into the adjoining washroom and turn the cold shower on them. Six of these unfortunate men died in one week. Only when he tried the same treatment on Fr. Brantzen on two successive nights without "success" were his methods brought to light. All the same, no disciplinary measures were taken, and he was allowed to remain in his job as nursing orderly.

Now and again, the SS staff doctor would turn up on a tour of inspection. None of us knew why he bothered to come, for although his visits were always preceded by fiendish activity in the form of cleaning, scrubbing, and polishing, absolutely nothing was ever done for the sick. There was only one doctor who really helped us. This was Dr. Blaha, a Czech prisoner who worked in the infirmary. He was indefatigable in his efforts on behalf of his Czech compatriots, but he was a wonderfully good friend to us Germans and Austrians too.

To this day, I do not know how I managed to survive the terrible fever. The days were long enough in the infirmary ward in the "care" of the atheist nursing staff, but the nights were a hundred times worse. Hounded by evil dreams, I would toss and turn, plagued by unrelenting thirst and by the bedsores on my back. I would thank God from the bottom of my heart every morning when the harsh electric light was switched on at five o'clock. My friend Fr. Fritz Seitz was a frequent visitor. When it looked as though there was no further hope for me, it was he who gave me Extreme Unction. But I did recover. Fr. Seitz was one of the infirmary porters, and he was loved and esteemed by the patients for his unfailing kindness and his grand sense of humor. He did valuable work among the sick in those dark days of the enteric epidemic, and it was largely due to him that the barrier between the priests and the atheist nursing orderlies was at last broken. Although it was a camp rule that Holy Communion could be administered only to the dying, Fr. Seitz brought the Blessed Sacrament to dozens of Catholic patients. He had to take the greatest care, of course, in this anticlerical stronghold, for there was always the danger of desecration.

In February, I received several parcels of food from friends at home, but most of the contents were stolen by the orderlies and my companions in the ward, particularly by the man in the next bed. He was a notorious criminal with deft fingers, and he would pick out all the best delicacies while I was asleep. And I needed the food badly, for I had no strength left.

To add to my misery, I developed erysipelas, but nothing was done to relieve it, and I was too weak to fetch the bottle of boracic lotion for myself.

No sooner had I begun to recover from the effects of the enteric than I was seized by severe abdominal pain and began running a temperature. Appendicitis! I was operated on by a highly competent Polish surgeon known in the camp as "Ali." This grand man had already saved countless lives in the concentration camp and will be remembered with gratitude by many.

The Sign of the Cross

The Cross was always before our eyes in Dachau, and I could recount hundreds of instances that prove the saving grace of the Sign of the Cross in time of danger.

"Cross of my Savior! Help me in this hour of need!" The man closed his hand over the little wooden cross that he had carved himself to take with him to his death. The camp SS guards dragged him off to the experimental station in Block 5. He was enclosed in a specially constructed decompression chamber. It was as good a form of murder as any, and no one had yet been known to survive this terrible experiment. The man told me further details of his experience when I saw him after the liberation in 1945. He still had his cross.

"I've spent forty-seven months in this place," a prisoner told a priest back in 1942. "They've given me the 'twenty-five' twice. I've been 'hung' five times. I spent three months in the punishment squad and a fortnight in the bunker. How have I survived? The cross was my refuge and my salvation! I wouldn't exchange one day of this suffering for the world — for here in Dachau, I found God. I've never been so happy in my life" (L. Arthofer).

Both in Dachau and in Gusen, I myself frequently used to make the Sign of the Cross when danger was near. I recommended my priest comrades to follow this act of confidence in God's providence, for I found it unfailing in many a perilous situation.

Over and over again, I made use of the prayer of exorcism in the camp. Never had the prayers and the Sign of the Cross seemed more fitting than in the midst of the hell of the prison camp, and an extraordinary sense of calm, of courage, and of confidence would come over me as a result of the power of the Cross.

Fr. Karl Schmidt recounts similar experiences in Sachsenhausen, where a notorious SS man used to subject his unfortunate priest prisoners to the most diabolical punishments. "We reached the point when we would literally tremble at the very sound of his footsteps," Fr. Schmidt told me. "One day, I agreed upon a plan together with a group of other priest comrades: each of us was to make an unobtrusive Sign of the Cross and silently pray the words of the exorcism whenever the man appeared. We were soon to have a chance of trying out our plan! The man stormed into our hut, roaring like a bull, his hand raised to hit us. But the next moment, his hand dropped suddenly, and he turned uncertainly and slunk out the door."

I have known the Sign of the Cross to stave off the pangs of hunger, to ward off sickness, and to ease pain. Miracle of the Cross of Christ! Miracle of Christ in Dachau! Many of the lay prisoners wore a homemade cross — at their own risk — confident that it would protect them, and many had rosaries they had made themselves out of beads and wire. The Sign of the Cross must have been made in Dachau thousands of times each day. In the darkness of the dormitories after lights-out and in the early morning, before and after meals, at work, in sickness, and at death. The Sign of the Cross gave us strength to meet every situation. In the chapel itself, the great cross above the altar was the open symbol of our faith. "By the Sign of the holy Cross, O Lord, shield Thy people against the wiles of all their enemies." "We adore Thee, Lord Jesus Christ, and praise Thee, for by Thy holy Cross and Passion Thou hast redeemed the world!"

The cross by the wayside

I was to hear the story of the cross by the wayside from Fr. Ferdinand Schönwälder many years later, in 1955. It is an incident worth retelling.

Priests were also used for work on the camp farm, Liebhof, which belonged to the SS. Every morning, a long column of workers would be marched off in the direction of this farm. The road led through the fields, and at a certain point stood an old, weather-beaten wooden cross such as are often to be seen in Austria and Bavaria. One of the SS guards who regularly escorted the prisoners to work used to take the greatest pleasure in kicking the cross every time he passed it. The cross was old, and the wood was rotten, and every time the man kicked at it, the cross seemed to groan.

Christ in Dachau

One day, as the column was on its way to the farm as usual, one of the prisoners was seen to break out of the ranks and run across to the cross. He was carrying three stout wooden pegs. He set about his work, using two of the pegs to support the cross and the third as a makeshift hammer.

The SS escort immediately called out for the column to halt. Everyone stared aghast at the young man working away under the cross. It was automatically regarded as attempted escape for a prisoner to break out of the ranks, and the guards were entitled to shoot. If they got their man, they were rewarded afterward by three days' leave, twenty marks, and an extra ration of cigarettes.

All the guards had raised their rifles, ready to shoot, but not one of them fired. The SS man was blue in the face with rage and raving like a madman.

"Get back into line, you swine, or I'll shoot you dead on the spot!"

He was about to hurl himself in rage against the cross, his jackboot raised for a vicious kick. But the young prisoner stood calmly in front of it, his arms outstretched in protection.

"No one shall damage this cross as long as I am here!" he declared, his voice firm.

The SS man was flabbergasted. He turned to the SS officer who had now appeared on the scene.

"This is nothing short of open mutiny!" he declared with a furious gesture. In the silence that followed, the young man's words could be heard quite distinctly by the whole column: "As a Christian, I refuse to allow the cross to be damaged!"

The guard would probably have shot him there and then if it had not been for a group of curious passersby who had stopped to see what was the cause of all the commotion. The officer in charge of the working party gave the command to move on.

The prisoners worked away in silence all that day. Even the SS guards seemed uneasy and left the workers in comparative peace. During the midday break, the commanding officer had the young prisoner brought in. He noted particulars of his name and number.

"I understand you're a student priest," he said sternly. "I shall have to report this affair. You must know that the penalty for mutiny is death! A pity you have to die for something so futile."

That evening, the young Jesuit was taken to the camp commandant. The whole priests' community began to pray for him. They went on to include the prayers for the dying, but they had barely finished the last of these when the door burst open and the young student appeared, his face shining.

"It's not possible! What on earth happened? For goodness' sake, tell us!" He was stormed with questions.

The young man shrugged and smiled.

"I just told him that it is our duty as Christians to protect the cross even if it means death," he said simply. "He listened to everything I had to say, and when I had finished, he told me to get hold of two other men and repair the cross properly tomorrow!"

1943: Typhoid year

January	Sunday sermons for the priest community officially permitted for the first time. Dying priests are now allowed to receive the Last Sacraments. Many priests are employed in the infirmary but also in other responsible positions in the camp.
January 25	Seven deaths from enteric in the priests' block alone. More Masses now allowed on Sunday. Lecture and discussion evenings arranged.
January 26	Bishop Kozal dies of enteric and exhaustion.
March 17	Camp chaplain Ohnmacht discharged. His office is taken by Fr. Georg Schelling as one of the most senior priest prisoners. Schelling has good contacts with the SS administration. Other priests are now also allowed to celebrate Mass.
April 25	Easter. Our Lady of Dachau arrives. A Paschal candlestick, about twenty-six inches high, is completed by Fr. Breitenberger; later, two sets of altar candelabra.

Christic in Dachau

May	Our Lady's altar decorated for May devotions. Capo Eisner, a gardener from the Tyrol, is of great assistance to us in the chapel.
July 2	We priests are crowded into two dormitories by the prisoner "bosses" who want to commandeer the extra room for themselves. Further evidence of the active hostility of the atheist fellow prisoners against us priests that characterized this year particularly.
July 16	Commandant Weiss puts an end to this all-too-independent order issued by the block personnel.
August	A. Wohlmuth, a carpenter from Styria, has done much useful work for us in the chapel this year.
September 14	The feast of the Exaltation of the Cross brings us a new cross for our altar.
November	Consecration of our new Stations of the Cross, the work of G. Fugel, by Father Guardian Hugo Montwe, O.F.M. Cap.
Advent	Christmas altar panel, painted in secret on the plantation by the Polish priest Fr. Sarnik, is completed. Two new lamps for the high altar received.
December 26	I celebrate Mass for the first time since May 18, 1940.

15

Christian Charity

Christ was waiting

After an absence of six months, I found myself back once again in the paper-bag commando. Those six months had been a real trial of strength — typhoid, erysipelas, appendicitis. My hair was suddenly much greyer, and I felt older. All the same, I had survived, and my heart was full of thanksgiving to God. I knew that He had work for me to do and that He alone had saved me. It was good to be back again among my priest comrades; above all, it was good to be able to visit the chapel and gain strength from Our Lord in the Blessed Sacrament for what lay ahead.

A new era now began for me in Dachau. It seemed as though God had sent me a special mission. No sooner had I fully recovered from the effects of the past months than I began to be besieged by prisoners in all kinds of physical and spiritual need. I never seemed to have enough bread to ease their hunger or to "buy" the clothing and other extras they needed to protect them against the weather. My heart went out to these unfortunates who came to me in their plight. So many of them never received a single food parcel from their relations or friends. Some of them had lost all their family — either in air raids or in the course of the long years of their own internment. Sometimes they had had no news for months, even for years. Some of their wives had left them or had died. Some had sons who had been killed at the front or were simply missing. And some of them had always been vagrants or gypsies with no place they could call home. They could expect no one to send them a food parcel or a warm scarf or a pullover. There were foreigners, too, poor wretches who were forced to exist on the meager camp rations, for the parcels from the Red Cross intended to ease their lot were a long time arriving. New prisoners came, in rags, half starved, in terror of what could lie in store for them. Day in and day out, I was confronted with such human misery. I thought of Christ's words as recorded in St. Matthew's Gospel: "As long as you did it to one of these my least brethren, you did it to me" (25:40). I knew that I must help them.

My sister, Sr. Norberta, a nun in a convent in Carinthia, was immensely good in sending me food parcels, and as soon as I had regained my strength sufficiently after my illness, I resolved to try to exist on the camp rations and use the contents of these parcels to help my less-fortunate fellow prisoners. There were many priests who thought the same way. Apart from the practical help that we were able to give, we wanted to try to set an example to the other prisoners: sermons and empty words were useless in the situation in which we found ourselves at that time, and we could see all too clearly that there were many who badly needed to be taught the lesson of loving their neighbor as themselves. The open greed and covetousness of some of the prisoners in the face of the misery of their comrades roused the righteous anger of all of us. But it was no good preaching — example was what counted.

We did what we could for the less fortunate. The contents of our food parcels not only helped to ease real hunger; they also helped to pave the way to a better job with lighter work and perhaps even an extra bread ration. They served to grease the palms of workers in the clothing depot and so obtained caps, pullovers, socks, jackets, and so on. We would save the best delicacies for those who had duodenal ulcers or chronic liver complaints that had been aggravated by the coarse prison food. The offer of a cigarette very often helped a diffident prisoner to overcome his shyness or even his shame and led him to open his heart to us. So many of them were grateful enough for a kindly word, for a friendly tip, or simply for the chance of pouring out their troubles to someone who they thought might understand. We found ourselves acting as arbiters, settling quarrels, visiting the sick and the dying, comforting the bereaved, baptizing the secret converts (many of these were Jews), and, of course, hearing confessions in the most extraordinary circumstances. It was all part of our work, and we were never happier than in those days when we felt we were really able to help in the name of Christ.

Most of our work and our "organization" had to take place in the evenings, after the labor in the camp was over for the day. We would often have liked to relax for half an hour with a good book or join in a stimulating discussion with our priest comrades. It would have been good, too, to have been able to visit the chapel for a while. But Christ was waiting. Outside, in front of our block, "the least of His brethren" were standing waiting, counting on our help.

We sometimes wondered how long we ourselves would be able to hold out. Our own work in the camp was often hard enough, and now that we had voluntarily reduced ourselves to the official rations, our strength sometimes failed. But we resolved to take no thought for the morrow, confident that God would help us to carry on.

Good comrades

All Christian love, devotion, and sacrifice must flow from the love of God. Works of charity that are not inspired by this love are worthless.

There were many good comrades in Dachau who gave proof positive of their love of Christ in a thousand ways in the help they gave us priests in the camp.

Carl Oesterreicher from Vienna was one of these. He was one of the clerks in the clothing depot and so had many valuable contacts there. He was indefatigable in his efforts to obtain clothing and shoes for our poorer prisoners, often risking the "twenty-five" and the bunker in his devotion. A selfless, kindly man, he was always ready to take on work to help his comrades.

As some of our comrades who professed to be atheists saw what we were doing for the others, they began to make their own contributions. They began to see for themselves that we priests were realists, concerned with providing practical help for the destitute; above all, they saw that our work was inspired by our love of Christ. Our example was the best possible means of convincing some of these hardened characters of the meaning of true Christian love. The emergency brought us nearer to one another, and it was not long before many of them were giving the others a fine example of their own self-denial.

My fellow priests helped me valiantly in my work, above all with contributions of bread for my various needs. Obviously, it would have been impossible to help all of those who came to us, but at least we could try to show our goodwill. It was all important to do what we could to restore the self-confidence of these unfortunates and their confidence in their fellow men. It was inevitable that some should exploit us, but this was relatively unimportant. After all, God was using us as His instruments; He accepted our sacrifices, and He will judge us accordingly. What we gave, we gave in His name.

There were, of course, some who viewed our work among these prisoners with suspicion, even with skepticism. The communists were only too ready to talk of our clothing and food action as "proselytizing," and on at least one occasion, they succeeded in setting the armed SS guards on the crowd of poorer prisoners who had gathered in front of the priests' block in the hope of assistance. For a time, it was forbidden to distribute clothing or food and even to visit the sick. But we had our own ways and means, and it was not long before we were back in action again. Christ was always waiting.

From those days, right up to the liberation, I had a tailor and a shoemaker working for me all the time in secret in the camp. We collected money where we could to pay these workers and to distribute among the poor. When the Americans arrived, they found thirty-one thousand prisoners in Dachau, from forty nations. Thousands of these were destitute. We did our best to help them in the name of Christ, our Brother. Sometimes ingratitude and fatigue were our only outward reward. But we were not concerned with gratitude. All that was important was the love of God.

Proof positive

We priests had chosen to follow Christ out of love of God, but, more important, Christ had chosen us; He had given us our vocation as His priests. Nowhere else in our lives before had we had the chance to bear witness so openly to this calling. We priests were a tiny community in the vast camp — only one-tenth of the total number of prisoners — but for all that, we could claim to exercise a tremendous influence in Dachau. We were the leaven, as it were, in the great mass of the camp, and it was significant that it was to us that most of the prisoners turned in their need. Our practical Christian charity was a thousand times more effective than the best sermon in proclaiming the love of God. We were there for our comrades. And they, in turn, knew that we would share what we had with them, apart from the help we could give them with their own special spiritual problems. No one in the camp could truthfully say, "I have no one" (see John 5:7). As far as their relationship with God was concerned, those who did not find their way to Christ in Dachau deliberately passed Him by of their own free will. The godless among us had no excuse for not changing their way of thought. They will have to answer their Judge at the Last Day, for Dachau offered so many chances to turn back to God, so many proofs of His mercy, and so many opportunities to find the right path through the offices of His Catholic priests.

One of the most active workers among the sick and the destitute in Dachau was Fr. Richard Frasl. He himself was to die of typhus on April 17, 1945, only a few weeks before the liberation. Georg Fraser, one of the lay prisoners who knew him well in Dachau, pays tribute to the will and the spirit of this good comrade. "I shall not easily forget those words he quoted to me from *The Imitation of Christ* on Christmas Eve 1943 as we were standing outside the hut under the starry sky," he writes. "He suddenly turned to me and repeated the words of Thomas à Kempis: 'My son, be not wearied out by the labors which thou hast undertaken for My sake, nor let tribulations cast thee down at all: but let My promise strengthen and comfort thee under every circumstance. I am well able to reward thee, above all measure and degree. Thou shalt not long toil here, nor shalt thou always be oppressed with griefs. Wait a little while, and thou shalt see a speedy end of thine evils. There will come an hour when all labour and troubles shall cease, for poor and brief is all that which passeth away with time.'"

The sick

Fr. Georg Schelling was often called across to the infirmary. The need of the sick grew. We priests gave them what spiritual consolation we could; above all, we brought them Christ in the Blessed Sacrament, either ourselves or through a "middle man," but there were many who were in desperate need of special drugs, of blood, of glucose, of fruit juices, biscuits, beef extracts, and so forth. The nursing orderlies, many of whom were priests after January 1943, would come to us for help for their sick comrades. We started a fund for the provision of these items, many of which could be obtained from outside after the order of 1942 permitting the sending of food parcels to prisoners had been introduced. Fr. Schelling put a notice on the door of the chapel, and he met with a fine response. Priests contributed generously, both with money and in kind.

Christ in Dachau

Lifesaving medicines and drugs, surgical instruments, disinfectants, floor polish, and invalid foods began to arrive — another proof of the power of Christian charity. Fr. Schelling often had to send back some of the contributions of food he received, for he knew that the donors had urgent need of them for themselves. He and Fr. Reinhold Friedrichs were responsible for the distribution of these items. The Poles had set up their own "charity committee," organized by "Ali," the redoubtable Polish doctor.

In the eyes of the SS, the sick were only an unnecessary financial burden, and they made little or no effort to alleviate their condition. Since the sick could make no contribution toward the war efforts and the maintenance of the camp, the sooner they died, the better!

It was strictly forbidden to visit the sick. Hard though this was, especially for us priests, the ruling was understandable in many ways. The risk of infection was too great. The infirmary was surrounded by a wire fence, and there was only one gate, with a sentry always on guard. The packets we sent across and our prayers were the only tokens we could give our sick comrades of our concern for them. At Christmas, we priests made a special effort with our parcels for the infirmary. One of the nursing orderlies told us that he had been able to distribute sixty parcels in his ward alone — all gifts from the priests' block.

In January 1945, typhus was rife in the camp. The unfortunate victims were crying out in their thirst, but there was nothing fit for them to drink. It was discovered that there was a large stock of mineral water in the camp canteen. But most of the sick prisoners had no money. One of the orderlies approached Fr. Friedrichs, and by roll call that evening, he had collected more than three thousand Reichsmarks to buy this soda water for the sick.

Certain incidents connected with the infirmary stand out particularly in my memory, as well as some of the men who were outstanding for the part they played in their care of the sick. Men such as the Polish doctor "Ali," "our Edi" (Dr. Eduard Pesendorfer, a high Austrian official who was a wonderful nursing orderly), Heini (another grand nurse), the Dutch priest Fr. Rothkrans, and many others. When the transports of wounded prisoners arrived from Augsburg in March and April 1944, every pair of hands was needed to deal with the truckload of mutilated bodies that were delivered at the gate of the infirmary enclosure. Hundreds of prisoners from Dachau had been sent to Augsburg to work in the Messerschmitt works. Absolutely no protection was provided during the frequent air raids — it was easy enough to obtain new slave workers from Dachau to replace casualties. As the bombing of industrial targets increased, hundreds lost their lives or were returned to Dachau, maimed for life. For days, the surgeons in the camp would be working overtime, operating, amputating, setting broken limbs, and attending to the terrible burns. Those were dark days indeed. We sent across hundreds of packets of glucose, pails of sugar, lemons, bottled fruit, and biscuits from our depot in the priests' block.

Even more important, however, was the help that priests in the infirmary were able to give to the dying. In December 1942, twelve Catholic priests had been patients in the infirmary. They offered to remain on there after their recovery, taking over all the most unpleasant tasks, such as cleaning the lavatories, emptying bedpans, disposing of dressings, and scrubbing floors. In this way, they could move about freely among the patients, and it was possible to help many in their last hours.

A mechanic from Vienna who had been a typhoid patient in May 1943 told me of his own experience. "I was quite exhausted from the terrible fever," he said. "I felt sure death was not far off. I sat up in bed with the greatest difficulty and began to pray: 'O Son of God, who died on the Cross for me, don't let me die in this place! But if it is Your will, then let me at least die a Catholic! Let me receive the Last Sacraments!' Suddenly I heard a voice in my ear. It was Fr. Alois Theissen, a Catholic priest. He heard my confession, gave me absolution, and then went to fetch the Blessed Sacrament, which was kept in Block 13 under the protection of comrade Wenzel Schulz [Prior of the Brothers of St. Vincent de Paul in Prague]. Fr. Theissen was so unobtrusive in all his movements that no one else in the ward had even noticed him."

By July 1944, the war had reached its peak and air raids had paralyzed the postal and rail communications. The flow of food parcels was reduced to a mere trickle. We were back again on hunger rations, and our store of reserves for the sick began to dwindle. There was, however, still one thing that we priests could continue to give unstintingly — our blood. From time to time, appeals for blood donors would be made, and the response was always heartwarming. "Although themselves often weakened by hunger and hard work, the priests continued to give their blood to those in need," writes Fr. Steinkelderer.

Christ in Dachau

Horror transports

The distress in the camp grew with the arrival of the crowds of new prisoners who came to join us. Many of these were in a pitiful state. After months spent in Gestapo prisons, the journey to the camp in the notorious cattle-truck transports was itself a nightmare experience.

In November 1942, a terrible transport reached Dachau — a transport of six or seven hundred young men and boys, most of them Russians, from a concentration camp near Danzig. All my life, I shall be haunted by the sight of the broken remnants of the transport, piled into the truck that delivered them at the gate of the infirmary. They were quite incapable of walking. We caught sight of their faces as they were driven past our block. We saw their eyes, like dark holes in their cadaverous faces. Terrible stories began to reach us shortly afterward, and they turned out to be quite true. The rations that had been provided for the journey had arrived intact in Dachau and had been confiscated by the SS. Many of the prisoners had died en route. Driven to desperation by sheer hunger, some of the prisoners had eaten the corpses of their dead comrades! A young Russian, the son of an officer from Orel, told us afterward that two corpses had been devoured, "gnawed to the bone, as though by rats." He had not been able to bring himself to eat human flesh, but he had been driven to eat his leather trouser belt. He was one of the few who survived that terrible transport, only to die of tuberculosis in January 1944.

Another appalling transport arrived in Dachau after an eight-day journey from France in July 1944 — 1,500 political prisoners, for the most part students, university professors, and high political officials. Packed into sealed cattle trucks, the prisoners were given neither food nor water. There was no ventilation or sanitary arrangements, and many died of suffocation. The corpses began to putrefy. Only once were the trucks opened, for a brief moment, for chloride of lime to be thrown in. They were then firmly shut again and resealed. When the prisoners began to cry out in their terror of suffocation and their unspeakable thirst, SS guards began shooting blindly into the trucks. More and more prisoners died, and many of the others went mad, killing their comrades in their own desperation. Of these 1,500 French prisoners, 483 died on the journey, and 550 died on arrival in Dachau. The putrefying corpses were raked out of the trucks by gangs of prisoners from Dachau specially detailed for the job and fortified with a special issue of cigarettes and "schnaps."

All through the winter of 1944–1945, transports arrived in Dachau under the most appalling conditions. Even one of the SS guards admitted after the arrival of one such train: "There were more dead than living, and those who were still living were more dead than alive!"

Many such transports came from the east, and it was these prisoners who brought the dreaded typhus with them to Dachau. The disease spread rapidly in the indescribably overcrowded and unhygienic conditions in the camp. Weakened by hunger, thousands fell prey to the fever. But the epidemic was to provide us with another opportunity to demonstrate what Christian charity really means. The Polish priests were the first to volunteer for nursing duties, but we others were not far behind them. Nearly all of us caught typhus; it was almost inevitable. Three priests were to die.

Book 4

God's Victory in Dachau

Christus vincit!
Christus regnat!
Christus imperat!

16

Preparation

Air raids

In the last year of the war, the Allied bombing of the German cities and industrial targets grew more and more concentrated. Dachau was not far from Munich, a vital railway junction and a highly important administrative center. What was more, there were several large industrial plants in Allach, only a stone's throw from the camp. Augsburg and the Messerschmitt works was not far away either. So we in the camp were never quite safe from the danger of bombing, although the Allies would never have bombed the camp deliberately. We had heard that both the Americans and the British had given the strictest injunctions to their bomber crews to avoid even flying over the camp, as far as this was possible, but even so, there was always the danger of stray bombs or incendiaries. In any case, the very sound of the wailing air-raid sirens, the deafening noise of the bombs exploding in the vicinity, and the thunder of the anti-aircraft guns was enough to set us trembling, for our nerves were badly frayed as it was, and we were desperately weak from hunger and privation.

We had no illusions as to what it would mean for us if a bomb should chance to fall on the camp. We were quite unprotected, for there were no such things as air-raid shelters. It was strictly forbidden to leave the huts after the sirens had shrilled the alarm, and we knew very well that the buildings, many of which were wooden, would have gone up like matchwood in the event of fire.

Christ in Dachau

June 13, 1944. It was a lovely morning, and visibility was perfect. We viewed the blue sky with an uncomfortable sense of foreboding as we set about our work that day. Shortly before nine, the sirens began to wail their warning of approaching aircraft. "Munich!" so we thought to ourselves. But suddenly, two of the glittering silver bombers dropped out of the flight and swooped down in the direction of the camp. Fourteen bombs were dropped that morning, aimed at the industrial installations in the external camp. The wife of the camp commandant was killed — as well as twelve unfortunate prisoner workers. This was the only attack that was actually ever made on Dachau. But our days and nights continued to be interrupted by the wail of the sirens and the thud of guns. Sometimes the sky would glow a sinister red in the darkness. Often enough, we would be out working on the plantation when the sirens sounded, and on more than one occasion, several priest prisoners were very nearly killed by flying bomb fragments. But our heavenly Father watched over us. No bombs ever fell on our part of the camp.

Nearer to God

Back in August 1943, I received a letter from my sister, the same nun who sent me such welcome food parcels from her convent in Carinthia whenever possible. She suggested that I should write about some of the ways I had found of drawing nearer to God in Dachau, as she felt this could be of assistance to her and her sisters. This gave me the idea for a book that I began to write in such spare moments as I had and which I called *Nearer to God*. By March 1944, I had completed the "first edition," a single typewritten copy with a suitable frontispiece, bound in a stiff cover.

On March 9, I was ordered to report to the camp director, together with several other priests who were known to be writers. We never discovered who had denounced us to the authorities. We found ourselves facing a special commission that had arrived from Berlin to investigate "leakage problems." It seemed that illicit letters and pamphlets had been finding their way out of the camp, and the authorities were concerned to discover the source. The affair could well have ended badly for me, but thank God, nothing happened. Strange though it may seem, I was even given back my book and received permission to continue my religious writing!

Preparation

The official inquiry was the result of an irresponsible action on the part of one of our priest comrades from Cologne who had been foolhardy enough to attempt to expose conditions in the camp in a book that he had then tried to smuggle out. Part of the manuscript had been found in the house of a discharged Dachau prisoner in Nuremberg. The affair had come to the ears of the party headquarters in Berlin. Countermeasures were taken immediately against the whole priests' community: our slightly better rations were withdrawn at once, and priests were removed from almost all the more responsible posts in the camp. It was a great pity that the whole community should have had to suffer for the irresponsible action of one unthinking man. Another lesson of camp life!

Most of my writing was done in the peace of the chapel. It was often bitterly cold, and I had to be ready to hide every evidence of my writing activity if an SS man should suddenly burst into my sanctuary. But I was never happier than during those brief periods snatched from my other work in the camp, and the spiritual training the work gave me was to steel me for what was still to come. I, too, drew nearer to God. Soon I had completed three books, each duly bound, and these were circulated in the camp. I was to hear from countless prisoners how much these books had helped them.

But although the commission from Berlin had given me permission to continue my work, the affair was not to end there. One day, I had the misfortune to cross swords with a man who was a declared atheist, a really tough criminal who exploited his comrades in every conceivable way for his own selfish ends. I tackled him about his deplorable practices, and from that moment, the man was my sworn enemy. Shortly afterward, he found a copy of one of my books in Block 27 and carried it off triumphantly to his SS master (among his other dubious activities in the camp, he was used by a certain notorious SS officer on the administration staff as a spy among his fellow prisoners).

"I'll bring you nearer to God!" grinned this same SS officer, who took exception to the title of my book. "You'll soon see how near to God you are after I've finished with you!" I already saw myself in a cell in "Death Row."

My book was produced at my hearing as "incriminating evidence," after which I was accused of having organized illicit clothing and food for the prisoners. Finally, I was charged with "dangerous language." These last charges were the invention of the man who had denounced me, but, libelous though they were, I knew perfectly well that, at that time, such "dangerous language" was punishable by death.

As far as my clothing organization was concerned, he accused me of having supplied 125 suits of clothing. I did not deny the charge, but I saw no reason to tell him about all the shoes, caps, socks, and mufflers.

"You'll tell me the names of the recipients before I've finished with you!" he said, his eyes narrowed menacingly.

"Not one name!" I declared stubbornly.

He could find nothing incriminating on my person, nor could the SS guard who was sent to search my belongings in Block 26 find anything.

I was marched off to Cell 56. They kept me there for sixteen days in solitary confinement, and I was convinced that each day was to be my last. I gave myself up completely to prayer and meditation, in readiness for the end. The SS man little knew how true his mocking words, in fact, were. He had indeed brought me nearer to God.

Punishment

But he had by no means forgotten my existence in the meantime. His scouts had finally succeeded in discovering the box in which I used to keep my notes and fragments of literary work. This was produced triumphantly at my next interrogation, and on the strength of what he read among these rough notes (they must certainly have been his first religious reading!), he had me sent to the punishment block.

Conditions here were indescribable. Poor wretches of all kinds — criminals, gypsies, Jews, and others — were herded together in the cramped quarters, half-starved human wrecks guarded by SS toughs and unscrupulous prisoner bosses. By an evil turn of fate, I found the very man who betrayed me in my dormitory. His mouth twisted into an unpleasant grin as he caught sight of me.

I was issued the dirty "zebra" clothing reserved at that time for the punishment block.

I had been sentenced to twelve days in the "standing bunker."

This was a unique experience indeed. A row of tiny cells, more like chimneys than anything else, had been specially built for this purpose. It was possible only to stand, to sit, or to kneel in them. A tiny hole for ventilation had been constructed in the outside wall and an empty tinned-food can served as a lavatory. A blanket or even an overcoat was verboten. The occupants received a cup of ersatz black coffee in the morning and a bowl of watery soup and a hunk of bread in the evening. There was no midday meal.

Once again, I found refuge in prayer. Those were valuable days.

I was allowed to return to the priests' block on the evening of December 17. I had missed the ordination of the young deacon Karl Leisner that morning.

A further disappointment was in store for me. Some weeks before, I had "commissioned" a crib for our block from a wood-carver who was known among the prisoners for his fine work. I now learned that the crib had been completed but that the craftsman had then destroyed his own work for fear of reprisals from the SS guards.

I was also to learn that my SS "judge" had had all my books destroyed. This was a bitter blow indeed. "Thy will be done!" was all I could say at that moment.

I had not seen the last of this man. He surprised us with a visit to our block on January 21. He caught sight of me at once and broke into a storm of abuse.

"You're a fanatic!" he shouted at me, his clenched fist raised threateningly. "But I'll get you yet, you cur! You won't be the first either!"

But he never came back again. Maybe he did not care for the atmosphere in our priests' block in Dachau.

"Blood donor wanted!"

On January 18, I was called across to the infirmary. I had volunteered as a blood donor in March of the previous year, and now they wanted someone with blood type A. The transfusion was needed for a young Austrian, the father of three children. Several transfusions were made during the next few days — with my blood. But I had not enough to give, and after the last transfusion, I lost consciousness. All the same, I learned afterward that the man had made a good recovery.

"Jesus, Son of David…"

That last winter in the camp was terrible indeed. Typhus was rampant, and between 100 and 150 prisoners died every day. Everyone knew that this dread disease was carried by lice, but it was quite impossible to get rid of the vermin in such unspeakable conditions. The overcrowding was now such that as many as five or even seven men were sleeping on two straw pallets. Many of the prisoners had no change of underclothing, for it was not always possible to get parcels sent from home, and not many had sufficient money to "organize" things in the clothing depot. The cold was intense, moreover, and no one could afford to be parted from such clothes as he had, however lousy these might be. And "delousing" was virtually futile, as things were.

We in the priests' block were slightly better off in this respect, for most of us did at least have a second change of underclothes. We did what we could to keep the vermin down with our daily "lice control," but we all knew that it was only a matter of time before the epidemic would reach our block too, no matter what precautions we might take.

One day in January 1945, I found that in the little tin box that I kept in the vest pocket of my tattered prison jacket there was still one of the consecrated Hosts left over after my visit to some of my protégés in the camp that morning. It seemed to me like a sign from Heaven. Jesus had healed the sick in Galilee. If it were His will, and if we had sufficient faith in Him, He could heal the sick of Dachau too.

I thought of Lourdes and of the numerous occasions in history when Christ in the Blessed Sacrament had been borne through the streets in times of pestilence and famine. Why should Christ not be carried through the Dachau camp? Fr. Schelling had nothing against my plan when I consulted him, and I decided to carry the Blessed Sacrament through the camp — in secret, of course — three times every day: in the morning, at midday, and in the evening. I held the little tin box with the Host firmly in my right hand, hidden inside my coat, and I made the Sign of the Cross again and again as I made my way through the camp.

"Lord, save us, we perish!" I prayed. "Jesus, Son of David, save us — the healthy and the sick, the living and the dying!" When I left the priests' block on February 14 to take up my duties again as an orderly in the typhus block, a young Bavarian priest took over and continued to bless the camp and the typhus victims.

On February 2, we priests began a Novena to Our Lady, imploring her aid for the sick and the dying.

Preparation

1944: An eventful year

January	Our Lady's altar and the credence are encased to conform with the high altar and are also used in future for Mass.
February 27	First Sunday in Lent. The new altar cross is consecrated.
March 9	Commission from Berlin arrives to investigate source of illicit letters and other literature.
March 19	The relief of St. Joseph is completed in the "carpentry commando" by Fr. Markarius Spitzig.
April 8	Holy Saturday — new lamps for the sanctuary.
May 1	On orders from Berlin, priests are withdrawn from all the better posts in the camp.
June 6	The first Allied landings on the Continent. Tremendous excitement in the camp.
June 13	Fourteen bombs are dropped in the external camp; twelve prisoner workers killed.
July 15	The new tabernacle and candelabra received.
July 19	Two fine Poles, the Kutera brothers, are executed. One of them wanted to study for the priesthood.
July 20	The plot to kill Hitler fails, and many of those involved are sent to Dachau.
August 15	Ivory-colored screens provided for the high altar and the altar of Our Lady.

Christ in Dachau

September	We are asked to volunteer to relinquish the chapel in order to provide additional accommodation for prisoners in the overcrowded camp.
September 24	Our Lady of Ransom is solemnly declared the patron of the camp. First performance of a new Mass composed by Dom Gregor Schwake, O.S.B. The French bishop Gabriel Piguet officiates at Solemn Benediction of the Blessed Sacrament.
September 25	Bishop Piguet joins Block 26. Miter, crozier, pectoral cross, ring, soutane, and so on are made for him in secret by camp craftsmen. Fr. Peter Bauer continues to work indefatigably as our tailor, despite hunger and weakness.
October 10	Fr. Georg Schelling is officially appointed dean of our community by the archbishop of Munich and is solemnly installed in the chapel on Sunday, October 15. That same evening, we are asked to volunteer for military service. We refuse on grounds of canon law.
October 26	Fr. Reinhold Friedrichs is appointed our first priest "block senior."
November	My SS interrogation. I am sent to the detention cells in the punishment block until November 10.
November 26	At long last, the chapel may be used again by the Polish clergy.
Early December	I am sent to the standing cells until December 17.

December 4	Fr. Karl Schrammel, rector of the seminary in Freudental, is transferred from Dachau to Buchenwald, where he is brutally murdered by the SS.
December 6	Overcoats are verboten.
December 17	Karl Leisner is ordained by Bishop Gabriel Piguet.
December 25	Feast of the Nativity with a Pontifical High Mass.
December 26	Fr. Karl Leisner celebrates Mass for the first time.
December 28	Choirs from eight nations join in carol singing in the chapel.

17

Typhus

The hardest decision of my life

By the early spring of 1945, it was clear to all of us that the war could not last much longer. It really seemed at last as though the Allied victory was not far off and, with it, so we hoped, our liberation. We began to plan for the future. All through those last terrible months, we were kept going by the thought of our freedom after all those long years, by the thought of being able to see our homes and families again, above all by the work that awaited us priests in a world ravaged by war. We knew well that it would not be easy for us, and what was more, there were far from enough priests to tackle the almost superhuman tasks that would have to be undertaken. But we longed to start work, for we who had endured so much misery in Dachau felt in all humility that a special mission awaited us in ministering to the homeless, the destitute, and the maimed; we felt that we were specially well equipped to preach the gospel of God's love to those who had lost all hope and all faith or whose hearts had been hardened by hate. This momentous task, undertaken with the help of God, would more than compensate us for the frustration of our imprisonment, and we could hardly wait to start on it. So we worked on in the indescribable conditions in the camp during the last months of the war, praying fervently that the day of our liberation might soon come.

God has His own ways of trying our strength. He sometimes confronts us with momentous decisions and places in our path obstacles that demand our last reserves of spiritual strength and faith if we are to surmount them worthily. Few of us have not been confronted with such a decision at some time during our lives. We priests in Dachau found ourselves in just such a situation in February 1945, at a moment when victory seemed so near and, with it, our freedom and all this entailed for us.

Typhus was raging in the camp. More than one hundred prisoners were dying every day, with no priests available to console them in their last agony. The quarantine regulations were so strict and the danger of infection for the priests' community as a whole was so great that it was impossible for any of us to risk trying to reach the sick. The situation was desperate, and Fr. Schelling's face was grave as he addressed the community after Mass on February 11.

He told us that the Polish priests had achieved the seemingly impossible and obtained permission from the SS authorities to work among the dying in the typhus isolation block. It seemed that the unbelievers (and there were many among the nursing orderlies in this block) had refused to stay on, for several of the orderlies had caught typhus and had themselves died. The camp administration was only too glad to have volunteers from the Polish priests' block. But among the Polish community, who had suffered so much in hunger and privation, there were too few men fit to undertake this strenuous work, and their chaplain appealed to us to help them. In asking for volunteers that Sunday morning, Fr. Schelling stated the facts quite plainly: the work was hard and extremely dirty, the conditions were indescribable, and by volunteering, we might well be volunteering for death — now, at this very moment when our freedom seemed so near! As he told us, it was up to each of us who was fit enough and capable of working in such conditions to weigh the decision carefully for himself. His announcement was followed immediately by a special Mass.

I found myself in a terrible state of spiritual conflict. Never had I longed so desperately for freedom and the chance to work again as a priest in the world than at this moment! Yet the sick and the dying were in a pitiable situation, and even if we could do little for their poor racked bodies, we could at least care for their souls. I felt strongly that I was destined to work for God in the postwar world. On the other hand, the plight of the typhus victims gave my conscience no peace. Who was I to judge, after all? Surely it was my duty to volunteer for the isolation block? Never before had I known such a state of indecision. So far, I had been saved from so many dangers, and I had escaped death through the mercy of God on so many occasions. Was He to ask the last sacrifice of me now, at the eleventh hour? I was suddenly overcome by real terror at the thought that God could ask me deliberately to walk into what might well mean death now.

"Thy will be done!" I prayed, as never before. "But give me some sign of Thy will!"

I offered myself up to God completely at Mass that morning as an instrument for Him to use as He willed. I placed my life and my will in His hands, dedicating everything to His service. I was nothing but His servant, and I prayed that He should tell me what I should do.

As I came out of the chapel after Mass, Georg Schelling was standing by the door. I took this to be the sign for which I was looking. He smiled encouragingly as he saw me.

"You can count on me for the typhus block," I told him as I passed, but my voice was toneless.

I did no more about the matter, and right up to the last moment, I secretly hoped that God would not ask this of me. Yet all the time, I kept telling myself that He had preserved me from such perils during the past five years: Why should He not save me from typhus too? I knew in my heart that my fears were unworthy of my priest's calling; it was just that I hoped so desperately that I would not be deprived of the chance of working for Him — outside.

"Nevertheless, not as I will but as Thou wilt!" I prayed.

The typhus block

The situation had grown, if anything, more critical, yet for some reason, only three of the many priests who had volunteered were granted permission by the camp administration to work in the isolation block — a Czech priest called Fr. Kos, Fr. Gleton from France, and I.

On the morning of Ash Wednesday, I packed my few treasured possessions and a change of underwear into a cardboard box and followed Fr. Schelling, who accompanied us to the gates of the isolation block. In saying goodbye to him, we knew we were also saying goodbye to the chapel, to Mass, to our books, to the hour or two that we had somehow always managed to find for prayer and meditation ...

A warm welcome awaited us from Fr. Felix Caminski, the Polish priest who had charge of Block 21. The senior nursing orderly in each of the four wards of this emergency hospital was a priest, the first Catholics to penetrate into what had hitherto always been a recognized stronghold of the unbelievers. These priests willingly undertook every kind of unpleasant and menial task in their untiring efforts to care for their unfortunate sick comrades.

It must have been about one o'clock when we arrived, and we found the naked corpses of the twenty or thirty prisoners who had died of typhus during the past twenty-four hours piled up in front of the hut. Our eyes were to grow accustomed to this sort of thing during the next few weeks. Other prisoners, themselves walking skeletons, had passed us, scarcely able to drag themselves along. The sun was shining, but somehow it served only to intensify the horror of those huts, spotlighting the sick and the dying on their filthy palliasses.

I was shown my bed in Ward 2. There was work enough to do all the afternoon and evening, and it was late that night before I fell, exhausted, onto the straw mattress. All the same, I could not get to sleep. The impressions of the hours before were still too new, too terrible.

My French companion, Fr. Gleton, had been assigned to work in what was known as the "death ward," Ward 4. But after only two days, he was overcome by a sudden and severe attack of diarrhea, so I took over his duties there. The next fortnight was to add ten years to my age, but all the same, they were the most worthwhile days of my life.

"One louse can mean your death!"

I had neglected to examine my bed that first night in Ward 2. "One louse can mean your death!" It was true that the notice hung everywhere in the camp in those days, for everyone knew that lice were the carriers of this dreaded disease, but I had been too tired and too dejected to take the necessary precautions. By the time I woke up the next morning, I found that I had been bitten at least thirty times. I knew very well that the six lice that I subsequently found in my bed were almost bound to be typhus carriers. I broke out in a cold sweat at the thought and rebuked myself for my own stupidity. I had volunteered as a nursing orderly, and the very first night, I had as good as dug my own grave — out of sheer carelessness.

There was nothing more to be done, however, and I decided that I must make the best use I could of the fourteen-day quarantine period. What happened after that lay in the hands of the Almighty. There was plenty for me to do in the meantime, and I threw myself into this work, conscious that this might be the last chance I would ever have of working as a priest in this life.

Work among the dying

I spent most of the day among the dying in Ward 4, administering the Last Sacraments and doing everything I could to comfort the unfortunates for whom death held nothing but terror. There were many who found their way back to God in those days, and I thanked Him in all humility for using me as His instrument. Apart from the strain of long hours of work in such conditions, the stench in the ward was almost unbearable — the terrible, festering smell of pestilence.

On February 18, Karl Gerike, the block senior, had the most serious cases brought into Ward 4 of Block 21; the less severe cases were concentrated in Ward 3; the light cases remained in Ward 2; and the prisoners who were merely in quarantine were confined to Ward 1. This helped to bring about at least some kind of order in the unspeakable chaos of the isolation block.

In the days that followed, I often had occasion to reproach myself for not having concentrated more on foreign languages during my priest's training. Now, in the isolation block, I found myself confronted with Poles, Russians, Czechs, Frenchmen, Belgians, Dutchmen, Spaniards, and many others, nearly all of them dying — and nearly all of them Catholics.

The morning I left the priests' block, I had chanced to find a small wooden crucifix lying on the table in the little room that served as our sacristy. On a sudden urge, I had pocketed this, and it was this crucifix — with the holy Names of Jesus and Mary — that was to serve as my interpreter in the Babel in which I now found myself. Prisoners who were dying would take the cross reverently and kiss the figure of Christ before making their confession in their own language while I knelt there beside them. They would beckon me to come over to them. They knew that there was not much time left, and they wanted to make their peace with their Creator. Only one dying man among all those hundreds sent me away.

And so I would make my way among the pitiable figures, lying on plank beds, three tiers high, and on straw mattresses on the dirty floor. The filth of these "beds" was unspeakable. Sometimes they had no mattresses at all, for there was often no alternative but to burn these revolting sacks, crawling with lice and covered with human excrement. The blankets had nearly all been collected for disinfection, and since most of the windows were broken, the cold was intense. Conditions in the wards reserved for the less severe cases were no better; indeed, here the situation was further aggravated by the criminal element among the men who had no hesitation in plundering the few miserable belongings of their comrades, and brawls over stolen mattresses and blankets were a frequent occurrence. Some of these men had knives in their possession and had no hesitation in using them.

Certain hygienic measures had to be taken as a precaution, both for the nursing orderlies themselves and for others. I washed my hands in Lysol water countless times while on duty, and four or five times each day, I would examine my clothing for lice. I usually found at least ten each time.

The authorities knew very well that anyone who had the misfortune to catch typhus was as good as doomed anyway, and they took no trouble to provide the sick with a suitable diet. We received the usual camp soup, usually made of turnips, for our patients, and certainly no diet could have been less suitable.

There was, however, one consolation for us priests in the squalor and misery of the typhus block. Nowhere else in the camp were we able to carry out our work as undisturbed as in the typhus wards. No SS man would have ventured to set foot inside the isolation block, and most of the atheist orderlies had long since fled. Such anti-Catholic orderlies as still remained did not trouble us, in any case. The fact that we had volunteered to work alongside them in the typhus wards had undoubtedly impressed them, and some of them began to revise their former opinion of "the black dogs." And so, although all forms of pastoral activity were strictly forbidden officially, we were able to minister to our flock without danger of detection.

Christ in the Blessed Sacrament — the pyx was a tin in which someone had once sent me butter — went with me in the midst of all the filth, sickness, and vermin to comfort the unfortunates dying of typhus, of dysentery, and, so some said, of cholera. Christ was there all the time to save their souls for life everlasting. I considered it a miracle that we were able to carry on as long as we did in those days. Yet another miracle of Christ in Dachau.

Typhus

Fr. Engelmar

One of the German priests who worked among the typhus victims in Dachau was Fr. Engelmar Unzeitig, a man who will never be forgotten for his utterly selfless work in the camp in the service of others. He had been arrested and sent to Dachau only a few months after his appointment as curate in a parish in the Sudetenland. His sermons had not been to the taste of the Nazis.

Fr. Engelmar labored untiringly among the poor and the destitute in Dachau. The Russian prisoners were his special protégés, and by his example of Christian charity and his teaching, he brought about several conversions among them.

He saw that he could best win these hardened cases by working alongside them in the daily grind of the camp, so he volunteered to join one of the notorious labor squads. He little realized with what new tasks he would be faced as he and his fellow workers were ordered to move across to new quarters in Block 23 — a typhus isolation block! Overcrowding had, by this time, reached peak figures in the camp, and there was no other accommodation available. The camp authorities had no compunction in allocating their prisoner workers to the isolation blocks. The order was as good as a death sentence, as the camp administration well knew, and before very long, Fr. Engelmar found himself caring for the physical as well as the spiritual needs of the many men who caught typhus. Many of them died.

We had no direct contact with one another, for I was working in the adjoining typhus block at the time, and in any case, the complicated quarantine regulations prevented communication. One evening, however, I heard a tap at my window. I found Fr. Engelmar standing outside. He had come to ask me for chrism, as his own supply had run out. One glance at his flushed face and at his eyes told me that he, too, had been stricken by typhus. I could see that his teeth were chattering, and he drew his thin jacket tightly across his chest to protect himself against the icy wind. I begged him to go to bed, but he only shook his head and smiled at my concern. There was still so much to do, so he said. As he reached through the window to receive the butter tin and the jar of chrism, my fingers touched his hot hand. It was the last time I was to see this heroic priest, who literally died on his feet in the service of others.

"So long as there are souls to save, so long as there is work to do," he had once declared, "I'll gladly endure imprisonment and everything it entails — for Christ's sake."

Christ in Dachau

No time to lose

On February 25, Karl Gerike, the block senior, fell sick himself. He asked me for the Last Sacraments, and he also asked me to take charge of his will. His wife was interned at the time too, in the women's concentration camp in Ravensbrück. His young son was later educated in a Jesuit school in Paris.

A few days later, a transport of prisoners arrived in Block 21, most of them Italians and Frenchmen, from the labor camp in Überlingen, near Augsburg. They must have endured terrible things in that camp, for the men looked like living corpses. Never shall I forget the pitiful procession dragging and staggering its way across to the isolation block in the thin sunshine of that February afternoon. Several of the prisoners had already collapsed in the roadway. I knelt beside them and gave them the Last Sacraments. I knew a little Italian and so was able to talk to these unfortunates, who received Communion with childlike devotion. A few minutes later, the others were kneeling before me. Nearly all of them were to die within the next few days, driven to death by hard labor, cold, hunger, and the lice.

Many of the prisoners in the isolation block were unable to walk, and since there were no such things as proper stretchers, there was nothing for it but for us to carry them on our backs. It was hard work, for we, too, were weakened by hunger and lack of sleep.

During the fortnight I spent in the isolation block, I baptized three Jews, at their own request, before they died. The last of these was a rich and extremely cultivated man, a Hungarian from Budapest. He told me that he had wanted to become a Catholic back in 1934 but that he had met with such violent opposition from his family that he had been obliged to drop his plan. His conscience had given him no peace, however, for he was convinced of the truth of the Church. On his deathbed, I was able to fullfil his dearest wish.

That same morning, I was forced to realize that I, too, had typhus. I knew the symptoms only too well. But I decided to keep on working as long as I could. There was nothing to lose and everything to gain. I was still needed to help the dying to find their way home to God.

One of my last patients was a young man of about twenty from Lithuania, a typical peasant boy. His great broad frame had been reduced to a skeleton, and his eyes were full of fear. He could hardly speak any German, but from his few broken words, I understood only too well that he was tormented by the idea that he would not be allowed into Heaven. He made his confession, and reverently and joyfully, he received Holy Communion. I promised to bring him Our Lord again next morning, but he shook his head with a smile.

"I no more there, Father!"

I found him dead the next morning, as if sleeping peacefully like a child, on his miserable bed of rags. There were twelve other corpses on the floor around him.

The harvest of death

It was usually eleven o'clock or later before I got to bed at night, and we were up again at five the next morning. After receiving Holy Communion, I would make my round of the "death ward," together with a grand Polish priest, Fr. Valkoviak, who was the head orderly. Every morning, we prayed together for those who had died during the night — and there were many. Their bodies would then be blessed before they were taken away to be piled up outside, ready for the truck that came around twice daily, stopping at each block to pick up the fearful remains of the typhus victims. These would be thrown into the back of the truck, like the carcasses of animals, and driven away, some to the crematorium, some to the Leitenberg, a hill near Etzenhausen, half an hour's drive from Dachau, for burial in the vast mass grave that had been dug there for thousands of the camp victims. The camp authorities had begun to save on coal for their crematorium. Official statistics give the number of those who died in the camp between January and April 1945 as fifteen thousand.

No adequate precautions were taken against the terrible disease that had most certainly been introduced by the endless transports of prisoners from the East. The highest death rate was recorded among the French, the Italians, the Yugoslavs, and the Czechs. The Poles and the Russians were less susceptible. There were no drugs available, and more and more prisoners were stricken, for accommodation in the camp during those last months was totally inadequate, and newcomers were very often allocated to quarters in the various isolation blocks.

From February 26 to 28, I continued to work in Ward 3. I wanted to administer the Easter sacraments to as many prisoners as possible. I knew very well that I would not be able to keep going much longer, for I already had a high temperature and my limbs were as heavy as lead.

Christ in Dachau

During the night of February 28, orders were received for the delousing and disinfection of Block 21. The prisoners were driven into the washrooms and stripped of all their clothing, which was then taken away for disinfection. This meant that they remained, completely naked, in the unheated washroom for ten to twenty hours. It was not surprising that many of them collapsed and died. I would have given much to have been able to be with them, to have done what I could to help them. But it was too late. I took my temperature again that evening. There was nothing for it but to go to the infirmary.

Thank God, they took me in, and for days and nights, I lay there delirious, ranting and raving in my fever-haunted dreams. This time, however, the nursing orderlies were far better, and I made a much speedier recovery than back in January 1943. The priests from Block 26 were wonderfully good to me too. Fr. Otto Pies was a frequent visitor. It was he who managed to obtain the drugs from outside that virtually saved my life and who collected such nourishing extras as were available for me from his priest comrades. I learned afterward that I had been given up for lost and that my friends had even decided who was to preach at my Requiem! But God willed it differently, and once again, I pulled through.

18

The End Draws Near

Back to Block 26

I returned to the priests' block from the infirmary — only too glad of the supporting arm of two of my priest comrades — on the afternoon of Holy Saturday, March 31, 1945. It was good to be back again, and I was given a heartwarming welcome. I felt as though I had been away for years. My hair was greyer, and I found that my eyesight and hearing were no longer as good as they had been before my illness, but these aftereffects gradually disappeared as my heart began to recover from the strain of the past weeks.

Easter had a very special significance for me that year. My heart overflowed in joy and thanksgiving to the Almighty for having saved me once again from what had seemed like certain death. The chapel rang with our Alleluias as we praised the victory of Christ over death. Our Easter anthem had, as it were, a double meaning for us, for it really did seem as though the day of our liberation was drawing near. What form this liberation would take we could not, of course, know, but even if the Nazis were to exterminate the camp before the end came — even if God were to demand the last sacrifice from us in the fulfillment of His plan — we knew that there was no question that the days of Hitler's diabolical regime were numbered. The dawn was breaking at last after all the past years of darkness. And so it was a wonderful Easter, despite the appalling conditions in the camp, in spite of death, disease, hunger, filth, and overcrowding.

Little did I guess on that Holy Saturday in Dachau that, on the same day, my father had lost his farm and everything he possessed. The countryside near

Christ in Dachau

our home in the Austrian province of Styria had become the scene of some of the bitterest fighting as SS troops tried desperately to hold out against the advancing Russian army. Whole villages were burned down and pillaged in the course of the next few weeks, and the civilian population was often subjected to unspeakable treatment. Already half drunk with victory, the Russian soldiers plundered the cellars of that wine-growing region, with disastrous consequences for the unfortunate peasants, particularly the women.

I begin a proper diary

In the chaos of those last weeks of the war, the SS had better things to do than to come searching our cupboards for incriminating documents, and I decided to start keeping a diary with a brief record of daily events in the camp. Everything was in utter confusion, and I was glad afterward for these notes.

The "special prisoners"

On the evening of April 16, the "special prisoners" were escorted through the camp to new quarters in Block 31, which had once been the camp brothel. Among other distinguished internees, we caught sight of Léon Blum, the French bishop Gabriel Piguet, a Spanish minister with his wife, two Russian generals, and our Austrian chancellor, Dr. Kurt von Schuschnigg with Frau von Schuschnigg; the latter had both been transferred to Dachau from Sachsenhausen concentration camp. That same evening, Bishop Piguet heard the confessions of his fellow internees, and Mass was offered the next morning in Block 31. Mass in the former camp brothel! Surely another triumph of Christ in Dachau!

Some of these "specials" had been interned for years in Dachau in a separate building behind the camp kitchens. We knew the names of only some of them. Among the dignitaries of the Church were the auxiliary bishop of Munich, Dr. Johannes Neuhäusler; the abbot of the Benedictine abbey in Metten; Bishop Gabriel Piguet who was transferred to this special block from Block 26; and the Protestant pastor Martin Niemöller. Other inmates included the well-known German industrialist Fritz Thyssen; the Hungarian president Miklós Kállay; Miklós Horthy Jr.; the whole of the Greek general staff; Lt. Vasily Vasilyevich Kokorin, who was a nephew of Vyacheslav Molotov; Capt. Churchill; and a number of leading German lawyers and prominent medical men. Various members of the families of men such as Count von Stauffenberg, Goedeler, Kaiser, and others were also interned. On April 23, the camp authorities transferred certain prisoners from the main camp to the special block, which they were planning to evacuate, for they could not risk letting these important hostages fall into the hands of the advancing American army. Thus, prisoners who had formerly been ordinary internees like the rest of us joined the distinguished group in the special building. These included Prince Xavier of Bourbon-Parma and the Catholic Prince Leopold of Prussia, ex-Vice-Chancellor Richard Schmitz, and Joseph Joos from Alsace, who had been a prominent figure in the German Catholic Centre Party.

Special prisoners had certain privileges in the camp. They received good treatment from their jailers and did not have to work. They were issued with the same rations as the SS and were allowed their own Mass every day.

On April 25, they were all packed into two large buses and driven off. Richard Schmitz told me about their experiences when I saw him in Vienna after the war. They were evacuated to a bleak hotel up in the mountains of the Pustertal in South Tyrol. After many adventures, they were finally rescued by the Americans and sent back home over roundabout routes.

Discharge?

On February 15, Fr. Schelling had been ordered to prepare a list of all German and Austrian priest internees "with clerical rank"; what was more, the authorities had demanded that the complete list should be ready within two hours. It was a momentous task to compile a list of some fifteen hundred men within so short a time, but Fr. Schelling somehow contrived to produce it. It seemed that by discharging priest prisoners from the concentration camp, the Nazis were hoping to obtain the favorable intervention of the Vatican on behalf of SS troops held as prisoners of war by the Allies. Our hopes rose as, by the middle of March, we learned that four discharge lists had already reached the political bureau of the camp from Berlin. This time, it was no rumor, and between March 27 and April 11, a total of 173 priest internees were discharged, most of them from the diocese of Munich. The 7 Danish and Norwegian pastors were discharged on March 23.

Christ in Dachau

"Our Block Father"

Among the members of the priests' community to be discharged during this period was Fr. Reinhold Friedrichs, who left Dachau on April 5. Everyone knew Fr. Friedrichs, popularly known among us as our "Block Father." He was indeed a truly fatherly man in his unforgettable devotion to his priest comrades, his unfailing Christian charity, and the peace that he seemed to radiate wherever he went — an inner peace derived from his close union with God.

Fr. Friedrichs came from Münster and had been an active member of the German Catholic Centre Party from 1922 to 1933. In the years that followed, his work as a chaplain to various schools, and to a military academy and a training college for the police force, brought him in close contact with young people — as well as with the various party officials who, at that time, were eager to infiltrate the youth of Germany with Nazi propaganda. Fr. Friedrichs was active in his opposition to the Nazi doctrine and refused to comply with many of the new regulations that encouraged young people to neglect their duties as Catholics and join the new Hitler Youth Movement. It was not surprising that he got into trouble with the Nazi authorities, and he was finally arrested on March 8, 1941. He spent months in various prisons before he was sent to Dachau in September of the same year. Today this fine priest is back working in Münster for Christ and His Church.

Back at work again

By April 18, I was back in the "paper-bag commando," wonderfully recovered from the effects of my illness. But in the typhus block, as many as twenty prisoners were still dying every day. Among these typhus victims was my good friend Fr. Richard Frasl, a fine priest from Lower Austria. Arrested after preaching a courageous sermon, he was sent to Dachau, where he was to die on April 17, 1945.

I heard that nursing orderlies were badly needed in Block 21, and I decided to volunteer again. I felt I would surely be immune this time, and I knew that it was my duty to go. God had protected me up until now, and He would continue to protect me. It would be hard to leave my comrades again, and I knew that I would miss the chapel and daily Mass, but the quarantine regulations were no longer so strict, and it would be easier to maintain contact with the priests' block.

I found many changes when I returned to Block 21 on April 21. All the Polish priests had caught typhus in the meantime, and most of them were still in the infirmary. Yet it was a remarkable fact that only three of the priests who had worked in the typhus block died.

It seemed to me that there was more work than ever to do. More and more prisoner transports began to arrive — terrible funeral processions of living corpses. It often seemed to me as though we must break down under the immense burden of sheer physical labor. But the knowledge of the help we were able to give these unfortunate human wrecks more than compensated for our fatigue. Two grand Polish priests and two French friars soon came to give me their help.

Slowly but surely, the typhus death rate began to decrease. The danger of infection was no longer so great. Soon the average number of deaths recorded each day was down to six or seven.

Evacuation?

Alarming rumors began to be circulated about SS plans for the mass evacuation of the camp — and even for its complete annihilation. All we could do was pray. I was grateful for my work among the sick, for although it was hard, it gave me little time to brood.

Rail communications in Germany had been disrupted by Allied bombing, and roads were crowded with refugees and evacuees from the bombed German cities. In the midst of this chaos, the Nazis began to evacuate many of their concentration camps, shifting long columns of broken prisoner workers from one camp to another. The point of these terrible forced marches across country and the dreadful rail transports was never clear. In these evacuation marches, men, women, and children were driven on by the brutal SS guards, in all weather, without rest, without food or drink, without shelter for the night. Anyone who collapsed on the way was automatically shot. Nightmare processions, the remnants of such long columns of prisoners, now began to arrive in Dachau, from Hersbruck, from Buchenwald, from Flossenbürg.

Similar evacuee columns were ordered to set out from Dachau too, senseless marches that ended in death for hundreds. Often, these columns would be forced back by bombing or the confusion of civilian and military traffic on the roads. On one occasion, two thousand Jews were evacuated from Dachau in a rail transport. The Americans bombed the locomotive in a well-intentioned attempt to prevent the deportation, and the Jews were brought back to Dachau on April 23, only to be sent off again. We learned afterward that they were all shot en route by the SS.

All these senseless mass-evacuation transports from one concentration camp to another were only one feature of the chaotic state of affairs in Hitler's Greater Germany as the war drew to an end.

Some extracts from my diary

April 26 — At nine o'clock this morning, orders were received for the total evacuation of the camp, with the exception of the sick and the invalids. Come what may, I shall remain with my sick comrades. What is going to happen to us? The SS will surely not leave these poor wretches for the Americans to find when they arrive, for this would be no recommendation for their model concentration camp!

April 27 — Hundreds of prisoners, including the German and Austrian priests from Block 26, were lined up on the parade ground this morning, waiting to start on their evacuation march, when there was suddenly a tremendous outburst of excitement. Prisoners started waving their caps, shouting and singing and climbing onto the roofs of the huts. Word had gone around that the Americans had arrived. But it turned out to be just another rumor.

April 28 — An evacuation transport from Buchenwald has arrived. One of the rooms in our block has been turned into a sort of dispensary in which we are trying to do what we can for these unfortunates. Some seven thousand prisoners — many of them old people, children, and invalids — started out on foot on this journey, which took nearly three weeks. Only a bare three thousand reached Dachau alive. A loaf of bread each and twenty potatoes was their ration for the whole journey! But their thirst had been even worse than their hunger. Anyone who had ventured to stop to fetch water from a stream or a pump by the wayside had been shot on the spot. It had often rained, and they had had to spend the nights out of doors. They tell us terrible things.

One of those who had come from Buchenwald was a man called Fritsch. He told me about a young Polish boy who had collapsed on his knees before a wayside cross. Weeping bitterly, he had cowered there, waiting for the guard to shoot him. He had buried his face in his cap so as not to see his murderer. And then, all of a sudden, he had leapt to his feet and run off in a last, desperate attempt to save his young life. But he did not get far. A few minutes later, he was lying in a pool of his own blood.

I did what I could for these poor wretches. Many had been shot in the arms and legs, their feet were wounded and blistered, their lips cracked and parched. Their ragged clothing was filthy and infested with vermin, and it was days before they could be bathed and disinfected. I spent hours in my emergency dispensary, working with my hands to relieve their bodily pain and trying to find a word to console and cheer each of them in his misery.

The "Death March"

The last of the mass evacuation schemes planned by the SS in Dachau was the forced march of more than 5,400 prisoners — among them, 88 priests — destined for the Ötz valley in the Austrian Tyrol. The long column set out during the night of April 26 — 5,400 men grouped into units of 100. The SS guards detailed to escort this trek had received orders beforehand to ensure that only 10 percent of the prisoners reached the destination and that no prisoner should fall into enemy hands. The guards did their best to carry out these orders as quickly as possible, and in fact, no prisoner ever reached the Ötz valley, for the trek broke up in chaos after a march of 62 miles, during which 1,000 of the prisoners had died or been shot.

When orders came to prepare for evacuation, we priests were faced with a difficult decision: Should we obey the command to join this trek, or should we remain behind in the camp? Many of us were incapable of marching long distances at the murderous tempo demanded by the SS. We asked ourselves whether this so-called evacuation scheme was not a trap and the SS intended to shoot us all in the cover of the woods. What would happen to us, on the other hand, if we remained behind? Would we be forced to join the evacuation column? Many of us decided to stay behind in Dachau at all costs, for we believed that this was God's will for us. We were needed there by the sick and by the dying. There was more than enough for us to do in the utter chaos of the camp in those last days.

Fr. Rieser's story

Fr. Georg Schelling was among the priests to be discharged on April 10, and he was succeeded as dean of the community by Fr. Andreas Rieser, a fine priest who had spent seven years behind the barbed wire of Dachau. Fr. Rieser was one of the thirty-eight priests who started out on the notorious "Death March" on April 26. Another priest comrade, Fr. Alfred Berchtold, later described this trek as worse than anything he had experienced during the seven years of his internment. Fr. Rieser sent me an account of his experience on this march, a shortened version of which is given here:

> For days beforehand, attacks by American aircraft on targets on the outskirts of Munich had hindered the start of the trek. Finally, we set out during the night of April 26. We were wearing the regulation wooden clogs and had been ordered to turn out with full pack. To march in such shoes and so heavily burdened was beyond the physical strength of most of the camp prisoners. All the same, they drove us on relentlessly all through the night.
>
> Fr. Otto Pies had been discharged from Dachau in March and had been working ever since as a sort of secret liaison officer between the Munich diocesan administration and his fellow priests still interned in Dachau. It was he who succeeded in locating the column — the heavy packs that many of the men had discarded by the wayside indicated the route they had taken. Disguised as an SS lieutenant, another Jesuit, Fr. Franz Kreis, found the camp, which had been pitched in the woods. At great personal risk, both priests then set about obtaining more than a thousand loaves of bread and some three hundred cans of meat from a depot in Munich, as well as supplies of schnaps and cigarettes with which to bribe the SS guards. They also brought along civilian clothing for some of the priests. The daring Jesuits succeeded in their plan, and during the night of April 28, they carried off ten Catholic priests in the truck belonging to the Jesuit seminary in Pullach. They returned the following night and took away a further party of nine priests and three Protestant pastors. Several other priests succeeded in escaping from the column alone. Another, whose parish was in Munich, was rescued and hidden by civilians.
>
> The road was blocked by the swarms of refugees, on foot and in carts, as well as by streams of tanks and armored cars, motorcycles, and horse-drawn vehicles. The noise was deafening as the last bridges were

blown up and bombs were falling on vital stretches of rail track in the vicinity. Machine guns were rattling ominously, and shots rang out all the time as the SS guards made short work of the stragglers. And the cries of the wounded and the desperate! Then, as though to add to our misery, it began to snow heavily. The SS soon saw that we were making no progress along the congested road, so they began to drive us across country, through the woods, across fields, up hills and down again. The confusion in the blinding snowstorm was indescribable. We priests tried to keep together as best we could. We offered up all our misery for the suffering world in silent prayer. We had all been through so much already during the past years in the camp, and we implored God not to let us die now, just as freedom seemed in sight.

In the vest pocket of my jacket was a tin box containing the consecrated Hosts that I had taken with me from the tabernacle in the chapel in Dachau so that I could administer the Last Sacraments to such priests who might die on the way.

The guards were shouting, their police dogs were howling, and in the snow, the going was even harder. The SS threatened to shoot if we did not keep the regulation distance from one another. And all the time, more shots and the terrible cries of the wounded and the dying. On and on without respite, until night fell.

We camped during the night of April 30 in a wood above Waakirchen, a village near Tölz. They had had to shoot one of the horses. The beast was literally torn apart on the spot and devoured by the ravenous prisoners. Some of them even ate the meat raw....

We implored Our Lady to come to our aid in our desperate situation. On the morning of May 1, Fr. Stumpf, a Dominican, began negotiations with one of the SS officers, who had learned, to his surprise, that there were priests among his group of prisoners. He had promised Fr. Stumpf that he would do what he could to help us to make a getaway. But it was late that night before we got definite news. We had begun to wonder whether the whole thing was not a trap.... We stood waiting in the snow at the edge of the wood and tried to find words to pray.... At last, we received word that it was safe to slip away. There were thirty-five of us — twenty-six priests, two seminarians, and seven lay Catholics. It was not long before we had reached the road to the village.

Trembling and weak from our exertions, we made our way to the rectory in Waakirchen. The parish priest could hardly believe his eyes when we told him we were escaped prisoner priests from Dachau. He took us in at once, and soon his sister had hot tea ready for us. They got a fire going in the stove in the sacristy and carpets laid on the floor of the church. No bed was ever more welcome! But before we lay down for the night, I transferred the Blessed Sacrament from the tin box in my pocket to the tabernacle on the high altar. *Te Deum laudamus!*

I offered Mass next morning in thanksgiving for our deliverance. Not long afterward, another prisoner who had escaped from the camp in the wood arrived to tell us that all the SS personnel had fled during the night.... Of the 5,400 prisoners who had set out on the trek five days before, there were still some 2,700 in the woods. Hundreds had tried to escape; many had died or had been shot. We returned to the camp, where we found 15 dead. We buried them in a field near the cemetery in Waakirchen. The villagers did magnificent work in caring for the crowds of half-starved prisoners.

Peasants with farms in the neighborhood came to offer us priests their hospitality. It was good to be able to wash and shave again. We felt like new beings. By midday, the Americans had arrived. Fr. Berchtold and I decided to make our way homeward to the Austrian border. We set off toward the south in the direction of the Alps.

On the way, we met a farmer who took us into his house for a meal. In 1938, he had replaced the cross that hangs in the corner of all peasant kitchens in Austria and Bavaria with a picture of Adolf Hitler. Now, in our presence, he solemnly restored the cross to its place of honor and acknowledged his guilt.

We worship Thy Cross, O Lord: and we praise and glorify Thy holy Resurrection; for behold, by the wood of the Cross came joy into the whole world.

19

We Are Saved at Last

Days of suspense

For the priests who had remained behind in Dachau, there was plenty to do. Prisoner evacuees from other camps continued to arrive every day — helpless human wrecks to add to the confusion and disorganization of the camp in these last days before the liberation.

It had long since become impossible to provide accommodation in the already overcrowded huts, and some prisoners began to camp out in tents and even to improvise primitive huts for shelter. The priest prisoners did what they could to help the problem of overcrowding. Fr. Schmidt had managed to get hold of a bale of heavy blackout material and had made a long curtain to screen off the altar with the Blessed Sacrament from the rest of the chapel, which we had turned into a workroom. Here, a group of priests was engaged all day in making tents for new arrivals and for many of the sick who had fled from the indescribable conditions in the so-called typhus block. Some hundred priests were sleeping on the floor of the chapel at night, leaving their quarters free for others. Three times a day, they cleared the chapel and drew aside the curtain: for Mass in the morning, for devotions at midday, and for Benediction in the evening.

Across in Block 21, where I was working, there were still many cases of typhus. There were other sick in this block too, for the infirmary had no more room in its overcrowded wards. There was never enough of anything — palliasses, blankets, food, and drinks to quench the tormenting thirst of the sick. The spring nights were cold, and the last days of April even brought snow. In the unheated huts, many of the men had to lie on the bare boards, often without any covering, racked by terrible coughs and whimpering with cold.

By now, there could be no doubt that the war was lost for Germany. Only the most unrealistic of the fanatical SS could continue to believe blindly in Hitler and to dream of the great victory he had been promising them for years. Despite the reassurances of the German radio and the eleventh-hour speeches of the Führer, the Allied advances were an open secret. In any case, we had our own ways of hearing the news, of keeping up to date with the latest developments in the fighting. We knew very well that it could be only a matter of days before American troops reached Dachau. But would they arrive in time to save us? That was the question we kept asking ourselves as we went about our work in the camp. I could read the question in the frightened eyes of the sick, and I could give them no answer as they asked me a hundred times over: "When will the Americans get here, Father?"

I, too, hoped and prayed that it would not be long before they reached Dachau, for every new day increased our fear and uncertainty. What, indeed, was going to happen to us? I awoke every morning with a sense of foreboding. And every morning I made a firm act of faith, placing my life and the lives of my sick comrades in God's hands and trusting in His providence.

Murderous plans

Although we felt sure that the SS never intended to allow us to be rescued alive, we still had no idea of how they would dispose of us when the time came. In his privileged office of camp senior, however, Oskar Müller had access to many of the administrative plans of the SS and so learned firsthand how the authorities planned to annihilate the camp and its inmates. It was he who managed to smuggle two men out of the camp with instructions to contact the advancing Americans. One of the men succeeded in getting through and delivering the SOS note describing the perilous situation of the prisoners in Dachau. The Americans arrived before the SS were able to put their murderous plan into effect.

We learned afterward what had been in store for us, though, one after another, the plans for our annihilation had failed.

First of all, they had arranged to blow up the crematorium — and, with it, half of the camp — on the night of April 26. They would most certainly have found some effective means of disposing of the rest. As it happened, one of the prisoners engaged in laying the charges, which were to be electrically detonated, had realized what would be involved if the plan were to be carried out and had cut the wires to the detonator.

Another plan was that of Gauleiter Giesler to have the whole camp wiped out by aerial bombardment from German planes. Fortunately, Commandant Weiter had consulted the former commandant of Dachau, Weiss, who succeeded in preventing the crime.

A wholesale massacre was then planned for the evening of April 29. The prisoners were to have been assembled on the parade ground and then mowed down by machine-gun fire. The camp itself, together with the sick and any other survivors was then to have been destroyed by flamethrowers. But the Americans arrived that very afternoon.

God had willed it otherwise.

"The Americans are here!"

April 29 was an unforgettable day for the prisoners of Dachau. Since daybreak, the white flag had flown over the administrative buildings of the camp. Thank God, the SS put up no armed resistance in the camp itself, though there was heavy fighting all around Dachau throughout that day. The atmosphere in the camp was tense. The excitement of the prisoners grew as an American reconnaissance plane began to circle slowly overhead. The chapel was crowded with priests and lay prisoners that afternoon, and it was here that the first jubilant shouts reached our ears.

"The Americans are here!"

It was true at last.

The prisoners went nearly mad for joy. Wherever an American soldier appeared, he was immediately surrounded by a crowd of riotous prisoners, laughing, cheering, and crying by turns. They could hardly believe that their liberators had come.

Never-ending horror

But there was a dark side to the story too. The Americans found terrible things in that camp of horror on that memorable day — the two trains standing on the spur line to Dachau, for example. The sealed cattle trucks contained a contingent of some thirty-five hundred prisoners evacuated from Buchenwald and Kaufering. Only thirty-two of them were still alive, and, of these, thirty died of typhus within a few days. Two survivors out of thirty-five hundred!

The righteous anger of the American general over this and other things in the camp itself was understandable. He gave orders for all SS troops taken prisoner in the camp to be shot forthwith and their bodies left where they lay for four days. He also ordered a two-hour reprisal bombardment of Dachau town by every gun that could be brought to bear. This was due to take place in three days' time, and only the intervention of the parish priest, the mayor, and other leading citizens, backed by the testimony of ex-prisoners, prevented the execution of the order.

Thanksgiving for deliverance

That evening, General Patek, who commanded the Forty-Fifth Division of the American Seventh Army, addressed the prisoners of Dachau assembled on the parade ground. He waved his steel helmet to them from the watchtower, the same tower from which the machine-guns had often rattled so ominously. The tumult below ceased as he motioned for silence.

"God is good," he said. "Here in this camp of horror He has sent you deliverance. It is only fitting at this moment that we should pray." And he then led the vast assembly in prayer and made the Sign of the Cross over the camp.

A thanksgiving service took place in the chapel that evening. The Te Deum was sung as never before by the priests of Dachau, and a moving address was given by the oldest priest of our community, eighty-two-year-old Fr. Stanislaus Pujdo from Lithuania. After Benediction of the Blessed Sacrament, the congregation broke into the anthem "Christus vincit," which we had adopted as our victory hymn in the chapel throughout the dark years of our internment.

The victory of the Cross

The feast of the Finding of the Cross on May 3 became for us the feast of the Exaltation of the Cross in Dachau. A great wooden cross had been made by the prisoners themselves and erected on the parade ground with the permission of the Americans. It stood there that May morning, the visible sign of the Cross that had triumphed in the hell that had been Dachau. An altar had been set up on a dais at the foot of the Cross, and it was here that Mass in thanksgiving for our liberation was offered. The altar was massed with wreaths and flowers, the candles burning palely in the sunlight. American soldiers provided an honor guard, and the grey expanse of the parade ground had been transformed by the colorful banners of countless nations. At the Consecration, the colors were all dipped in salute to Christ, King and Victor. The priests' choir led the vast congregation in a solemn Te Deum. It was an unforgettable occasion.

Our victory was sure, the victory that had inspired us throughout all those years: the victory of the Cross.

The next day, a Requiem Mass was celebrated at this same altar for the many thousands who had died or been murdered in Dachau. May they rest in peace.

Order out of chaos

The Americans had arrived. The war had ended with the capitulation of May 7. But for us, a new era of work had just begun. For weeks, we had lived in suspense in the midst of utter confusion, for even the rigorous SS camp organization had broken down in the general chaos that accompanied the last stages of the war. The SS had had their own ways of maintaining law and order in the camp, arbitrary though these were. Now that their discipline was lacking, the criminal element in the camp — unfortunately numerous — took the chance it had been waiting for to give vent to the urge for vengeance and plunder. An emergency camp police force of some nine hundred of the more reliable prisoners had been set up as a precautionary measure but proved quite inadequate to deal with the events of the next few days. It was not long before the criminals had reduced the SS quarters and their stores to a shambles, robbing and despoiling whatever they could lay their hands on. Their mad desire for revenge and for destruction for its own sake drove them to every kind of unbridled conduct. In this way, much that might have been used to ease the plight of the sick and the destitute was, in fact, destroyed.

We did, however, manage to salvage some items from the SS stores. Among them were rolls of bunting, and before long, the colors of all the nations interned in Dachau were flying bravely on the various buildings. The priests' block was no exception, and we soon had the papal flag hoisted proudly above Block 26 alongside the Polish eagle and the other national flags of the priests' community.

An international committee was set up to deal with matters of camp administration. The chairman was the Russian general Michaelov, who had himself been interned in Dachau. National Committees were also soon established to cope with arrangements for the ultimate discharge and repatriation of their own countrymen.

The sick still had to be cared for. I continued to work every afternoon in my makeshift dispensary, trying to deal with the endless procession of the sick, the lame, and the maimed, the pitiful remnants of the futile evacuation treks. Although many of these men had been in Dachau for days, they had not been bathed or deloused, let alone clothed. The machinery of the camp administration had all but broken down. The redoubtable Oskar Müller kept things under control as best he could, but it was a superhuman task, and he had far too much to do.

Although for the first few days after the arrival of the Americans there had been a noticeable improvement in the food, this sudden change to a rich diet had been too much for the digestion of the prisoners. There were many who even died as the result of intestinal disorders caused by the unaccustomed food after months or even years of semi-starvation. It was not long, however, before we were back once again to hunger rations, for there was no longer any kind of discipline in the camp kitchens, and here again, the criminal element had no hesitation in seizing what it could at the expense of the others. I was often forced to go across to the kitchens and fight for a bare minimum of food and, above all, for drinks for my sick comrades. The warm sunshine of those first weeks of May proved the best cure for the patients who had been suffering from diarrhea, and many of them now developed voracious appetites. But we had scarcely anything to give them. I trailed in vain from one national committee to another, to the Red Cross, and to the office of General Michaelov himself in the hope of obtaining some sort of food for them.

By this time, Dachau was more like a gypsy encampment than a concentration camp, with prisoners living in tents in the roadway and cooking over fires such food as they could get hold of. The weather was kind, and even the sick (some of them with high temperatures) were lying out under the open sky.

Ever since the first days of the liberation, war correspondents and photographers were to be seen in the camp, and movie cameramen soon appeared to record the terrible reality of Dachau. It was not long before their reports were featured on the front pages of newspapers and magazines all over the world.

Organization

Many of the members of the priests' community were kept busy in the camp offices writing interminable lists in duplicate, one for Allied HQ and one for the Vatican. Lists of those deported or evacuated, of those already discharged, of those still interned in the camp, of the missing and the dead . . .

Jan Domagala, the Polish camp clerk, managed to save the card index with records of the priests interned in Dachau before these could be destroyed by the SS. According to these files, 2,720 priests were interned in Dachau concentration camp, 1,034 of whom died.

Work among the sick in Block 21 was made even more difficult by the attitude of the Russian block orderlies, who suddenly lost all sense of discipline and responsibility and turned on those from whom they had been only too glad to accept help in the past. A few months before, they had gladly taken our bread and cigarettes with assurances of their eternal gratitude. Now they were breaking out in open mutiny, refusing to work and robbing us systematically of everything we possessed. My own shaving gear disappeared overnight. When they threatened to cut my throat, however, I took their warning seriously and moved across to the chapel dormitory to sleep. In that kind of mood, I knew they were capable of anything.

Most of my priest comrades from Austria had already moved across to the external camp organized by the Americans in what had formerly been the compound reserved for the SS. Since May 15, they had been urging me to join them, but as long as the typhus block was still open, I felt it my duty to remain with my sick. I kept on impressing upon the new camp administration the futility of all their efforts to organize the chaos of the camp as long as this "festering sore," as I called the typhus block, remained in its present form. Block 21 was a breeding ground for new cases of typhus, and I could see that all the precautionary measures the Americans had introduced with their DDT and typhus inoculations would be unavailing as long as it was still open. Nevertheless, it was a long time before the block could be closed. Only gradually could the patients from the camp infirmary be transferred to the new sick bay that the Americans had set up in the external camp, thus freeing beds in the infirmary for the occupants of Block 21. It was May 22 — more than three weeks after the arrival of the Americans — before the last of my patients could be transferred and the block finally closed. Only then was I able to join my fellow Austrians with a clear conscience.

And so the various complex administrative problems were gradually being solved. Arrangements went ahead for the care of the sick and the destitute and for the discharge of prisoners fit to travel. But it all took time.

Burial for the dead

The Americans had ordered the neighboring farmers to cooperate in the removal of the dead from the camp. The liberators found some seventeen hundred corpses piled up outside the crematorium, thrown together, a ghastly heap of skeletons. Up until mid-1940, bodies had been taken to Munich for cremation, but the authorities soon built their own crematorium in Dachau camp, and they enlarged the building in 1942. The crematorium had an annex that housed the notorious gas chamber (with the misleading notice "Shower" on the door), an "interrogation room," and other "special installations." The building was situated not far from the priests' block, half hidden behind a copse of fir trees, and the stinking smoke that poured out of the high chimney often hung in the air for days.

But coal was short toward the end of the war, and more and more bodies were buried in the mass graves on the Leitenberg, a few miles from Dachau. For days after the American liberation, peasant carts arrived in the camp each morning to transport the dead to the new cemetery in Etzenhausen. Graves of non-Jewish prisoners were marked with a cross. Once a week, the American Episcopalian chaplain collected a Catholic priest and a rabbi and drove over for prayers in this cemetery. I accompanied him on two occasions. A cross and the star of Zion now marked the mass grave that was the last resting place of the six thousand prisoners who had died during that last winter.

We hope for a "Church of Atonement"

The surviving Polish clergy were the last priests to remain in the actual prison camp in Dachau, and when they were finally transferred to the former SS barracks in Freimann, near Munich, at the end of May, Christ in the Blessed Sacrament went with them in the tabernacle from our prison chapel. The first primitive altar, with the original cross, tabernacle, and candlesticks, was removed to the rectory in Dachau town and later set up to the right of the altar in the parish church.

On July 28, 1945, the Bavarian daily *Münchner Zeitung* reported that Cardinal Michael Faulhaber, archbishop of Munich, had proposed to General Eisenhower that a monastery should be built on the site of Dachau concentration camp, a monastery that would at the same time be a fitting place of pilgrimage for Christians from all over the world. The report quoted Fr. van Gestel, rector of the Jesuit house in Maastricht, as the source of this information.

A "Church of Atonement" in the Dachau camp was the wish of all Catholics who had been interned in the camp and of those who recognized the victory of Christ in that place of horror. Plans were submitted for a church in Baroque style, large enough to accommodate a congregation of two thousand. A special committee met on September 1, 1945, to consider the design. But lack of funds prevented the realization of this original plan. It still remains the fervent hope of all of us, however, that a worthy Church of Atonement will one day be built and that the statue of Our Lady of Dachau, which brought such consolation to the prisoner priests, will find a fitting place of honor there.

1945: Year of decision

January 1	New Year's Day. Fr. Schelling, as dean of the community, celebrates Solemn High Mass.
January 11	Fr. Augustin Rösch, S.J., is sent to Dachau and transferred the next day to Berlin.
January 22	Bishop Gabriel Piguet transferred to the "specials" block.
End of January	Seven blocks in typhus quarantine. Polish priests volunteer as nursing orderlies.

February 2–11	Priests' novena to Our Lady to save the camp from typhus.
February 11	The Blessed Sacrament is exposed for one hour — as a symbol of our Forty Hours' Devotion.
February 12	The chapel is turned into a workroom for two hundred priests. Fr. Karl Schmidt installs the black curtain, which now screens off the sanctuary. The chapel serves as dormitory for a hundred priests who sleep on the floor. Mass is no longer possible before roll call, but an evening Mass is introduced for the priest workers.
February 14	Several of the priests from Block 26 join their Polish comrades as orderlies in the various typhus blocks.
February 15	A list of all priests — with clerical rank — demanded immediately by the camp administration.
March 14	Special devotions in honor of the Holy Father, Pius XII, with an address by Fr. Adam Ott.
March 27	The first large-scale discharges begin — on March 27, 28, and 29 and April 3, 4, 5, 9, 10, and 11.
March 31	Room 4 of Block 26 is turned into a ward for the typhus convalescents — living skeletons with an insatiable appetite.
April 1	Easter.
April 3	Fr. Karl Schmidt takes secret photographs of many of the priest prisoners.

April 7	SS guards arrive suddenly in Blocks 26 and 28 during the night. We priests think we are about to be shot. (Himmler had issued a "shooting order" only a few days before!) But they only search the blocks for hidden arms.
April 8	The Austrian chancellor, Dr. Kurt von Schuschnigg, is brought to Dachau from Sachsenhausen camp via Flossenbürg.
April 9	Feast of the Annunciation. New moves in an attempt to ease the acute accommodation problem. In Block 26, the German priests from Room 3 join the Austrians in Room 2. Rooms 3 and 4 now house the remaining 846 Polish priests from Block 28. More than 1,000 prisoners arrive from Flossenbürg in a pitiable condition. They are first herded into the chapel and finally allocated to Block 28. Once again, we manage to save our chapel!
April 10	Fr. Georg Schelling is discharged. He is succeeded as dean by Fr. Andreas Rieser.
April 15	Second Sunday after Easter. At the suggestion of Fr. Rieser, Mass is celebrated for the first time today at the altar of Our Lady. Later, the credence table ("St. Joseph's Altar") is also used. More than fifty Masses are now said each week in the chapel.
April 26	The "special prisoners" are evacuated.
April 27	The "Death March" begins.
April 28	9:00 a.m. — SS sirens in the camp give the alarm "Enemy in sight!"

April 29	The white flag is hoisted. 6:00 p.m. — the Americans arrive.
May 1	International rally on the parade ground.
May 2	We learn from Fr. Pies, in person, of his rescue work among the priests on the "Death March."
May 3	A cross and an altar are set up on the parade ground. A Solemn High Mass is offered in thanksgiving for the liberation, followed the next day by a Requiem Mass.
May 4	Fr. Karl Leisner, our newly ordained priest, is removed by Fr. Pies to a convent sanatorium in Planegg.
May 11	The statue of Our Lady of Dachau is removed to Dachau rectory.
May 13	Austrian prisoners — including priests — are transferred to the former SS quarters in the outer camp.
May 22	Block 21 — the typhus block — is closed.
End of May	The last of the Polish clergy are transferred to the former SS barracks in Freimann, near Munich. The Blessed Sacrament from the camp chapel goes with them.

20

The End Is Only the Beginning

The sick still remained

When I returned to Dachau in June, after my pilgrimage visit to Altötting, I was able to distribute more than five thousand Reichsmarks among the sick and destitute prisoners still waiting in Dachau camp for their transfer to the hospital or for their repatriation. The people of Altötting had responded most generously to my appeal for help. I received further assistance in gifts in kind from the citizens of Dachau town. Just as they had helped us in secret in the past, they rallied around now. In those days after the capitulation, when everything was in short supply, it meant real sacrifice to part with food and clothing. The parish priest of Dachau, the late Msgr. Friedrich Pfanzelt, and the kindly parish priest of Herbertshausen were always ready to help where they could.

In this way, I was nearly always able to give my protégés some kind of material assistance when I visited them in the camp. Apart from what I could bring them, however, I was grateful that I was often able to help them when they asked my advice concerning the many problems with which they were confronted after having been cut off for so long from the outside world.

Fr. Leonhard Roth had been appointed official camp chaplain, and I, too, received a letter from the diocesan authorities in Munich in which I was asked to look after such former prisoners as still remained, particularly the sick, and to care for the spiritual needs of the military prisoners.

On July 20, these military prisoners were transferred from Dachau to another camp, and their place was taken in our old quarters in the concentration camp by twenty thousand SS prisoners.

Christ in Dachau

"We won't treat them badly," declared the American camp commandant. "We've no intention of using Hitler's methods!"

For two months, I continued to work in the camp. By July 31, however, practically all the sick had been transferred to hospitals in the district, and only those who were too ill to be moved remained.

It was time for me to leave Dachau at last, and on August 3, I started on my journey home to Austria.

The Dachau Trials

Several months later, I was to return to Dachau, together with Fr. Konrad Just, for the Dachau Trials, which took place there in November 1945. The American general John Lentz was president of the court. The Americans had questioned Fr. Just and me before the trial opened on November 15, and this hearing revealed that many of the SS due to stand trial for crimes committed were, in fact, unknown to us. What was more, the Americans did not seem too interested in what had taken place in the camp before the end of 1942 — that is, before America entered the war. In the circumstances, we were of no use as witnesses for the prosecution. Toward the end of November, we were, however, called upon to give evidence for the defense of Weiss, von Redwitz, Lippmann, and Kick.

By the end of the trials, three of the men accused had been sentenced to ten years' hard labor and one to life imprisonment. Thirty-six men were condemned to death by hanging, among them Böttger, Eisele, Hintermayer, Jarolin, Kick, Lippmann, von Redwitz, Ruppert, Schilling, Trenkl, Wagner, Weiss and Welter — and three former prisoners: Block Senior Becher, Capo Knoll, and Capo Mahl.

Fr. Roth was chaplain to the SS prisoners in Dachau and also acted as chaplain to the condemned prisoners.

Many of them are beginning to come to their senses at last [he told me]. They're gradually finding their way back to God. There are twelve Protestants among them. As far as the Catholics are concerned, five of them are hardened cases, deaf to all reasoning, particularly Dr. Hintermayer and the "murder Capos" Mahl and Knoll. Weiss is a different case, but I still feel there is hope for him. All of them appeared at Mass, with the exception of Weiss. He was so against the Church in the past, I imagine he is too ashamed and proud to change his attitude — in public at any rate....

Camp Director Ruppert was the first to turn back to God — none of the others show such deep faith. Dr. Klaus Schilling, the malaria professor, is a broken man. He is quite unable to understand how a medical man of his standing, a scholar of repute, can be condemned to death.

The malaria station in Dachau, which had *been run by* this celebrated doctor, was known to us all in Dachau. Some 120 of the Polish clergy had been selected as human guinea pigs for his experiments. More than 5,000 prisoners were "treated" in this experimental station. Of these, some 1,200 died.

Other medical tests were carried out on the inmates of the camp by the various staff doctors, but not all these things had been known to us at the time. Although I had been interned in Dachau for more than five years, the trials revealed terrible facts and crimes, many of which I heard about then for the first time.

Many of the condemned prisoners seemed incapable of believing that they had been sentenced to death. They refused to believe that this was possible. The Nazi doctrine had so blunted the consciences of these men that they could not bring themselves to admit their guilt, certainly not in public. All of them had pleaded not guilty when the trial opened, but ten days later, von Redwitz was to declare: "We are all guilty!" But his spontaneous words met with vigorous protest by his fellow prisoners.

All the same, there were some who changed their minds in the end. These included Fritz Becher, Dr. Eisele, Kick, von Redwitz, Dr. Suttrop, Trenkl, Wagner, and Welter. Schilling was one of the last to change his way of thinking.

No such thing as collective guilt

The Dachau Trials showed that many of the crimes committed in the camp had taken place behind the scenes, unknown to the prisoners and very often unknown to the rank and file of the SS themselves.

Unscrupulous propaganda and the regime of terror enforced for so long by the Nazis had led to disastrous consequences. It often happened that the helpless individual was caught up against his will into the terrible party machine. Not all of those who joined the party — very often in mistaken idealism — or happened to be members of the SS could be branded as criminals. So much happened without the knowledge, let alone the consent, of the general public or even of the "little Nazis" that it would be absurd to think in terms of "collective guilt." It seemed to me that this was something that those who had not themselves lived under the Hitler regime in the so-called Greater Germany could hardly be expected to understand.

The proceedings at the Dachau Trials prompted me to draw up a memorandum in which I pointed out that it was futile to hold the whole German nation responsible for the terrible crimes committed in its name during the Nazi era. I completed this memorandum on November 25 and requested a higher clerical authority to ensure that this document reached the American commission conducting the trials.

Dachau priests' reunion, 1953

A reunion of the priests who had been interned in Dachau took place in the Abbey of St. Florian from July 13–15, 1953. This lovely abbey in the province of Upper Austria was a fitting setting for this memorable occasion.

Fr. Georg Schelling, now a parish priest in Vorarlberg, celebrated the Requiem Mass for those who had lost their lives in Dachau. This was preceded by an address by a German priest, Dom Maurus Münch, O.S.B., from Trier. This fine priest, who had himself suffered so much, was especially concerned with the problem of the responsibility of the German nation as a whole for the events of the past dark years. His moving words from the pulpit of the abbey church seem to me a fitting epilogue to the story of Christ in Dachau:

> I feel it to be my sacred duty here on this solemn occasion to examine the attitude of Germany toward the events of the Nazi era and to tell you what she feels today. What happened to all of you here — what happened to millions — was never the will of the people of Germany. Nevertheless, these things were unfortunately done "in the name of the German people."
>
> For all that, as you know yourselves, those who were guilty of these murderous crimes were never authorized by the German nation as a

whole to commit such acts in their name. The majority of our people always abhorred and condemned such methods. Those who remained true to themselves and refused to be blinded by the Nazi ideology were always on our side. Their prayers were constantly offered for us, and their thoughts were with us in brotherly love. We all felt this so often. It was always the grave concern of all right-thinking Germans that there could be men and women in our country so blind that they were capable of inflicting such unspeakable suffering upon their fellow men. I ask in their name for your forgiveness.

After my release from Dachau in 1945 and my return to the Rhineland, I addressed many vast congregations of men who came to hear me speak about Dachau. In speaking from the pulpit about the concentration camp, it was far from my intention to preach a sensational sermon. I was not appealing for vengeance, nor was it my wish to stir up hatred. I was simply following the example given by the prophets of old in rousing my people to atone for their sins. I was urging my fellow countrymen to begin a new era of love after all those years of hatred. I appealed to them to show the world, which for so long had seen only a distorted picture of the German nation, what was the real Germany — the other Germany, the Christian Germany.

I am convinced that millions of my fellow Germans are behind me as I speak to you now. Millions of Catholics, together with our Protestant brethren, as well as those who stand outside the Church, join with me now as I bow my head in honor before you and your dead and all the innumerable victims of these terrible years. I speak in the name of the German people in asking for your forgiveness.

Terrible years followed for Germany after the capitulation: years of hunger, years of misery. Millions found themselves homeless overnight, and millions of our soldiers faced privation and death in the prison camps of Russia.

Christian Germany bore the burden of these years, bowed but unbroken. This sorrow and suffering have been borne in the spirit of faith, in the spirit of penance, in the spirit of atonement for our own guilt and the guilt of our erring German brothers. And it is in this same spirit that we go forward to undertake the work of reconstruction that awaits us. In this spirit, we shall work for the spiritual revival of our people.

It is my conviction that out of this broken world, a new Christian Germany will emerge, born out of the suffering endured by so many of our compatriots, for, as history has shown throughout the ages, every genuine and worthwhile revival has always grown and developed out of the sacrifice of the nation as a whole.

We have only to look at the frescos here in this Church of St. Florian. There the saint stands awaiting judgment. Here we see him beaten and scourged. Here he is being thrown from the high bridge into the river below. His body is broken; his life is ended. But here we see him again, this time transfigured, radiant, and triumphant before the throne of God. He is wearing the martyr's crown.

Are not our brothers standing there before us too? Martyrs for Christ! They are not vanquished but victorious. They are victors because they gave their lives for Christ.

Whenever Cardinal von Galen, "the lion of Münster," received news of the death of a priest in Dachau, he would have a votive Mass said in honor of the holy martyrs, a triumphal Mass with festive red vestments.

It would be fitting here on this occasion to celebrate such a Mass, a Mass in honor of the martyr victors. But the victory song of the Church can be heard all through the Requiem Mass too, as we hear of peace and of life in God, the only life worth living, the only life worthy to be called life!

So let us celebrate this Requiem Mass in this spirit, remembering in honor all those who died and who have entered into the glory of their Lord.

The lessons of Dachau

But the story does not end here. Even when there are no more events to be recorded, the story will continue in the minds and hearts of those who lived through it; it will continue in the lessons it has taught them, lessons that they, in turn, try to pass on to their flocks. For the lessons learned in Dachau have still, and always will have, great significance in the unceasing struggle between good and evil.

The story of Dachau is a story of suffering. What has to be learned from this suffering? Perhaps, first of all, something that all of us know in theory but seldom realize in practice — that suffering cannot be equated with evil. As Maritain says, man is a creature who inevitably bears the stigmata — either the stigmata of the old Adam or the stigmata of the New Adam, the Crucified. All men have a cross to bear. For those who bear it willingly, in union with Christ, it is a grace, and the Cross sustains them; for those who rebel, it is a burden that will crush and destroy them. There were, unfortunately, plenty of godless people interned in Dachau, and in their case, suffering could be equated with evil, for without the grace and the light of God, their suffering served only to plunge them deeper into the darkness of godlessness. For those, however, who recognized the loving hand of God and could accept the suffering as His will, their internment in Dachau proved to be a time of instruction and improvement, a prolonged and painful retreat, but a retreat crowned with the greatest rewards for those who made it.

And while we learned in this hard school to recognize that suffering comes from God, even when it is inflicted by the hand of His enemies, we also learned a lesson in humility in the recognition that the everyday good things of life also come from Him. We had taken so much for granted in the past. Suddenly we found ourselves deprived of everything in the way of rights and possessions. Those who had perhaps once complained of a meal overcooked or grown cold now gratefully accepted a dirty piece of raw turnip. We learned the joy of gratitude for everything. And, for the first time, we learned the real value of freedom.

With these lessons came two thoughts. The prisoners of Dachau had lost everything; those who accepted this sacrifice as the will of God learned to know an inner peace and joy that no amount of cruelty, starvation, and disease could banish, and they enjoyed a freedom that took no account of barbed wire. Sleeping on boards, often on mattresses infested with lice, with insufficient covering, cramped and overcrowded, ill, exhausted, and bitterly cold, we nevertheless slept "the sleep of the just." How different might things be, we thought, if Hitler and his henchmen could for one night of conscience-ridden material luxury barter one night of the peaceful luxury of the soul!

The second thought concerned the future. We all knew that with the capitulation of May 7, 1945, the battle was not won. The war between good and evil is coextensive with time, and we knew that new battles must soon be fought. We had experienced much, learned much, and lived through much in Dachau. To what end? Were we to go back to our parishes, monasteries, and schools and resume the daily round as before? Were we just going to sit down and write books and give lectures about our experiences? Were we simply going to look back to the past? No! The fact that so many of God's priests had learned these lessons and had survived must have some greater significance than that. For God does not temper our spiritual weapons to no purpose.

Of the 2,700 clergy who were interned in Dachau concentration camp, 1,034 died as opponents to the Nazi pseudo-religion. Christ called us survivors to proclaim His love and His mercy and the truth of the Catholic Church, the eternal Church that He Himself founded. Let us go forward, then, in this spirit and preach the gospel of God's love. May we attain life everlasting, together with "all men of good will."

Appendices

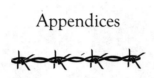

Appendix A

List of Gifts for the Catholic Chapel in
Dachau Concentration Camp

See of Breslau — May 1941: 100 large and 16 small breviaries, each in four parts; July 1942: 4 sets of vestments, 3 albs, 1 ciborium, 1 chalice, and more.

See of Branitz (Silesia) — 1 set of gold-colored vestments, including chasuble, 2 dalmatics, 1 cope, 1 velum; 2 surplices, 2 frontals; Easter 1943: the statue of Our Lady.

Dachau parish — Summer 1941: 1 harmonium; later 2 albs, 1 altar cloth with lace, 1 picture of Our Lady.

Ettal Abbey — December 1942: 1 white chasuble, 1 alb, 1 chalice, 1 censer, 1 set of cruets.

See of Cologne: 1 set of vestments, white Gothic; 1 set of vestments, red Roman; 2 stoles, 1 alb, 3 surplices, 1 chalice, and more.

St. Matthew's Abbey, Trier — 4 sets of Gothic vestments (red, green, violet, and white), 1 alb, 4 lectern cloths, 2 stoles, 1 chalice, and more.

Fr. Moser (Diocese of Linz) — Stations of the Cross, 3 lace cloths for the altar, 1 ciborium veil, 1 alb, 1 biretta, 1 green velum, 2 chalices, 1 stole (white and violet), 1 set of cruets.

Münster (Men's sodality) — February 1944: large cross for the altar.

Munich (obtained through Fr. Muhler): 2 stoles, 3 Communion stoles (white and violet).

Schönstatt (from the nuns) — 1 tabernacle, 1 tabernacle veil, 2 burses for the Blessed Sacrament, 3 chalices, 2 sets of surplice laces.

Christ in Dachau

Candles and altar wine were obtained through the good offices of various priest prisoners, including Frs. Adams, Averberg, Heinzl, and Steiner. The parish priest and parishioners of Dachau were unfailing in the help they gave us. Other items that reached us, very often hidden in food parcels, included 1 large chalice with paten; 1 censer; 1 custodia; 2 small chalices, each with 1 paten; 2 ciboria; several large pyxes; 1 aspergillum; bells; and several small metal crosses.

Appendix B

Memorial Chapel of Christ's Agony
Consecrated in Dachau

The memorial Chapel of Christ's Agony was consecrated in Dachau concentration camp on Friday, August 5, 1960, in a moving ceremony that was one of the main features of the Thirty-Seventh International Eucharistic Congress, held during that week in Munich. The solemn consecration took place appropriately at 1:30 p.m. — the hour of Our Lord's agony on the Cross — and was performed by Dr. Johannes Neuhäusler, suffragan bishop of Munich, who was himself interned in special custody in Dachau.

The chapel, which is built of roughly hewn grey stones from the bed of the nearby River Isar, is designed in the form of a round, towerlike fortress, open in front to symbolize final liberation from captivity. A spiked crown of thorns is suspended above this opening, which reveals the great cross over the altar. In its impressive simplicity, it is a fitting memorial in this terrible place, and it has been fittingly named, for only a stone's throw away, thousands upon thousands endured their own agony of death or suffered torment and starvation at the hands of their Nazi jailers.

The papal legate to the Eucharistic Congress, His Eminence Cardinal Gustavo Testa, was among the many distinguished guests who attended the ceremony. Many high dignitaries of the Church from all over the world were present; representatives of the German federal government, diplomats, public officials, and journalists were all there. But even more impressive than all the scarlet and purple, all the uniforms and decorations, was the vast crowd of "old Dachau" comrades and the long lines of ex-Dachau priests.

Christ in Dachau

Bells began to toll solemnly as a slow procession of more than three thousand Catholic youths made its way down the crowd-lined road through the camp. These young people — all of them far too young to have had any part in Dachau and its tragic history — had made a voluntary four-hour "March of Atonement" from Oberwiesenfeld to the former concentration camp, carrying a great oak cross flanked by the banners of their various youth organizations. During this significant pilgrimage to Dachau, seven special intentions had featured in their prayers and meditations: persecution during the Hitler era; persecution throughout the world today; the persecution of the Jews and all forms of racial hatred and intolerance; the peace of the world; hunger and disease in the world; the unity of Germany; and finally, prayers for themselves.

Three former inmates of the camp — Leopold Figl, the postwar Austrian chancellor and present speaker of the Austrian Parliament; the Polish archbishop Adam Kozłowiecki, now in Northern Rhodesia; and the French minister of justice Edmond Michelet — made short but moving speeches, alternating with readings from the Passion of Our Lord. An address by Dr. Franz Hengsbach, bishop of Essen, preceded the ceremony of consecration. The following passage is taken from the bishop's sermon:

> We are gathered here in this place at the hour of Christ's agony, remembering not only Our Lord's agony, but also the agony and terror of death endured by suffering human beings. We can only fully realize the relation between these if we consider the meaning of Christ's own words: "As long as you did it to one of these my least brethren, you did it to me" (Matt. 25:40). If we think of Dachau in this way, we must realize that wherever human beings suffer the fear of death, Christ's own agony is present too. He suffered here. He endured hunger. He was beaten, hanged, shot, and burned. He called out to His Father in Heaven: "My God, my God, why hast Thou forsaken me?" (Mark 15:34). For He identified Himself with all those who were the victims of inhumanity.
>
> It is therefore impossible to remember His agony and His death without at the same time remembering the agony and death of all those who bear His name. Golgotha was as real and present in Dachau as Dachau was part of Golgotha.

And for this reason, we cannot participate in the Holy Eucharist, in which the death of Our Lord is renewed in the unbloody Sacrifice of the Mass, without remembering in Him those whose suffering and death were given a new meaning, a new significance, through His own death.

Appendix C

The Wisdom of the Cross

An extract from Cross and Sorrow, *a pamphlet by Fr. John M. Lenz*

1. To all who are in the state of grace the Cross brings a greeting from God Himself: "I love you! I care for you! I, your Creator and Redeemer, will lead you *certainly and surely* straight to Heaven!" Infinite love, wisdom, and justice lie behind all earthly sorrow.

2. Borne patiently, your cross will lead you *high* into Heaven. A "God's will be done!" said once in time of sorrow is certainly worth more than self-appointed works of penance or a hundred prayers said in time of prosperity and happiness. If we someday want to be multimillionaires in Heaven, then here is the way to reach our goal!

3. Borne patiently, the cross will lead you *quickly* to Heaven after death. Your stay in Purgatory is, because of your cross, very much shortened or even eliminated altogether. The infinitely great God Himself suffered death upon the Cross for our redemption.

4. In the eyes of God, the very carrying of the cross is in itself a *mighty act of intercession*. Do not complain that you can do nothing for yourselves and for others, for whoever suffers gladly in God's name or for the love of God and his fellow men can achieve tremendous things.

5. The cross shows us the way to *imitate Jesus,* who, in His infinite love for us, went on before us carrying the heaviest Cross of all. And the cross leads us to Mary, the Mother of Our Lord, who, after Him, suffered most. Surely you want to be a disciple of Our Lord Jesus Christ?

6. The cross bears the inscription "*God's will.*" My cross has been laid upon me in infinite wisdom, love, and justice. Our Father in Heaven, who knows always what is best for us, forgets no cross, whether large or small, that is borne out of love for Him and for the saving of souls.

7. The cross is the best *preventive* against sin. It leads us ever nearer to God — and whoever has a heavy cross to bear in this world will not be unduly attached to life. It is all the easier to obey God's call into the eternal bliss of Heaven.

8. The cross is an excellent *means to sanctity.* For the cross makes us humble, courageous, and unselfish. It teaches us how to practice many virtues. It teaches us to pray. We are worth no more than our own prayers. If you know how to pray, then you will always be able to master life.

9. To bear your cross with patience is also *holy prudence.* No child of Adam is spared his cross. To struggle against your cross and to curse like the bad thief is only to make your cross even heavier. This is a cross borne to your temporal — and eternal — torment.

10. Who knows what may lie behind your cross? It is the *cross of God's providence*, intended to spare you from far heavier crosses. God alone distributes His crosses. And God knows what He is about — and all the consequences. "God is our Father; God is good; everything that He does is good."

11. The cross bears the inscription "*Sorrow is but temporary; joy is eternal.*" Make your choice. There are other short-lived pleasures for the price of eternal damnation. Choose instead to follow God's will, for that alone is what makes man truly great. "To serve God is to rule."

Appendix D

The Riches of the Cross

An extract from Cross and Sorrow, *a pamphlet by Fr. John M. Lenz*

1. Sanctifying grace is divine life in the soul. God in three Persons is present in us. We are children of God, brothers and sisters of Christ. That is infinitely more than to be an emperor on earth or a king or a president. We live in God's own family, with Mary, the angels, and the saints.

2. Sanctifying grace brings about a true friendship and indescribable love of God toward us. In the sight of God, we are worth more than all men without this grace — yes, more than the whole cosmos itself. We are infinitely richer than the richest men in history who did not possess this grace. All our works receive in this grace an infinite value in the eyes of God and for all eternity.

3. In this grace is to be found the highest science, true freedom, and the greatest progress. In this grace, the Holy Ghost gives us His life and His gifts and the theological and moral virtues. God Himself, as the God-man, offered His life on the Cross for our grace life. God Himself nourishes our grace life with His own Flesh and Blood in Holy Communion.

4. By means of this grace, our soul is an exalted temple of God. The glory of Heaven shines in the soul of the child of God. There can be no true happiness without this grace. God, the Lord, helps and protects us, His children, above all. The angels of God are especially assigned to our service and protection.

5. This grace prepares us in a truly wonderful fashion for the eternal, manifold glories of Heaven. It is the purchase price of this soul-satisfying happiness and, through it, makes us heirs of God and co-heirs of Christ.

Photos

1. General Dwight D. Eisenhower, as commander in Chief of the Western liberating armies.

2. The late General George S. Patton Jr., general commanding the U.S. Seventh Army, which liberated Dachau town and concentration camp. Mr. McCloy and General Stimson.

3. The late bishop Dr. Michael Kozal, Poland.
4. Dr. Josef Beran, archbishop of Prague.

5. Dr. Johannes Neuhäusler, auxiliary bishop of Munich.
6. The late bishop Dr. Gabriel Piguet, France.

7. Fr. Georg Schelling, Austria; our dean.
8. The late Fr. Titus Brandsma, O. Carm., Holland.

9. Fr. Andreas Rieser, Salzburg, Austria.
10. The late priest brothers Prabutzki, Poland; from left:
Boleslaus, Alois, and Paul (our first camp chaplain).

11. Archbishop Dr. Adam Kozłowiecki, S.J., Poland; missionary bishop in Africa (1941–1945 in Dachau).
12. Msgr. Reinhold Friedrichs, Germany; our "Block Father."

13. The late Msgr. Dr. Carl Lampert, Austria.
14. The late Msgr. Dr. Heinrich Feuerstein, Germany.

15. The late Fr. Fritz Seitz, Germany.
16. Fr. Dr. Gregor Schwake, O.S.B., Germany.

17. Fr. Joseph Kentenich, S.A.C., now United States.
18. Fr. William Bock, O.S.A., Austria.

19. The late Fr. Karl Leisner, Germany; ordained in
Dachau concentration camp, December 17, 1944.
20. The late Fr. Rector Karl Schrammel, Silesia, Germany.

21. German Protestant pastors, September 11, 1955.

22. The late Msgr. Friedrich Pfanzelt, Dachau town (left); Fr. Peter van Gestel, S.J., Holland; Fr. Otto Pies, S.J., Germany (right), June 1945.

23. The paper-bag commando or "Cathedral Chapter."

24. Prisoners' living quarters in Dachau concentration camp.

25. Building used for drying purposes on the plantation.

26. Entrance to the camp, with a view of the parade ground.

27. A moat, a wall, and high barbed-wire fences surrounded the camp.

28. View of the plantation and the pepper mill.

29. "Execution Hill," near the crematorium.

30. Our first military Mass kit.

31. Our Lady of Dachau.

32. Corporals made of paper.
33. Relics, formerly in Dachau concentration camp, now in Dachau parish church.

34. Altar cross and tabernacle.

35. The chapel decorated for a feast day (1945).

36. Priests assembled for Pontifical High Mass, Easter Sunday.

37. Major General William B. Arnold, chief of Chaplain Corps,
U.S. Seventh Army, May 31, 1945.

38. Some of the priests from the Czechs' block, with
Msgr. Stašek (second from the left).

39. Priests at work on the plantation (from left to right): Alois Sindler, Kurt Habich, Benno Scholz, Richard Schneider, Hermann Quack.

40. "Our angel": a little girl from Dachau town brought us clergy vestments and a chalice.
41. Fr. Alois Langhans was in charge of the SS rabbits.

42. The photography commando: Fr. Paul Wasmer, Fr. Karl Schmidt (with camera), W. Schibailow (Poland), Fr. Franz Sales Hess, O.S.B.

43. Dr. Leopold Figl, speaker of the Austrian Parliament.
44. Duke Max von Hohenberg, son of the
former heir apparent to the Austrian throne.

45. Dr. Heinrich Gleissner, governor of Upper Austria.
46. The late Dr. Friedrich Funder, celebrated Catholic journalist.

47. Dr. Eduard Pesendorfer, a high official in Austria.
48. Dr. Emmerich Zederbauer, university professor in Vienna.
49. Fritz Eckert, Catholic politician, Vienna.

50. Oskar Müller, social minister in Hessen, Germany.
51. Dr. Franz Blaha, Prague.
52. Franz Olah, trade union president, Vienna.

53. Fr. Leopold Arthofer, Austria.
54. The late Fr. Leo Roth, who remained as parish priest in
the former concentration camp in Dachau until 1960.
55. Fr. Ludwig Hiller, Germany.

56. Fr. Engelmar Unzeitig, Austria.
57. Fr. Klaus L'Hoste, Austria.
58. Fr. John M. Lenz, the author.

59. Here "lived" and died the sick and invalid and the typhus victims in Dachau concentration camp.

60. Bodies awaiting the Dachau "hearse," end of April 1945.

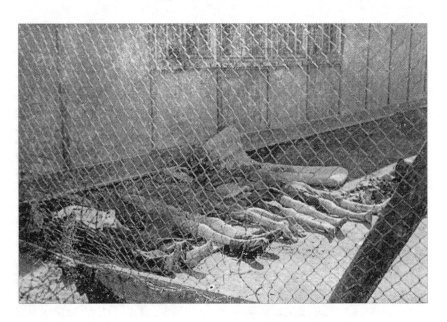

61. Bodies of typhus victims lying in the roadway.

62. Crematorium and a pile of about 1,700 bodies.

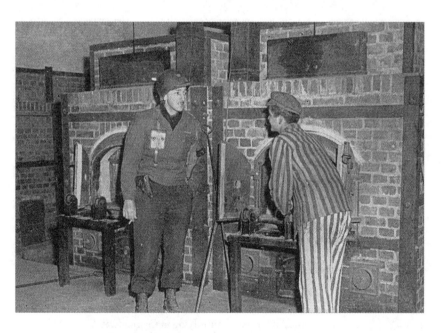

63. A former prisoner shows the crematorium furnaces to
Colonel Walter P. O'Brien, XV Corps, U.S. Seventh Army.

64. Berghof Hitler, a luxury apartment.

65. Hitler without a mask, a drawing by an Austrian prisoner.

66. Cheers for the liberators, April 29, 1945.

67. Ceremony to celebrate the liberation on the parade ground.

68. The Dachau Trials, November 15 and December 13, 1945.

69. The accused, in the center, Dr. Schilling.

70. The ashes of the thousands of unknown dead.

71. *The Prisoner* (monument).

72. The camp Madonna is transferred to Dachau parish church,
September 11, 1955.

73. Procession of regular clergy.

74. Procession of clerical dignitaries: Msgr. Pfanzelt and
Msgr. Ott, followed by Abbot Niedermoser (with pectoral cross) and
Fr. Emil Muhler, Msgr. Friedrichs, and Msgr. Baumjohann.

75. Procession of secular clergy.

76. Reunion in St. Florian of Austrian priests interned in Dachau.

77. Dachau, a romantic old town on the Amper River.

78. Model of the Chapel of Christ's Agony, built in the camp in 1960 and consecrated during the Eucharistic Congress in Munich, August 5, 1960.

79. The lovely model proposed by Mr. V. Hammer (Vienna):
"Father, forgive them, for they know not what they do" (Luke 23:34).

About the Author

After being imprisoned for his faith from 1938 to 1945, Austrian Jesuit priest Fr. John M. Lenz (1902–1985) traveled widely and visited thirty-three states in America in 1958–1959. His other books include *Die Himmel rühmen* and *Reise ins Weltall*.

Sophia Institute

Sophia Institute is a nonprofit institution that seeks to nurture the spiritual, moral, and cultural life of souls and to spread the gospel of Christ in conformity with the authentic teachings of the Roman Catholic Church.

Sophia Institute Press fulfills this mission by offering translations, reprints, and new publications that afford readers a rich source of the enduring wisdom of mankind.

Sophia Institute also operates the popular online resource CatholicExchange.com. *Catholic Exchange* provides world news from a Catholic perspective as well as daily devotionals and articles that will help readers to grow in holiness and live a life consistent with the teachings of the Church.

In 2013, Sophia Institute launched Sophia Institute for Teachers to renew and rebuild Catholic culture through service to Catholic education. With the goal of nurturing the spiritual, moral, and cultural life of souls, and an abiding respect for the role and work of teachers, we strive to provide materials and programs that are at once enlightening to the mind and ennobling to the heart; faithful and complete, as well as useful and practical.

Sophia Institute gratefully recognizes the Solidarity Association for preserving and encouraging the growth of our apostolate over the course of many years. Without their generous and timely support, this book would not be in your hands.

www.SophiaInstitute.com
www.CatholicExchange.com
www.SophiaInstituteforTeachers.org

Sophia Institute Press is a registered trademark of Sophia Institute.
Sophia Institute is a tax-exempt institution as defined by the
Internal Revenue Code, Section 501(c)(3). Tax ID 22-2548708.